CHILDREN
AND THE
DEATH OF A PRESIDENT

Children
and the
Death of a President

MULTI-DISCIPLINARY STUDIES

Edited by
MARTHA WOLFENSTEIN
and
GILBERT KLIMAN

Doubleday & Company, Inc.
Garden City, New York
1965

"Choice of Defenses Used by Prelatency Children in Reaction to the Assassination," by Augusta Alpert is reprinted from Volume XIX of *The Psychoanalytic Study of the Child*, by permission from International Universities Press, Inc. Copyright 1964 by International Universities Press, Inc.

"Diagnostic and Therapeutic Utilization of Children's Reactions to the President's Death," by Othilda Krug and Cynthia Fox Dember is reprinted from *The Journal of the American Academy of Child Psychiatry*, October 1965, by permission from International Universities Press, Inc. Copyright 1965 by International Universities Press, Inc.

ACKNOWLEDGMENTS

At the beginning of April 1964, we held a conference at the Albert Einstein College of Medicine on "Children's Reactions to the Death of the President." Researchers who had been gathering material on this subject came together to discuss work in progress. Their studies in fuller form are brought together in this volume.

We should like to acknowledge the help we received in holding the conference out of which this book emerged. Dr. Joseph B. Cramer, Director of the Division of Child Psychiatry at the Albert Einstein College of Medicine, played a decisive role in planning and organizing the conference. We are grateful to him for his unfailing interest, encouragement, and many valuable ideas. We owe much to the colleagues from a variety of fields who participated as discussants in the conference: Dr. Lenin A. Baler, Dr. Henry Barnett, Dr. Barbara Biber, Dr. H. Robert Blank, Dr. Sybille Escalona, Dr. Maurice Friend, Dr. Robert Furman, Dr. Helen Gee, Dr. Harry Gordon, Dr. Mary O'Neil Hawkins, Dr. Mildred January, Dr. Reginald S. Lourie, Dr. Rhoda Metraux, Dr. Fritz Redl, Dr. Julius Richmond, Dr. Milton Rosenbaum, and Dr. Edwin A. Weinstein. A contribution of Dr. Arthur J. Brodbeck was, to our regret, not revised in time to be included in this volume. We wish to acknowledge his valuable presentation at the conference.

We are grateful to the Ross Laboratories, whose support made the conference possible, and to their medical director, Dr. L. J. Filer, who gave tireless and sympathetic assistance on that occasion. The Albert Einstein College of Medicine was generous in providing facilities and hospitality.

We wish to thank Mrs. Ruth Warren for her devotion and care in preparing the manuscript.

CONTENTS

CONTRIBUTORS

AUGUSTA ALPERT, PH.D.
Associate Director, Child Development Center, New York City

CYNTHIA FOX DEMBER, PH.D.
Chief Clinical Psychologist, Child Guidance Home;
Assistant Professor of Psychology, Departments of Psychiatry
and Psychology, University of Cincinnati

SYLVIA GINSPARG, PH.D.
Psychologist, The Menninger Foundation

FRED I. GREENSTEIN, PH.D.
Associate Professor of Government,
Wesleyan University, Middletown, Connecticut

GILBERT KLIMAN, M.D.
Clinical Instructor in Psychiatry,
Albert Einstein College of Medicine, New York

OTHILDA KRUG, M.D.
Director, Child Guidance Home and Child Psychiatry Division,
Department of Psychiatry, College of Medicine; Professor of
Child Psychiatry, University of Cincinnati

ROBERT E. LANE, PH.D.
Professor of Political Science, Yale University

ALICE E. MORIARTY, PH.D.
Psychologist, The Menninger Foundation

LOIS BARCLAY MURPHY, PH.D.
Psychologist, The Menninger Foundation

CAROLYN PRATT
Ph.D. candidate, Department of Political Science, Yale University

ROBERTA S. SIGEL, PH.D.
Associate Professor of Political Science,
Wayne State University, Detroit

MARTHA WOLFENSTEIN, PH.D.
Associate Clinical Professor of Psychiatry (Psychology-Child
Therapy),
Albert Einstein College of Medicine, New York

JOAN J. ZILBACH, M.D.
Staff Psychiatrist, Judge Baker Guidance Center, Boston

PREFACE

This book on children's reactions to the death of the President was not born without pain. Its authors had to overcome their own shock and distress, and could not avoid feeling uneasy in approaching as a subject of scientific inquiry an event so personal to all of them, despite their confident belief that the effort deserved to be made. When in April 1964 researchers from different fields who had been working on this topic were convened, we wanted to discuss a moving event at a time when the feelings it had evoked were still fresh in our minds. It was also our purpose to facilitate exchange of findings and ideas on work in progress, relating to a subject little studied before. The conference, like the researches reported, required planning at an accelerated tempo. Arranging this was made possible because Dr. Lloyd J. Filer, medical director of the Ross Laboratories, shared our feelings and gave us generously of the resources of his corporation.

We wanted to make sure that a view of the disaster from the standpoint of behavior, of development, and of the unconscious forces of the mind would be a part of its history. At the same time each of the researchers approached the event from a background of interests in related studies. For our own staff the context was that of investigating the impact on children of a death in the family. For others it was the meaning of political events to the growing generation, or the ways of coping with difficulties of various kinds in the course of development. For still others it was an interest from a clinical point of view in picking up the immediate effects of disturbing occurrences. We found through our colloquium that we were recording the impact of an historic event from our special points of view and adding to our understanding of human development by analyzing the rich and varied data that we shared.

This book and the discussions at our April conference* reflect a cooperative effort among scientists which the complexity of those problems of today that need our interest requires. Through this documentation we express our recognition of the complexity of man and his environment, of the need for humility and also for increased sophistication, and of the benefits our disciplines afford to one another.

JOSEPH B. CRAMER, M.D.
Associate Professor and
Director of Child Psychiatry
Albert Einstein College
of Medicine

* The discussions at the conference were recorded in full. A condensed version will be distributed by Ross Laboratories.

INTRODUCTION

Our purpose in this introduction is to place studies of the impact of a national tragedy in a larger context of research. We are concerned with a terrible event which has affected us in many different ways. The researches in this volume are intended to clarify our understanding of these various reactions. Our focus is on the growing generation, children and adolescents, into whose life experience the murder of the President intruded. In part these studies are historical documents of the immediate meaning of a major national event to those who experienced it. They are records of a sort rarely made before. The specific concern with the growing generation, and the significance of this event for them, also has few precedents.

However, we speak here as social scientists rather than as historians. We are oriented not to chronicling a unique event but to placing it in a context of related experiences. This context includes a range of stressful situations, from those of personal bereavement to large-scale disasters. We shall indicate some of the lines of research that form the background of our studies, and to which they in turn aim to contribute. Since we are concerned with children and adolescents, we will also indicate the larger context of developmental studies which provide a framework for our researches.

I

Among the many reactions to the assassination of President Kennedy were those of a number of people who started almost immediately to gather observations on the impact of this event. The pursuit of such research is related to psychological needs in the individual and to certain trends in research in the human sciences. The researcher who occupies himself with gathering data in such circumstances can in part master his own distress in this way. We know from the field of disaster research that the disturbing impact of such events is moderated for those who keep very busy immediately afterward, occupying themselves with others who have been affected.[1] Following the assassination there was also the need, expressed by many persons, from the age of adolescence on, to think very intensely and continuously about what had happened. This need to think had multiple motives. The murder of the leader tended to evoke feelings, fantasies, and memories from deeply repressed layers of the mind, reaching down, one might say, to the totem-and-taboo level. For those so affected there was a kind of inner turmoil of conflicting thoughts and feelings, which called for an effort of reorganization. The image of the external world was also disrupted, and required reordering. For those who pursued researches at this time, their work afforded a way of coping with a complicated emotional malaise.

There have been, until now, very few studies of reactions to a leader's death. Some of the great dramas in our literature, such as *Oedipus Rex* and *Hamlet,* have evoked the tragic repercussions of the murder of a leader. Poets have been traditionally occupied with grief for loss, including occasions when a leader dies. Freud has speculated on the profound emotional consequences of the murder of a leader in human prehistory and in biblical times.[2] Historians have recorded the deaths of leaders, often by execution or assassination, and tried to reconstruct what their immediate and long-term effects may have been. But there have been very few systematic, empirical studies undertaken shortly following the event, attempting to ascertain what its impact really was on those who had just experienced it.

Among the rare earlier studies we find Fairbairn's, written in 1936 after the death of King George V, reporting the reactions of a few analytic patients;[3] de Grazia's paper relating to the death of President Roosevelt, based also on observations of patients in analysis;[4] and Orlansky's study of public reactions to Roosevelt's death, based on newspaper reports and informal interviewing.[5]

But within hours of President Kennedy's assassination, a substantial number of researchers in a variety of disciplines were moved to undertake studies of reactions to it.[6]

This can be partially explained by certain developments in the human sciences within the last twenty years which have been preparing researchers to investigate the impact of extreme events. World War II alerted us to how little we knew about how people really react to extreme situations. In England, before the war, the government asked experts to predict the probable consequences of the bombing of cities. Their anticipations of mass panic, precipitous flight from cities, and great increase in the incidence of mental illness proved, in the event, to be fantastically in error.[7] After the war observations of its impact on civilian populations were collated,[8] and an increasing number of research projects was initiated to make field studies of the effects of a variety of peacetime disasters.[9]

The possibility of a future nuclear war has given a sense of practical urgency to disaster studies. Research on how people react to all the phases of a disastrous event, from anticipation to aftermath, has interrelated theoretical and practical implications. The impact of extreme events reveals the vulnerabilities and the resources of individuals and community organizations. Information about, and understanding of, such reactions provides a realistic basis for practical planning for a wide range of exigencies, from deciding how warnings of danger should be issued to helping those damaged or deprived by a disaster to achieve maximal recovery.

The National Opinion Research Center was one of the forerunners in the field of disaster studies, in training teams that would go into the field at short notice. So it is no accident that the NORC carried out the most comprehensive study of adult reactions to the assassination of President Kennedy.[10] There will be repeated references to their findings in the course of this book.

Antecedent disaster studies not only prepared us for immediate research activity in a time of sudden crisis, but also helped us to recognize many characteristic responses. The impact of the sudden, violent death of a leader resembles other disasters that affect large numbers of people simultaneously. People react differently to such large-scale events than they do to more exclusively individual or familial catastrophes. In a large-scale disaster the individual does not feel singled out by fate as he may when misfortune befalls him alone. He feels to some extent sustained by the realization that many others have been affected by the same event, that he is sharing in a common experience. In our culture it is generally felt to be somewhat reprehensible to complain or demonstrate distress about personal suffering.[11] We tend to feel, however, that it is more permissible to experience and express unhappy feelings about events that concern us less personally, whether they occur in the larger real world of which we are a part or on the stage or movie screen. Such emotion is considered more noble, since it includes a component of sympathy for others.

The death of the President evoked many of the reactions found to be common in other disasters: the initial reaction of being stunned, dazed, or shocked, which has been characterized as the "disaster syndrome";[12] the feeling of disbelief, which is closely associated with this; the apprehension that other disasters will ensue; the tendency to recapitulate the disastrous event repeatedly, in an effort to assimilate it and master the disorganizing distress it has caused; and thoughts and fantasies of how the disaster could have been prevented or how such disasters could in the future be forestalled. Large-scale catastrophes recurrently pose the problem of evil, since they challenge latent or explicit beliefs about the benevolent ordering of the world. And following a disaster people frequently feel they have been brought closer together by what they have commonly undergone, and resolve to do better from here on. These phenomena, familiar from the study of other disasters, will be variously illustrated in this volume.

The situation following the President's death, however, differs from that precipitated by other disasters that have been studied. In such disasters as the wartime bombing of cities, or peacetime floods, tornadoes, or earthquakes, there is the need for immediate action. The expression of emotion is postponed by absorption in the urgent work of rescuing and caring for survivors. Adults, especially in our culture, also feel that they must exercise emotional control, they must keep calm; a major reason given is that they must not upset the children.[13] After the President's death, there were no practical steps to be taken, nothing that most people could do but watch on television the recapitulations of the terrible event and its sequels. Thus children were confronted with the unaccustomed sight of their parents, ordinarily active, restrained, and cheerful, here immobilized, weeping, and depressed.

Another development in the human sciences that has sensitized us to the importance of attending to the immediate impact of disturbing events is that of preventive psychiatry.[14] Clinical findings have shown that damaging experiences often produce delayed reactions, a latent vulnerability that leads to breakdown under subsequent stress, or subtle, covert disturbances, which may manifest themselves in acute form years later. For instance, studies have shown that there is a significantly greater incidence of having lost a parent in childhood among adults who suffer severe mental illness than among the rest of the population.[15] Often, at the time that a child undergoes such a loss, the damaging effects are not immediately apparent. But in many instances the potential for emotional adaptation has been so impaired that there is a likelihood of later more serious disturbance.[16] An objective of preventive psychiatry is to intervene promptly in such life crises, with the hope of working through the immediate repercussions and forestalling later, more malignant consequences. At the same time we may add to our theoretical understanding of the range of reactions at different ages to different kinds of stress.

Both disaster research and preventive psychiatry focus attention on situations in which there has been a sudden disruption of major relationships.[17] Psychoanalytic investigation has contributed a background of understanding of emotional reactions to the loss of loved persons.[18] Particularly relevant here are John Bowlby's recent formulations[19] which postulate three phases of reaction to loss. The first phase is one of protest, in which the feelings of a young child at separation from his mother are re-evoked. The separation from the loved person is felt to be intolerable, and there is a clamorous demand for the person's return. In this phase the reality of the loss is vehemently denied. The second phase is one of disorganization, precipitated by some realization that the loved person is not coming back. Many feelings of distress and disturbance characterize this phase. It constitutes a transition from the way of life predicated on the presence of the loved person to a life in which he can no longer play a part. Much pain is involved in detachment of feelings from the lost person and the abandonment of habits and expectations that were associated with him.

The third phase is one of reorganization, of going on with life. In this phase the loss of the loved person has been assimilated and no longer occasions traumatic repercussions or deep distress. In this phase the transfer of feelings to other persons who can more or less take the place of the one who has died is of major importance. Feelings for the lost person have not been obliterated, but are reduced in amount and intensity. The survivor is reconciled to his loss and can think of the lost person without pain. These phases are of varying duration in different individuals, and in some cases there is a fixation on the first or second phase, where the individual remains unable to master the loss he has suffered. We shall see these phases variously illustrated in this book.

There is a strong need in human nature to maintain that the dead have not really died. While this is partially a denial of reality, it also expresses an important psychological truth. Freud has pointed out the tendency to internalize, to bear within oneself the image of a beloved person who has died.[20] This is a complicated phenomenon, susceptible to many alternative manifestations. In the special circumstances of the murder of a leader, there is a tendency, according to Freud's speculations, for the followers to make the principles he embodied more binding upon themselves in posthumous obedience.[21] The influence of a murdered leader on the formation of ideals and conscience in those who witness his death and in later generations is no doubt related to how clearly and strongly he embodied important and novel principles. Thus Lincoln has contributed to our national heritage of ideals as McKinley, for instance, has not. What image of President Kennedy will be borne in the minds of Americans we do not yet know. For the present generation, we might expect it to vary with the age of the individual at the time of experiencing the impact of the assassination.

On another level there are the prevailing attitudes in our culture toward death, funeral rites, and mourning customs.[22] We tend to ward off awareness of death, to curtail funeral ritual, and to minimize or eliminate formal mourning observances. Geoffrey Gorer has suggested that the reduction of mourning forms, which give social recognition to the state of the bereaved, imposes great emotional hardship on the mourner, who must work through his distress secretly and in isolation.[23] The death of the President was an exceptional event and evoked corresponding responses. There was widespread preoccupation with the loss, overshadowing all other concerns, and most of the people in the country, through the medium of television, participated in the elaborate and impressive funeral ceremonial. The mourning family of the President became for millions objects of warm and painful sympathy. It is probable that for many whose grief for personal losses had been subdued, suppressed, or curtailed, this provided an occasion for release of feelings of uncompleted mourning for their own dead.

While the need to gloss over the facts of death has been prominent in our culture, there are signs of a recent countertendency. This may be seen in the increasing concern of parents with how to tell their children about death when it occurs within the family circle.[24] American parents make an unusually high demand on themselves to spare their children painful experiences. This valiant effort cannot always succeed. We know from the study of children's reactions to the death of a parent how negatively children react to being told little and belatedly about this event, to being excluded from funeral observances.[25] At the present time parents seem to be increasingly aware of the need not only to spare children distress, but, when this is impossible, to help them to tolerate and work through it in an optimal way. Perhaps Mrs. Kennedy's inclusion of her children in the funeral ceremonies for their father will serve as a valuable precedent in this respect.

Another wide area of research relevant to our subject is that of attitudes toward authority figures in general and political leaders in particular, political and other group allegiances, and traditions of transmission of power. Of particular significance here is how awareness and feelings in these matters develop in young people.[26] Orientation in this context will be supplied by the political scientists contributing to this volume.

The field of communication research provides yet another context in which the assassination and its sequels may be viewed. Television played an exceptional role in keeping millions of people in touch with the course of events and including them in the funeral ceremonies. A new social ritual was improvised, which we might call the television wake. Mourners across the nation were helped to work through their distress by having images of the man they mourned repeatedly re-evoked, the circumstances of his death presented over and over till disbelief gradually gave way to acceptance of painful reality, and by having their feelings released and relieved by participating at a distance in the protracted funeral rites.[27] The multiple functions of communication media following the assassination are dealt with in a volume by Greenberg and Parker.[28]

II

As we have said, this book is concerned with the impact of the President's death on children and adolescents. This focus exemplifies an important trend in the social sciences. In 1950, in his Introduction to *Childhood and Society,* Erik Erikson observed: "One may scan work after work on history, society, and morality and find little reference to the fact that all people start as children and that all peoples begin in their nurseries."[29] In 1954, in the Introduction to *Childhood in Contemporary Cultures,* Margaret Mead wrote that children are "newcomers in the social sciences."[30] In the present volume political scientists have joined with clinicians and researchers in child development to study the impact of a major national event on the growing generation. The child experts, more habitually occupied with studying children in relation to their immediate environment, have here widened their scope to see their subjects in a national context. This linking, from both sides, of children with a major event in the society at large implies a growing awareness that, if we are to understand human nature in any of its manifestations, we must acknowledge the long course of development by which the mature human being is formed. Conversely, to understand the developing individual we must see him also in the wider social world in which he lives.

A basic frame of reference for all our studies is that of phases of development. Each phase of emotional growth has its characteristic resources, conflicts, and alternatives for disturbance or resolution.[31] Concurrently there is the process of intellectual maturation, marked by a sequence of modes of reasoning and comprehension.[32] The process of socialization, in which the child gradually comes to approximate the prevailing attitudes of the adults in his culture, is far from being a simple inscribing of messages on a *tabula rasa.* What the child is being taught is subjected to selection, translation, misinterpretation, substitution, and distortion in accordance with the emotional preoccupations and ways of thinking of his age. Anna Freud has recalled how, in the early days of child analysis, high hopes were expressed that much could be changed for the better if adults would tell children the truth about the facts of life instead of fobbing them off with fairy tales or evasions. But subsequent observation showed that the children so enlightened tended to revert to their own childish sexual theories, which were more in keeping with the typical feelings, fantasies, and experiences of their phase of development.[33]

The significance of any event will vary depending on the phase of development on which it impinges. The subjects of our various studies range from children of four through college students. In terms of phases of development they would be expected to exemplify the oedipal phase, the latency period, prepuberty, and early and late adolescence. We shall not here attempt to recapitulate the complex emotional content of these phases. However, we should note that, while each phase is marked by focal problems and modes of coping with them, there is also a carry-over or periodic re-emergence of themes from antecedent phases, which complicates the picture. Also age is no sure index of the emotional status of the developing individual. The possibilities of fixation on a phase usually associated with earlier years, or regression to such a phase, may operate to make an older child emotionally approximate a much younger one. The impact of decisive experiences in one or another phase may lead to keeping the typical preoccupations and traits of that phase dominant in the character formation of the individual.

While we cannot here present a comprehensive account of phases of development, we would like to give a few illustrations of the kinds of susceptibilities characteristic of different phases that we would expect to be relevant to differential reactions to the assassination. In the beginning years of life the major anxiety is separation anxiety. The small child is almost totally dependent on the care of his parents, particularly his mother, and becomes anxious in their absence. While susceptibility to such anxiety normally decreases as the child's capacities for independent activity and relationships outside the family develop, it continues to make itself felt intermittently, usually with reduced intensity, over many years. For children who, because of age or the exigencies of their own experience, were particularly susceptible to such anxiety, the fact that the father of young children had died might be selected as the most disturbing aspect of the assassination.

In the oedipal phase the wish to eliminate one parent in order to gain exclusive possession of the other is predominant. This wish brings with it fears of retribution in the form of bodily damage and loss of love. For children in this phase we might expect that the murder of a very important man would have the emotional significance of the carrying out of their secret wishes. The precedent of such an act might intensify their forbidden impulses. But since these impulses are opposed by the forces of love and fear we would expect it also to intensify their struggle against their impulses. The assassination of a leader corresponds to the oedipal fantasies of boys. We shall have to see whether girls translated the event into their own oedipal terms.

Oedipal conflicts are typically revived in adolescence, and we would expect some of the responses to the assassination in this phase to be related to them. We may say, however, that emotions belonging to the oedipal phase haunt the human mind from this period of life on. In the latency period they are normally repressed to a considerable extent, but a powerful experience fraught with oedipal significance may stir them up. In later life, oedipal feelings, though normally reduced, leave their latent residue in the depths of our minds. They reverberate again when, for instance, we watch *Hamlet* on the stage, or when we experience in real life an event peculiarly suited to evoking them.

Conflicts over aggressive impulses and related ideas about crime and punishment are manifested in many different ways in the course of human development. Fantasies of violent acts and equally devastating retribution characterize the oedipal phase. In the latency period, aggressive impulses are being brought under control, moderated, and sublimated, for instance, in the occupation with games played according to rules and requiring a sportsmanlike attitude toward the opponent. In prepuberty, aggressive impulses tend to break through again in a more unruly way. The impact of the murder of the President and the subsequent murder of his assassin might be expected to vary according to the phase of the battle against his own aggressive impulses which the child was living through at the time of these events. We would expect that in cases where conflicts over aggression were emotionally central for an individual, he would be more affected by the criminal aspects of what had happened than by a sense of loss of a beloved person.

A major change that occurs in the course of adolescence is the gradual and difficult withdrawal of feelings from the parents and the quest for new love objects and ideal models. It is at this time that a whole range of glamorous figures—heroes and idols from beyond their personal world in time and place—engage the emotions of young people. In this phase one would expect the transfer of some strong feelings to the President. Thus we would anticipate a sense of loss and grief for his death more in adolescents than in younger children.

While the framework of phases of development is central to our studies, numerous other variables are relevant to the understanding of our findings. The assassination and the events that followed were very complex. Each individual could select from them or elaborate on them in imagination according to his prevailing emotional preoccupations. There were many individual differences in reactions, related to different life experiences. Sex differences and differences related to class background, race, religion, and political affiliation also played a part. The children studied in this book varied also in respect to mental health; the subjects include both normal and emotionally disturbed children.

III

The contributors to this volume have used a variety of methods in their several studies. We may summarize these methods as follows: 1. Observation in situations of everyday life. This includes observations made by the researchers and those reported by parents and teachers in interviews, written reports, and in response to questionnaires. 2. Interviews with children and adolescents, individually and in groups. 3. Clinical material, from cases of the researchers and cases reported by co-workers and therapists in supervision, as well as in response to questionnaires. Clinical data on parents of the subjects were also used when available. 4. Questionnaires addressed to children and adolescents. 5. Essays written at school. 6. Projective techniques. Background information on the subjects varied widely in the different studies, from bare identifying data to intensive life histories.

Sylvia Ginsparg, Alice Moriarty, and Lois B. Murphy in Topeka have investigated the impact of the President's death on a group of children with whom they have been long acquainted. These children, now in early adolescence, have been subjects of a study of normal development extending over many years. Their reactions to the assassination and its sequels, elicited by an open-ended questionnaire, are analyzed in the context of their antecedent life experiences and characteristic ways of functioning.

Roberta Sigel has used a highly structured questionnaire to study a large sample of school children in Detroit. The subjects range in age from fourth-graders to seniors in high school. The findings are compared and contrasted with those on adults obtained by the National Opinion Research Center. Differences related to sex, class, race, and political affiliation are also considered. Interpretations are offered on the varying degrees of socialization shown in attitudes toward political authority and the administration of justice.

Martha Wolfenstein is concerned with the psychology of grief and mourning in relation to stages of development. She analyzes children's reactions to the death of the President against a background of research on children's reactions to the death of a parent. She draws on clinical material, interviews with normal children, teachers' observations, and on essays by young adolescents that were particularly revealing of strong grief for the murdered President.

Othilda Krug and Cynthia Dember report on the impact of the national crisis on child patients and the staff workers caring for them in a residential treatment center in Cincinnati. Individual differences in the children's ways of reacting are related to their antecedent disturbances and life experiences. Observations continued over a period of months. Findings from specially devised projective tests, given three and a half months after the event, reveal the effects of emotion on memory.

Augusta Alpert has analyzed reactions of young child patients as observed by their therapists and teachers in a combined nursery school and treatment center in New York. She is concerned with the changes in modes of psychic defense in these children as they struggled with the emotional distress provoked by the assassination.

Gilbert Kliman has used clinical material and interviews with normal subjects to show how the assassination was fraught with oedipal significance for children and adolescents. Among the themes dealt with are: death wishes, incestuous motives, identification with the assassin, identification with President Kennedy, and rescue fantasies. Dr. Kliman also presents material from his cases antedating the assassination to show the difficulties in assessing the impact of a particular event.

Joan Zilbach reports on children, adolescents, and their parents, as seen in a child guidance clinic in Boston. She discusses how the children's reactions varied with age and sex. The question of how much the children's feelings corresponded with those of their parents is considered. The problem of how therapists should deal with a crisis that affects both them and their patients is also discussed.

Carolyn Pratt and Robert Lane have investigated reactions of students of both sexes in colleges in Connecticut. They focus on the issue of emotional acceptance of the fact of the President's death. Their findings are derived from a questionnaire administered shortly after the event, and again two months later, asking whether students still found it hard to believe what had happened. Interpretations are offered of prompt and delayed acceptance in terms of sex and personality differences and other variables.

Fred Greenstein interviewed groups of students in a men's college in Connecticut during the days immediately following the assassination. In these discussions we see something of what a young and brilliant President, cut down in mid-career, meant to young college men, who also express their feelings about his wife and his successor.

NOTES

1. Wolfenstein, 1957.
2. Freud, 1913; 1939.
3. Fairbairn, 1936.

4. de Grazia, 1945.

5. Orlansky, 1947. Also cf. Johannsen, 1946.

6. A survey of research projects on reactions to the assassination of President Kennedy, compiled by the Bureau of Social Science Research, Inc., Washington, D.C., as of April 1964 listed 39 such studies.

7. Titmuss, 1950.

8. Janis, 1951.

9. Baker and Chapman, 1962.

10. Sheatsley and Feldman, 1964.

11. Zborowski, 1952.

12. Wallace, 1956.

13. Wolfenstein, *op. cit.*

14. Caplan, 1961; 1964.

15. Hilgard, 1963.

16. Unpublished research on children's reactions to the death of a parent, conducted by the editors of this volume, in the Division of Child Psychiatry of the Albert Einstein College of Medicine. One of our repeated findings has been that children's reactions following a parent's death tend to be muted and covert. Often, to those around them, the children do not appear disturbed or even noticeably sad.

17. Studies of the effects of radical interruptions of parent-child relations include the following: A. Freud and D. Burlingham (1943; 1944) on young children separated from their families in wartime nurseries; I. Hellman (1962), a follow-up study on one of these children; A. Freud and S. Dann (1951) on concentration camp children; E. L. Gyomroi (1963), the later analysis of a concentration camp child; R. A. Spitz (1946) on infants in the first year separated from their mothers; and J. Robertson (1958) on young children in hospitals.

18. Freud, 1917; Abraham, 1924; Lindemann, 1944; Mahler, 1961; Fleming and Altschul, 1963.

19. Bowlby, 1961a; 1961b; 1963.

20. Freud, 1917.

21. Freud, 1913; 1939.

22. Feifel, 1959.

23. G. Gorer, *Death, Grief, and Mourning,* New York: Doubleday, 1965.

24. Mohr, 1952; Wolf, 1958.

25. Unpublished research on children's reactions to the death of a parent, referred to above.

26. Hess and Easton, 1960; Greenstein, 1965.

27. We might suggest that, among other meanings of the television at this time, it served as a homely, familiar object to hang onto. It had something of

the consoling effect that a favorite blanket has to a lonely and anxious child. Cf. Winnicott (1951) on transitional objects.

28. Greenberg and Parker, 1965.

29. Erikson, 1950.

30. Mead, 1955.

31. Freud, 1905; Fenichel, 1945; Erikson, 1959; Blos, 1962.

32. Piaget, 1926, 1928; Inhelder and Piaget, 1958; Wolff, 1960.

33. A. Freud, 1954.

LIST OF REFERENCES

Abraham, K. 1924. "A Short History of the Development of the Libido, viewed in the Light of Mental Disorders." In *Selected Papers on Psychoanalysis*, pp. 418–501. London: Hogarth Press, 1942.

Baker, G. W. and D. W. Chapman. 1962. ed's. *Man and Society in Disaster*. New York: Basic Books.

Bowlby, J. 1961a. "Processes of Mourning," *International Journal of Psychoanalysis*, XLII, 317–40.

———— 1961b. "Childhood Mourning and its Implication for Psychiatry," *American Journal of Psychiatry*, CXVIII, 481–98.

———— 1963. "Pathological Mourning and Childhood Mourning," *Journal of the American Psychoanalytic Association*, XI, 451–73.

Blos, P. 1962. *On Adolescence*. Glencoe: The Free Press.

Caplan, G. 1961. ed. *Prevention of Mental Disorders in Children*. New York: Basic Books.

———— 1964. *Principles of Preventive Psychiatry*. New York: Basic Books.

de Grazia, S. 1945. "A Note on the Psychological Position of the Chief Executive," *Psychiatry*, VIII, 267–72.

Erikson, E. 1950. *Childhood and Society*. New York: Norton.

———— 1959. *Identity and the Life Cycle*. New York: International Universities Press.

Fairbairn, W. R. D. 1936. "The Effect of a King's Death upon Patients undergoing Analysis." In *An Object-Relations Theory of Personality*. New York: Basic Books, 1954.

Feifel, H. 1959. ed. *The Meaning of Death*. New York: McGraw-Hill.

Fenichel, O. 1945. *The Psychoanalytic Theory of Neurosis*, pp. 33–113. New York: Norton.

Fleming, J. and S. Altschul. 1963. "Activation of Mourning and Growth by Psychoanalysis," *International Journal of Psychoanalysis*, XLIV, 419–31.

Freud, A. and D. Burlingham. 1943. *War and Children*. New York: International Universities Press.

—————— and D. Burlingham. 1944. *Infants Without Families*. New York: International Universities Press.

—————— and S. Dann. 1951. "An Experience in Group Upbringing." In *The Psychoanalytic Study of the Child*, VI, 127–68.

—————— 1954. "Psychoanalysis and Education": Freud Memorial Lecture, New York, May 1954. Abstract in *The Psychoanalytic Study of the Child*, IX, 9–15. New York: International Universities Press.

Freud, S. 1905. *Three Essays on Sexuality*. Standard Edition, VII, 125–43. London: Hogarth Press.

—————— 1913. *Totem and Taboo*. Standard Edition, XIII, 1–161. London: Hogarth Press.

—————— 1917. "Mourning and Melancholia." Standard Edition, XIV, 237–58. London: Hogarth Press.

—————— 1939. *Moses and Monotheism*. New York: Knopf.

Greenberg, B. S. and E. B. Parker. 1965. eds. *The Kennedy Assassination and the American Public: Social Communication in Crisis*. Stanford: Stanford University Press.

Greenstein, F. I. 1965. *Children and Politics*. New Haven: Yale University Press.

Gyomroi, E. L. 1963. "The Analysis of a Young Concentration Camp Victim." In *The Psychoanalytic Study of the Child*, XVIII, 484–510. New York: International Universities Press.

Hellman, I. 1962. "Hampstead Nursery Follow-up Studies: 1. Sudden Separation and its Effect Followed over Twenty Years." In *The Psychoanalytic Study of the Child*, XVII, 159–74. New York: International Universities Press.

Hess, R. D. and D. Easton. 1960. "The Child's Changing Image of the President," *Public Opinion Quarterly*, XXIV, 632–44.

Hilgard, J. R. and M. F. Newman. 1963. "Early Parental Deprivation as a Functional Factor in the Etiology of Schizophrenia and Alcoholism," *American Journal of Orthopsychiatry*, XXXIII, 409–20.

Inhelder, B. and J. Piaget. 1958. *The Growth of Logical Thinking from Childhood to Adolescence*. New York: Basic Books.

Janis, I. 1951. *Air War and Emotional Stress: Psychological Studies of Bombing and Civilian Defense*. New York: McGraw-Hill.

Johannsen, D. E. 1946. "Reactions to the Death of President Roosevelt," *Journal of Abnormal and Social Psychology*, XLI, 218–22.

Lindemann, E. 1944. "The Symptomatology and Management of Acute Grief," *American Journal of Psychiatry*, CI, 141–48.

Mahler, M. S. 1961. "On Sadness and Grief in Infancy and Childhood." In *The Psychoanalytic Study of the Child*, XVI, 332–51.

Mead, M. 1955. "Theoretical Setting—1954." In *Childhood in Contemporary Cultures*. Edited by Margaret Mead and Martha Wolfenstein, pp. 3–20. Chicago: University of Chicago Press.

Mohr, G. J. 1952. *When Children Face Crises*. Chicago: Science Research Associates.

Orlansky, H. 1947. "Reactions to the Death of President Roosevelt," *Journal of Social Psychology*, 235–66.

Piaget, J. 1926. *The Language and Thought of the Child*. London: Routledge and Kegan Paul.

———— 1928. *Judgment and Reasoning in the Child*. New York: Harcourt Brace.

Robertson, J. 1958. *Young Children in Hospitals*. New York: Basic Books.

Sheatsley, P. B. and J. J. Feldman. 1964. "The Assassination of President Kennedy: A Preliminary Report of Public Reactions and Behavior," *Public Opinion Quarterly*, XXVII, 189–215.

Spitz, R. A. 1946. "Anaclitic Depression." In *The Psychoanalytic Study of the Child*, II, 313–44. New York: International Universities Press.

Titmuss, R. M. 1950. *Problems of Social Policy*. London: His Majesty's Stationery Office.

Wallace, A. F. C. 1956. *Tornado in Worcester: An Exploratory Study of Individual and Community Behavior in an Extreme Situation*. Washington: National Academy of Sciences–National Research Council.

Winnicott, D. W. 1951. "Transitional Objects and Transitional Phenomena." In *Collected Papers*. New York: Basic Books, 1958.

Wolf, A. W. M. 1958. *Helping Your Child to Understand Death*. New York: Child Study Association of America.

Wolfenstein, M. 1957. *Disaster: A Psychological Essay*. Glencoe: The Free Press.

Wolff, P. H. 1960. *The Developmental Psychologies of Jean Piaget and Psychoanalysis*. New York: International Universities Press.

Zborowski, M. 1952. "Cultural Components in Responses to Pain," *Journal of Social Issues*, VIII, 16–30.

CHILDREN
AND THE
DEATH OF A PRESIDENT

1

Young Teen-agers' Responses to the Assassination of President Kennedy: Relation to Previous Life Experiences[1]

SYLVIA GINSPARG, ALICE MORIARTY, and LOIS B. MURPHY

Peggy is a thirteen-year-old girl who, like nearly all Middle Western children, heard about the assassination of Kennedy at school shortly after it occurred. Three days after the funeral she sent her account of her reactions in a questionnaire; it was a report of feelings that were similar at many points to those of other young teenagers in the predominantly Republican Middle Western area where she lives, while at other points her feelings and thoughts were uniquely her own. The following is a verbatim record of her report (including her misspellings):

I thought the girl that had told me was joking and I started laughing but when I found out she wasn't I thought how horrible it was that it should happen in our country and I wondered what kind of maniac would do a thing like that.

I had an empty feeling like when you try hard to win something and then lose. I wanted to talk to somebody to see how they felt about it, and to see if other kids my age were as concerned about it as I was, if they realized what I what a horrible thing this was to the entire world. (I was in office work and there is only one other boy with me and he didn't have much to say.)

In sixth hour most of the kids around me were in tears. We talked about it the whole hour and they were worried about whether Kruchev was behind this or not and how easily it would be for Castro to take over the government.

I think that little John didn't exactly know what was going on but Caroline is just alittle younger than I was when my mother died and I know that she feels a deep loss and knows that she'll never see her father again but she doesn't realize how deeply this will affect her for the rest of her life. I feel Mrs. Kennedy being deeply relegious has taken it as a devout Christian but also with pride, that he died doing a job for his country.

I feel *Oswald should of had a trial and be sentenced by a jury.* To me he should be put to death either by an electric chair or hanging but lots of kids thought up all sorts of tortures to put him to.

My first thought was now the Russians and Castro won't believe that he did it since he wasn't tried and they will say that an extreme rightest killed him.

I feel *Ruby should be tried and sentenced.* In a way I don't blame him but he sure did mess up things!

I watched TV about 15 hours.

I felt that Kennedy was just one person and that because he was president was no reason to stop other people's enjoyment. After all they don't stop all programs on Sunday. Sunday is God's day and God is *much greater* then *any* President.

This will make me appreciate the president (any president) more even if I won't like the way he runs the country.

It will make the (American) people wonder what our country is coming to and help everyone be more patriotic.

It will show (the people of the world) that although our leader dies our system of government won't die but a new president will take his place, and that we will join together even more as a nation instead of falling apart with everyone grabbing for power like there would be in Russia.

It made me want to be a better citizen, to be more patriotic, and not talk about someone unless I know both sides of it.

Similarities to and differences from the replies of other children will be apparent as we review the latter. Peggy's report is one of approximately 2500 received from children in this area. Fifty-seven came from normal children whose development has been studied from infancy,[2] and it is this group with which we are concerned here, together with records from disturbed children receiving in-patient treatment at the Children's Hospital.

After the assassination of Kennedy on November 22, 1963, our research staff wondered what had been the reactions of the approximately 60 normal young teen-agers (aged 13 to 15) we had been following for more than a decade. We know a great deal about the thought processes, coping styles, defense structure, and adaptation patterns of these children. We have numerous reports on their reactions as individuals and as groups of preschool, latency, and prepuberty-aged children to environmental disasters (such as floods and tornadoes), to family experiences and stresses (birth of siblings; death, illness, or divorce of parents; accidents resulting in physical injury or discomfort; moving to new neighborhoods or communities, etc.). We thought that the assassination of the President might have been more dramatic and potentially more threatening than anything else that has happened to most of the children in the normal group.

The death of a President was in a sense more removed from them than personal family losses through illness, death, or divorce, yet reactions to this immediate situation and the events following it might well give us more understanding about their deeper reactions to loss as well as their feelings on a range of topics including authority, law and order, capital punishment, and issues of personal responsibility in a complex world. Along with this, we felt that the personality of John Fitzgerald Kennedy and his family was so vivid and well publicized through the media of radio, TV, and newspapers that no child could be unaffected or without some feelings and thoughts about these events. The very facts that the President and Mrs. Kennedy were approximately the same age as their own parents and that there were two young children in the White House might make the presidential home more meaningful and closer to children, particularly because reporters kept the public aware of a variety of small details and everyday occurrences: the Kennedy baby had died a few weeks earlier; Caroline had a pony named Macaroni and numerous pets; little John John was allowed to play under his father's desk and saluted soldiers at Arlington; Mrs. Kennedy had conducted a tour of the White House on television; Mr. Kennedy liked sailboats and sat in a rocking chair; and so forth. Regardless of positive or negative feelings about politics and religion, Mr. Kennedy might have been as real to Topeka children as their teacher or pastor.

It was with these thoughts in mind that we drew up a questionnaire which we hoped to administer to our small sample, whose reactions could be checked against years of personal history, test results, and conference notes, and also to a larger child sample which might then serve to highlight differences or similarities in the reactions of the experimental sample and other children (of comparable ages) from public and parochial schools and from a Children's Hospital for Disturbed Children. As noted above, this report deals chiefly with the responses from the intensively studied, normal sample.

The questionnaire was mailed on Monday, the day of the funeral, and reached the Topeka children the next day. Fifty-seven responses—of 60 questionnaires mailed—were returned within approximately ten days.

The Questionnaire

A review of the questionnaire, item by item, will explain the purpose of the questions and some of the most general trends of the answers. These trends will help to set in perspective details of individual answers.

1. How and when did you first hear that J.F.K. was shot?

    This was an entirely factual item not calling for the expression of feeling. It simply oriented the child toward the task at hand. Barring illness, we could assume that most children first heard the news at school. This proved to be true.

2a. How did you feel about the news that John F. Kennedy was shot?

2b. How did you feel when you later learned that J.F.K. was dead?

    Here we were seeking a measure of the emotional impact, first of hearing the news that the President was shot and second of hearing that he was dead. For many children, these questions were treated as a unit, but for some children answers to the first question reflected room for hope or denial. Denial was still a possible reaction to the definite news of death, but hope was no longer possible. Assuming there was an emotional response, we can then ask about its form and quality.

3. How did the student sitting next to you or the person you met feel upon hearing the news?

4. How do you think Mrs. Kennedy and the children feel?

    These questions were designed to explore the child's feelings through his projections as to what an acquaintance of his or the family of the murdered man might have felt. Where differences appeared, we might see some distinction between conscious and unconscious feelings. We were especially interested to see whether the children overtly identified with Mrs. Kennedy or the children or both or were unable to identify with either.

5. Question 5 was concerned with feelings about the killer. There were three parts to this item:

a. What do you think should have been done with the killer?
b. How did you feel when you learned that he had been shot?
c. How should the killer's assassin be treated?

Here we were seeking to learn something about the children's attitudes in regard to law and order, sense of justice, capital punishment, and perhaps appreciation of mental health problems. We wondered whether these feelings were general or whether they varied in relation to the specific case. Were feelings different about the appropriate treatment of an assassin who deprived the world of a well-known figure and the murderer of an unknown, apparently disturbed, individual? How much did the children identify with Ruby, who perhaps committed an act they might have condoned or even wished to commit themselves? The lawlessness and lack of control in Ruby's retaliation may have been especially upsetting to many, especially if they experienced or felt anger at any level.

6. Did you listen to TV and/or radio broadcasts? How much? (Estimate the number of hours.)

This was on the surface a factual question but the number of hours spent in listening to newscasts might reflect intensity of concern, curiosity about the series of events, including the funeral, the attitudes of the parents or guardians, or other nuances of motivation.

7. How did you feel when many usual programs or activities were canceled?

We included this specific question after hearing from one of our subjects that he was angry when his usual TV programs were discontinued. We wondered whether this was general or the feeling of only a few children.

Questions 8, 9, and 10 were designed to investigate maturity of thinking and feelings of responsibility.

8. What do you think will be the effect of the President's death a.) on you, b.) on the country, c.) on the world?

We wondered to what extent the child moved beyond his immediate feelings toward a consideration of the larger implications of the tragedy. How did he see his own role in society as related to these issues? Was there a sense of guilt? If so, how was it expressed? Did the child feel that the effect was temporary or pervasive and probably would be of long duration?

9. Did you feel that you wanted to do something after hearing of the death of the President? If so, what?

This aimed at seeking information as to ways in which the child coped with the feelings he had. It seemed to us that with some children feelings might have been expressed or held in control by actions. We wondered how much children sought reassurance from their parents or from their religion. We were also interested in determining whether children preferred to be alone, with their friends or family, and how much they sought verbal interchange.

10. Do you think the President's death could have been prevented? If so, what could have prevented it or what should have been done?

Here we were mainly interested in the degree of concreteness of the replies. Beyond this, it seemed to us that such a question might be an indication of feelings of guilt and individual responsibility. We wondered whether the children, like many adults to whom we talked, made efforts to shift the blame for the assassination to groups representing feelings or values different from their own.

11. Were there things about Mr. Kennedy as a person which you did not like to see in him?

This question was disapproved by several adult administrators with whom the questionnaire was discussed. Presumably there was some feeling that it was unwise or lacking in taste to report anything negative about someone dead. From a strictly logical point of view, criticisms if valid in life should be valid after death. Thus, inability to respond to a question such as this suggested that there might be unhealthy repression or denial. We wondered specifically whether children might be able to isolate aspects of Mr. Kennedy's personality or background that were negative in their eyes, such as his religion, his politics, or his liberal tendencies.

12. Give one word or a short phrase which best describes Kennedy as you saw him.

By this question we hoped to get at positive or negative feelings about the President and beyond this we were interested in the terms in which these were expressed.

Comments on the Questionnaire

Our study focused primarily on *feelings* about Kennedy's death, the assassin, the killer of the assassin, Kennedy's family; impulses and ways of handling feelings; expectations about impacts on self, the nation, and the world; ideas about how it could have been prevented.

The children's responses are of interest from several points of view:

1.) To help us understand how these young adolescents experienced the President's death, as one addition to our view of the involvement of the young in matters of national welfare.

2.) To provide an additional source of data on the personalities of children whose emotional and mental health we had been studying—data unique in that it came from a sudden disturbing event to which all the children were exposed in a more or less similar way.

3.) With our group whose emotional development had already been studied, the data could throw light on precursors of, or factors contributing to, certain typical or unusual individual differences in reaction.

Group Results

Typical feelings reported as arising after the first announcement of the attack were negation, or disbelief with a reality-testing quality, shock, sadness, anger, and denial as a defense after the fact was established. Abhorrence of the aggressive act or shame that it happened here were also frequent; more rare were reports of initially feeling sick or numb, or a sense of personal loss. Feelings experienced after the President was reported dead included: disbelief (33⅓ per cent), while more than earlier (another one third) reported sadness; several "felt like crying" and more reported that others cried. One girl commented that "some kids were crying and not ashamed to show it," implying that others might have cried if not inhibited by the need to appear grown-up and controlled. The low proportion who admitted crying contrasts with the NORC report on adults. In an earlier psychiatric interview one girl had regarded feelings as messy and could not let herself cry because crying made her feel worse.

In this group of 57, children who did not interpose reality testing, and/or denial mechanisms, between their initial hearing of the report and accepting it were a minority. Half a dozen children who reported direct acceptance of the news of Kennedy's death appear to be, if anything, too ready to believe bad news. All but one of these children had experienced loss of a parent by death or deprivation due to the mother's severe or prolonged illness, or deprivation of attention from the mother when too many babies came too fast. They knew from bitter experience that trouble is part of life.

Children who expressed "disbelief" and those who defined their feelings as "shock" with little or no elaboration might seem to be falling back on clichés to define their reactions. Most of the children, however, gave highly individualized descriptions of their feelings, among which were the following:

> I felt very sad to think how civilized our country is and to know that someone killed the leader of our country.

> I was completely shaken, it took me several days to get used to the fact that he was no longer alive.

> I felt sorry for Mrs. Kennedy and the two Kennedy children.

> When I heard that the president had died I felt *a great sense of loss,* was very sorry.

> When I heard that J.F.K. was dead I was filled with sadness and disgust. I hated the man who did it.

> Everything was obliterated but the voice on the radio and the possibility that the report was wrong. It took me nearly a week to fully assimilate the fact, however.

> It was such a shock. I really felt bad. No one really knew to much about it and I just felt the U.S. was coming to its end.

> Terrible nightmare. I thought, oh well, it couldn't be true, but it was. That is my honest opinion of how I felt at the time. I felt kind of scared too, but I don't know why.

> There was a hollow empty pit in the middle of my stomach. I was just numb and stunned.

> I felt as if a living part of me had died.

> I felt awful and thought that it might lead to war but I still couldn't believe it.

> When I heard that J.F.K. was dead, I was very grieved and perhaps a little angry that a thing like this could happen in my country.

> I felt so funny on the inside when I heard President Kennedy was dead. It was as if someone had taken my breath away.

> When I heard he was dead I was sad and felt like crying but I didn't.

> I had a very strange feeling, of a sort of shock.

The concrete and vivid detail of the children's replies, each in his own words—made possible by the open-ended questions—

communicates a sense of validity. Cliché responses were few although the essential content of many responses was similar.

When asked how their neighbors or friends reacted, about half of the children reported sadness, while 28 per cent indicated shock, and slightly more, anger. This suggests that it is easier for young teen-agers to recognize or to admit deep feelings in others than in themselves.

Seventy-five per cent attributed grief of varying degrees to Mrs. Kennedy, and over half of the children (31) showed some identification with both Mrs. Kennedy and the children. One boy (an only child whose father died before he was born) discussed only Mrs. Kennedy's loss. The majority of the group felt the Kennedy children had suffered an irreparable loss.

In contrast with Nemtzow's findings,[3] none of our children explicitly identified with Oswald; a few wanted to catch the killer. Sixty-three per cent, however, emphasized *justice* or normal legal procedures in dealing with the killer, while most of the others emphasized punishment or execution; in a few instances, suffering, or severe punishment by slow death, was suggested. Disturbed children (from the Children's Hospital) suggested bizarre punishments aimed to extend suffering.

The majority regretted Oswald's murder, most frequently because he *should have had a trial,* or because more could have been learned about his motivation. Six children felt that he should have suffered more (one of them, Ida, said he should have been "brainwashed"). Nine (16 per cent) were glad of the murder; two of them had previously mentioned that he deserved death. For Oswald's killer, *72 per cent emphasized the need for justice;* over one fourth felt he deserved maximum punishment, while a few minimized his crime.

One eighth of the children felt the experience would have a far-reaching effect on them, or cause an improvement, and almost a third simply felt it would make a lasting impression, while over half foresaw little or no change. *Almost half of the children felt it would have a far-reaching effect or cause improvement in the country, and the world, bringing peace, better feelings and relations,* more closeness between Negroes and whites, etc. Almost one sixth had pessimistic forebodings: it might lead to war; it might give other countries the impression that we're a bunch of nuts; it might lower our stature in the world, it might bring nuclear war closer, etc.

Almost half of the children felt there was nothing to do about the disaster and entertained no wish or impulse to do anything, and among these, six felt emotionally overwhelmed. But 51 per cent of the children expressed active impulses: with nine children there were *vengeful* feelings of wanting to catch or kill the assassin, or attack the schoolmates who were hostile to Kennedy; nine others wanted to comfort or *help* the family. All but two of these teen-agers with vengeful impulses were girls; no boy in the group had "helpful" impulses in the sense of offering comfort; two boys wanted to kill the assassin. Five boys and one girl wanted to *pray*. One girl who also wanted to kill the assassin "wanted to die": "I felt there was no reason for living. It seemed to me that life was over for everything." Five boys by contrast wanted to find out more about it and to *understand*.

There were differences between children who were overwhelmed and those whose feelings were contained or suppressed; children who hoped for constructive results from the event as opposed to those with pessimistic views about its impact, and children whose ideas of how it might have been prevented implied a wish for external protection as contrasted with those who felt the individual should protect himself.

In some children, the event seemed to evoke deep conflicts and to loosen defenses; this helped us to see residues of early emotional experiences: feelings of sorrow, anger, tenderness, despair, or shame. In other children, there were impulses of retaliation, sadistic revenge; or wishes to comfort, help, pray, or try to learn more and to understand. Disorganizing tension in certain children contrasted with the swift mobilization of active wishes, hopes, or impulses in others.

Some Factors Involved in Feelings of Loss

Before discussing broader or deeper developmental or characterological factors in responses of individuals whose reported reactions differed from the main trend, let us look briefly at some factors involved in the few explicit expressions of loss. Of the children who specifically mentioned such feelings, half fell into the "helpful" group while *none* was found in the vengeful group, suggesting that the aggressive angry feelings of revenge allow no room for either feelings of loss, suffering, or need, or the empathic projection of such feelings which evoke corrective impulses to comfort or to help.

Anita, who said first that she wanted to kill the assassin, then that she felt like dying, is a striking example of the close association between the wish for aggressive revenge and feelings of helplessness or despair. Ida, who felt helpless and abandoned as a year-old infant when a sibling was born before she was able to manage for herself, revealed a similar association of vengeful and helpless feelings.

There was some evidence that girls experience loss differently than boys (or that girls have lower thresholds for experiencing loss) although this needs to be checked on a larger sample. It was a girl whose parents had recently been divorced who said, "I felt as if a living part of me had died." Another girl whose mother works full time and is relatively unavailable, usually appears comfortable on the surface, but was among those expressing a sense of personal loss at the death of the President. Another girl who also felt loss had moved recently, losing friends in the process.

In keeping with the stoical defenses of denial and proud self-control maintained by the boys who, as we saw, referred crying to the girls, only one boy specifically mentioned a sense of loss. His parents had threatened divorce at one time. Two boys and one girl who had suffered intensely from the loss of a parent by death or divorce some years earlier did not mention feelings of loss. One of these children had attempted to master his feelings by consciously "trying to forget," while another had eagerly attached himself to the substitute parent, and the third had developed a massive resentful constriction after a previously reserved but dependent relationship with his mother. With these children defenses against actual personal loss were so firm and massive that no room was left for experiencing a new loss.

Individual Patterns of Response

The full individual quality of the experience of the event is reflected in a digest of several questionnaires:

Wayne is one of five children in an intact Catholic family. His father is a carpenter. This boy's concise phrases revealed intense feelings of retaliation, although his answers showed no disorganization, no anticipation of long-term severe effects, and no other evidence of disturbance in reaction to the tragedy:

> One of my teachers told me in school about 1:30 . . . I thought that he was shot in the arm or leg . . . I didn't think my teacher was telling the truth . . .
>
> (Person next to me?) He acted as if it were a joke.
>
> (Kennedy family feels?) Mrs. Kennedy was probably horrified but the children probaby did not understand it.
>
> (Done with killer?) I think he should be *electricuted*.
>
> (Done with Oswald's assassin?) As any other killer.
>
> (Watched TV?) About 25 hours.
>
> (Feel about cancellation of programs?) I thought it a wonderful tribute but I wanted to see the football games Sat. and Sun.
>
> (Effect on you?) I don't think there will be any effect on me.
>
> (On country?) Its a great loss to the country but he is being replaced by a capable leader.
>
> (On the world?) Other countries will now protect their leaders better.
>
> (Felt like doing something?) I felt that I wanted to kill the president's assassin.
>
> (Any way to prevent it?) No. If someone would risk their own life to kill him they could easily kill the president.
>
> (Criticisms?) No.
>
> (Opinion of J.F.K.?) A great American leader.

Neal is the oldest of three children whose father is in life insurance; this is the family in which the parents talked of separation but did not carry it through. As a preschool child Neal found it much harder to separate from his mother than Wayne did, although in his cautious reactions to new situations Wayne seemed quite similar to Neal. Neal's emotional responses as reported by him were pervasive, with deeper sadness, a fantasy of restoration, a warmer, more elaborated appreciation of Kennedy, and a capacity to balance his sadness with thoughts of gratitude for what Kennedy had done:

> When I heard that President Kennedy had been shot I was very unhappy and could not see why anyone would want to shoot President Kennedy. When I heard that the President had died I felt a great sense of loss, was very sorry.

(Others felt?) They felt the same way I did, some with tears in their eyes.

(Kennedy family feels?) The children do not understand very well but I think Mrs. Kennedy was hurt more than any of us.

(Done with the killer?) I think the killer should have been imprisoned for life or be put to death.

(Feel about Oswald's killer?) I was not happy but did not want him to be shot by a civilian. I think the killer's assassin was partially insane and should be imprisoned. The killer could also be a Communist and killed Oswald to keep him from saying anything more.

(Watched TV?) Yes, for about 22 hours in all.

(Feel about programs canceled?) I did not care because I wanted to find out as much about the President's assassination as possible.

(Effect on you?) I will always feel unhappy at the President's death.

(On country?) I think our country will always be thankful for President Kennedy.

(On world?) I think the world will always remember President Kennedy and the work he did.

(Felt like doing something?) Yes, I wanted to, although I couldn't, bring the president back to life.

(Any way to prevent it?) Yes, by putting up the bullet-proof top in his car although he did not like it.

(Criticisms?) No, there were not any that I can remember.

(Opinion of J.F.K.?) Great President. I think he was one of the best presidents of the United States for the help he gave the Negro and for the preservation of peace between the major powers of the earth.

Roger responded less with a sense of personal loss, and more with sadness that such a thing could happen here; he reported more than average preoccupation with TV but kept himself differentiated from the events and anticipated no long-term effects:

(Feel when learned he was shot?) I couldn't believe it, that some *gey* would go and shoot President John F. Kennedy.

(Feel when learned he was dead?) I felt very sad to think how civilized our country is and to know that someone *kild* the leader of our country.

(Others felt?) He did not look like he felt *to* good.

(Kennedy family feels?) I think they felt very very sad.

(Done with killer?) I think that should *by* sent to the electric chair as *some* as they *gethered* all the evidence they need to prove he was guilty.

(Feeling when learned killer was shot?) I felt that the *gey* who shot Oswald was part of the killing of the President and he didn't want Oswald to tell what he knew.

(Done with Oswald's assassin?) I think he should be *sentence* to life in prison.

(Watched TV?) Yes, I *watch* it about 25 hours.

(Feel about cancellation of programs?) I didn't mind it because they would be on next week.

(Effect on you?) I don't think it make an *efect* on me because I think Johnson will take his place *farely* well.

(Effect on country?) I think won't have *to* much of a *efect* because they have a well *qualifed* leader, Johnson.

(Effect on world?) I don't think of any *efect* as long as we still have a President.

(Felt like doing something?) No.

(Any way to prevent it?) Yes, I think that if he had his bullet-proof car in the parade, that he would not have been shot.

(Criticisms?) No.

(Opinion of J.F.K.?) Thoughtful.

Chris's reiteration of feeling "a little sick," difficulty in accepting the fact, projection of "feeling a little sick" to Mrs. Kennedy, very high preoccupation with TV, and wish to have actively gone to the funeral, all point to far more personal involvement, with a diffuse psychosomatic reaction:

(How and when heard of shooting?) I didn't think it had really happened. I didn't think that it could happen.

(Feel when learned he was shot?) I was a little sick that some person would do such a thing.

(Feel when learned he was dead?) I didn't really believe it even though I knew it happened.

(Others felt?) Most people in my English class were quiet. My English teacher cried after she heard he was dead.

(Kennedy family feels?) I think Mrs. Kennedy feels like most of the people in the World and is a little sick and sorry.

(Done with killer?) I think he should had a trial and if found guilty sentenced to a slow death.

(Feeling when learned killer was shot?) I was glad he had been shot.

(Done with Oswald's assassin?) I think he should be tried IF found guilty sentenced to prison (10–15 years).

(Watched TV?) Out of a total of 72 hours I listened to radio and t.v. 49 HOURS. app.

(Feel about cancellation of programs?) I was a little disappointed although I knew it (TV) would.

(Effect on you?) I was a little sick and mostly sick.

(Effect on country?) *Fiancel problems.*

(Effect on world?) I haven't thought much on world *situcation.*

(Felt like doing something?) I would have liked to have gone to his funeral.

(Any way to prevent it?) I think that if *he* bubble had been used it might have been prevented or at least he wouldn't have been hurt as badly.

(Criticisms?) No!

(Opinion of J.F.K.?) A great and *intellegent* person who could have helped the United States a great deal.

While Brad showed a temporary somatic response, this was neither so diffuse nor so persistent; he maintained a thoughtful perspective on the situation, differentiating between his immediate and later responses, and his current as opposed to his anticipated future feelings:

When the news of President Kennedy having been shot came over the P.A., I felt shocked and couldn't believe it. . . . I felt so funny on the inside when I heard President Kennedy was dead. It was as if someone had taken my breath away.

(Others felt?) Everyone in my class was quiet. Between periods and after school its usually noisy in the halls, but after the announcement everyone was quiet.

(Kennedy family feels?) I imagine the children and Mrs. Kennedy are very sad about the death of father and husband.

(Done with killer?) I first thought the police should of hunt this man down and shot him, but after thinking it over I thought he should be given A FAIR TRIAL.

(Feeling when learned killer shot?) I first felt he got just what he deserved but now I know that this will hurt our country more than the assassination.

(Done with Oswald's assassin?) I feel he should be given A FAIR TRIAL.

(Watched TV?) I listened to both T.V. and radio during this tragic time. I would estimate the time to be around 23 hours not counting the day of the funeral and around 29 hours counting Monday, the day of the funeral.

(Feel about cancellation of programs?) I feel the broadcasting companies paid a wonderful tribute to the President.

(Effect on you?) I believe the effect of the President's death will effect me when I'm older. Now it is the idea of losing a great man and leader.

(Effect on country?) I believe this event will either bring our countrymen closer together or perhaps weaken us. I think it will depend on how our people support President Johnson.

(Effect on world?) I think the world is going to observe our country and us more carefully than ever. I imagine these people are wondering even more what kind of people we are and if we are going to give up because our President was assassinated or if we are going to support and follow our new President.

(Felt like doing something?) Yes, I wish I could of met President Kennedy personally and after his death I would have liked to of *payed* my respects at his funeral.

(Any way to prevent it?) No, I don't think the President's death could of been *provented*.

(Criticisms?) I admired President Kennedy very much and can *fine* nothing I disliked about him.

(Opinion of J.F.K.?) I saw President Kennedy as a brilliant man and leader. I thought President Kennedy was more common than most Presidents.

Up to this point we have illustrated both such general trends as the frequent reports of shocked, sad feelings reported by many children and the deeply rooted cultural values reflected in the children's emphasis on justice; and also nuances of individual experiences. There were variations in the intensity of feelings as well as in content. While some children reflected the political and religious identifications of their families, many children's responses differed at certain points from those of their mothers. A separate report will deal with these relationships.

Factors Contributing to Individual Differences in Response

Individual differences in the quality of feeling varied with differences in temperament; in deeply established tendencies to use certain defense mechanisms including reaction-formation, projection and displacement as well as denial; in incompletely resolved conflicts, and unconscious needs. To understand such personal variations in the patterns of response we must consider the backgrounds of the children's emotional orientations; specifically, precursors of tendencies toward vengeful or helpful reactions.

For some children, perhaps, the distance of the event, the fact that the loss or threat was shared with many others, that it did not immediately threaten their personal lives, that the adults they observed did not try to hide their distress, loosened the barriers against expressing their feelings. Thus, in some instances we were shown emotions that they had not shown us during the years we had known them. This appears to be the case with Anita, who said she "wanted to die and felt there was no reason for living— it seemed that life was over for everything," an expression of a mood never directly communicated to us in any other situation. On the surface this seems to be an extreme response for a girl who had not, like some others, lost a parent by death or divorce— a girl who had been active in school, church, and other teen-age activities and had made very active and successful efforts to correct special physical blemishes, thus apparently both using opportunities and coping vigorously with her problems.

But her response can be better understood when we review her infantile vulnerability—an unplanned, puny, poorly functioning baby whose mother already had handsome, successful teen-age daughters and interesting sons. What little security Anita had probably came from her father, and, according to her, from the family of a neighboring playmate, a girl to whom she was still attached after years during which both families moved to other cities. The following is a digest of the sequence of her responses with comments:

Anita, fifteen, tenth grade

2. a. "I didn't know the seriousness of the injury, so I didn't feel too upset."

   b. "It was such a shock. I really felt bad. No one really knew *to* much about it and I just felt the U.S. was coming to its end." (She seems to have pushed aside the possibility of real danger to President Kennedy at first, perhaps as part of a pattern of attempting to maintain a sensible point of view. But when the fact of his death was inescapable her reaction was one of the most extreme among these children. She felt *shocked* and severely disturbed about the consequences she assumed would ensue for the country.)

3. She felt others shared her feelings. "We all felt sorry for Mrs. Kennedy and her two children." (She is capable of sympathy, though this seems weaker than her later reported feelings of loss and her impulse toward direct aggression. Note responses to questions 5 and 8.)

4. "I think they *fell* terrible, like its going to be very hard to go on living without someone they love and need." (Emotional impact here is great; loss of love and protection emerges as a threat so great as to imperil living.)

5. a. Oswald "should have been questioned to find out what motivated him in doing such an act. He should have gone through
the suffering of *intarigation,* and later execution." (She would
like to know the origins of aggression, perhaps the more so because she has suffered a good deal of verbal barrage from her
mother.)

b. Killing of Oswald: "I was just sick. I didn't want him to get out
of it so easily. . . . The U.S. looks like a fool to the rest of the
world. It was very foolish for the Dallas police to let anyone be
around while he was being moved." (Her feelings are so strong
as to produce physical sensations of illness. Inadequate control
by the police causes loss of status. One should stay alert to possible aggression. These statements need to be seen in relation to
her own struggles with her siblings, particularly the next older
brother from whom she needed protection.)

c. "He [Ruby] should be executed, and I wish they'd get it over.
I can't stand to *here* about it all the time." (Along with a wish to
punish, there is a limit to her tolerance for discussion of the aggressive event. If feeling cannot be avoided, then let it be brief;
feelings of this intensity can be overwhelming, especially when
the stimuli are so immediate and persistent. Note misspelling of
"hear"; it is not only the sound that threatens, but the immediacy.)

6-7. She listened to newscasts less than average probably because her
feelings were too intense to allow her to maintain her surface poise.
Furthermore she was "bored" (another way of expressing her
limited tolerance of repeated discussion) and longed to "go on as
if nothing happened."

8. Effects: a.) personal—"I just wish it hadn't happened." (Then, her
feelings would not have been brought to the surface.)

b.) Greater precautions would be taken in the future and guilts
will be assuaged by memorials to Kennedy.

c.) "Everyone has lost someone they really liked. I think there will
be more of a strive for peace." (Strong sense of personal loss with
some possibility of unification through shared tragedy.)

9. (Want to do something?) "I felt I *wanted to kill* the person who
had done it (but I'd have waited until it was *time* for his execution). I also *wanted to die.* I felt there was no reason for living. It
seemed to me that life was over for everything." (Aggressive urges
come to the fore, but she modulates these in fantasy to achieve a
modicum of appropriateness [in contrast to Ruby's impetuous ac-
tion]. There are also strong pervasive feelings of discouragement,
depression and defeat.)

10. She is critical of Secret Service. (Her own strong feelings are handled in part by projecting blame.)

Anita's replies are complex. She is capable of some sympathy, but she is angry and vengeful toward aggressors who not only inflict physical harm, but hurt emotionally. Hence, they should suffer in kind through verbal barrage, emotional torment, and loss of life. She feels deprived of love and attention and would strike out, but she is also depressed, doubtless guilty at a deeper level about her impulse to retaliate and, in a sense, defeated. Hence she would like to retreat with ultimate finality, i.e., to die. She can recover some equilibrium through projection of blame and through identification with strength and wisdom, returning in the end to surface poise and avoidance of strong feeling through denial.

Incidentally, Anita's even, legible writing reflects her efforts to appear poised and is a concrete example of her characteristic motor restraint of underlying anger and depression.

In other children in the vengeful group we see similar combinations of early sensitivity and physiological discomfort, but with certain kinds of deprivation secondary to *restriction,* met by feelings of frustration, anger, and aggression. Ida, the most extreme of the vengeful girls in regard to the Kennedy assassination and also perhaps one of the most frank, had been extreme as a three-year-old who actually bit off the head of a celluloid baby doll in a play session. A frail premature baby, handled with exaggerated protectiveness and elaborate display as an infant, she had experienced both chronic and periodic strain and stress in an unstable family setting, with repeated shifts in alliances and moves from one home to another as each of five siblings was born in rapid succession. (She also felt "sick" at the Kennedy news; she had actually been nauseated and ill at the birth of each except the last of five siblings.) Here, as with Anita, it seems probable that this sudden distant event, with an implication of loss and deprivation, uncovered a deeper level of feeling than any of the usual research methods had revealed to us—a feeling doubtless determined by a multiplicity of factors including diffuse infantile rage in the earliest months, frustration of an actual need for the mother, and anger at the sibling responsible for Ida's initial "loss" of her mother.

A review of the sequence of Ida's responses reveals the persistence of the degree of intensity of the initial impact, but with the added note of disgust at first, then hate. Soon a compensating note of idealization, repeated several times through the report, is expressed through her admiration for Mrs. Kennedy, and virtual apotheosis of the former President himself—her reference to an almost perfect person seems to imply that he was almost Christ-like. The alternation of feelings of disgust and hatred on the one side, and adulation on the other, recurs as if reflecting a deep undercurrent in Ida herself, of self-loathing for her extreme impulses and fantasies of hostility and disgust compensated by an ego-ideal of exaggerated perfection. This combination of drives and defense can be partially understood in terms of the early deprivation she suffered at the arrival of a sibling just at the period when she was moving from an oral to an anal phase of psychosexual development; her chief gratification prior to the birth of the baby had been the narcissistic and perfectionistic grooming her mother gave her. At the age of six to seven years we have records of the unusual intensity of her religious preoccupations, loaded with anxiety and fear of purgatory and hell, doubtless exaggerated by her deep sense of guilt regarding her intense jealousy.

(How and when first heard J.F.K. shot?) In science at about 1:30. When I first heard about it I felt all sick in side. I just could not believe that the president was really shot. When I heard that JFK was dead I was filled with *saddness* and disgust. I hated the man who did it.

(Kennedy family feel?) The children are really too young to know what is really happening. I think Mrs. Kennedy is very sad but she does not show her emotions in public. I admire her greatly for this.

(Done with killer?) I think the killer should have been brainwashed.

(Feeling when killer shot?) I felt very sad and disgusted.

(Killer's assassin be treated?) I think he should get a term for life in jail.

(Watched TV?) I watched T.V. for about 10 hours.

(Feeling about programs canceled?) I think they should have been cancelled. Any decent American would rather watch reports on Kennedy than regular programs.

(Effect on you?) I think we have lost *one of our greatest men,* and everyone will always remember him.

(Effect on country?) Our country will not be run as well as if Kennedy were still here.

(Effect on world?) The world lost a man of much respect and *never will anyone be respected as much as Kennedy.*

(Feel you wanted to do something?) My heart was filled with hatred and I wanted to kill the assassin.

(Criticisms of J.F.K.?) I found no faults in Kennedy. To me he was almost a perfect man.

(Opinion of J.F.K.?) The greatest American that ever lived.

Not all children who had such a vulnerable infancy responded in the same way; others revealed helpful or comforting rather than vengeful impulses. Beth, for example, was a girl extremely susceptible to infection and, like Martha and Ginger, had a mother who had shown depressive tendencies when Beth was an infant, so that she experienced some early deprivation. Beth's warm wish to "take Jackie and the children in her arms to comfort them" seems to be an externalization and then meeting of her own earliest longings for comforting contact (some of which had been met by her father). In three other instances we found the urge to provide comfort and help, which was probably a mobilization of feelings growing out of *periods* of warm gratifying experiences in girls who, we had learned, experienced other periods of difficulty and deprivation. (This process was also seen in Beth, whose deep belief that bad things can turn into good things evolved partly from her experiences of being comforted by her grandmother at times of stress.)

These are Beth's specific responses:

I was in English class at school. We were giving book reports. Our principal said over the loud speaker, "Important announcement, (he repeated it), President Kennedy and Governor *Connaly* of Texas have just been shot."

I was stunned and shocked. I was not sure I had heard straight. . . . My jaw dropped several inches and I just sat motionless, dazed.

(Other persons feel?) Just as shocked and unbelieving as I did; sad.

(Kennedy family feel?) I should think that Mrs. Kennedy is still too dazed and numbed to know the full impact of what has happened. I do not think that the children understand what is going on or that their daddy is not coming back. Caroline might understand partially, but little John is too young to understand and will probably ask for his daddy one day soon.

(Done with killer?) I think they were going about things as best they could and I think they should have tried to shock him into realizing the terrible thing he had done.

(Feeling when learned killer shot?) I felt shocked that such a thing could happen with all those police around. I think it was a foolish thing and that Ruby gained nothing but trouble.

(Killer's assassin be treated?) I think that he should stand trial as any other killer would and should be treated as any other killer would.

(Watched TV?) Yes, I listened to the radio and watched tv a lot. Approximately 44 hrs. (quite a bit isn't it?)

(Feeling about programs canceled?) I thought that this was a good idea. He was our President.

(Effect on you?) It will make me think more.

(Effect on country?) It will make people wake up and better our country.

(Effect on world?) I hope it will make better feelings and relations.

(Feel you wanted to do something?) *Yes, I felt as if I wanted to take Caroline, John, and Jackie into my arms and comfort them.*

(Could it have been prevented?) Yes. If he had been more careful, had looked ahead, and had had his bubble top up he would still be living.

(Criticisms of J.F.K.?) No.

(Opinion of J.F.K.?) He was a good man and he had lived a good life.

Reviewing this sequence of responses we can see, on the one hand, the full awareness of her own intense feelings and their physical expressions, and the persistent urge to hold on to and to implement "good" and "better" aspects and sequelae of the traumatic event. "Comforting" the Kennedy family is thus not only an impulse to extend warm support, but part of a broader pattern of selecting, accenting, helping to make or create positive outcomes. In contrast to Anita, Beth makes no direct criticisms, nor does she offer any criticism at all of the authorities. It was Kennedy himself who should have been more careful. It might be added that six months after the Kennedy assassination, following the traumatic death of a sibling, it was Beth who actively supported and comforted her mother during the funeral and subsequently commented on her mother's need for this and inability to comfort her sorrowing children. This was a positive demonstration of the strength of such supportive patterns in Beth.

Findings like this from our exploration of a few individual cases prompted us to scrutinize more carefully the entire pattern of differences between the "vengeful" and the "helpful" group. Thirty-one children (56 per cent) handled their feelings by overt expression of anger or revenge or attempted to cope with compassionate feelings or wishes to help in ways that seemed personally meaningful. In addition to the examples already cited there were also these answers to the question "Did you feel you wanted to do something?":

Vengeance

PENELOPE: I felt as if I would like to do something to make some of the loudmouths at school be quiet. They were claiming they had killed President K., and some of them were saying ya! I don't think they really *ment* it.

AUDREY: Yes, I wanted revenge.

WAYNE: I felt that I wanted to kill the president's assassin.

CASSY: I don't know what maybe I wanted to catch the killer or retract what had happened and warn the president.

LEIGH: I felt like catching the man who did it.

DENNIS: I felt like hitting the assassin good and hard.

Helpful or Respectful Feelings

MARTHA: Helping and *confering* the two children because I love children.

LORI: I would of liked to make it easier for Mrs. K. and the children.

CLAUDIA: I felt like I wanted to be there and do something for Mrs. K., but I knew this was impossible. I felt absolutely helpless. [Note that Claudia felt both sympathetic and helpless.]

CORLISS: Anything that would be of help.

MILLY: I would have liked to have gone to Washington.

PATRICIA: I felt like sending Mrs. K. a letter showing my sorrow.

BRENDA: It made me want to be a better citizen, to be more patriotic and not talk about someone unless I knew both sides of it. [Possible guilt here; B. was very outspoken about what she had disapproved of in President Kennedy.]

GINGER: I didn't know. I don't think there's much I can do. More than anything I want to go straighten out this mess of a country, but I'm afraid I'd put it in a even more perilous position. [Feelings of insecurity are intermingled here and possibly some anger.]

Differences and similarities between the two groups included the following: On hearing that the President was shot, two thirds of the vengeful group responded in this manner, but there were also references to feeling of loss, injustice, and more emotional response.

These groups were similar in their tendency to perceive others as responding with some form of affect, two thirds of each group giving this response. While there was little difference between the two groups in their patterns of identification with the Kennedy family, the "vengeful" group showed a much greater tendency to attribute feelings of sadness and irreparable loss to Mrs. Kennedy and the children (seven of the nine giving this response).

There was far less homogeneity in the "helpful" group with only one third of this group expressing feelings of irreparable loss.

When asked what they thought should have been done with the killer, two thirds of the "helpful" group placed emphasis upon the need for *justice* or the normal course of legal proceedings. There were none who recommended execution without any need for trial. Two thirds of the vengeful group placed emphasis upon some form of punishment for the killer; four mentioned execution, and two the need for him to suffer.

The greatest difference between the groups was in response to the question "How do you think the killer's assassin should be treated?" While five of the nine in the "vengeful" group felt the crime merited *maximum punishment,* seven of the nine in the "helpful" group again emphasized the need for *justice*. The "vengeful" children in the majority of instances sought not only punishment of the assassin, but of his killer also. More than two thirds of the "helpful" children, on the other hand, emphasized the need for justice and the usual legal procedures in the treatment of both the assassin and his killer. This was in line with the trend seen in the group as a whole.

The attitude of the two groups toward the cancellation of usual programs or activities also differed. While five of the nine in the "vengeful" group considered the cancellations a "necessity," the same number in the "helpful" group expressed a *preference* for watching the history-making events.

On the effect they thought the President's death would have upon them personally, five of the nine in the "vengeful" group felt that the President's death would produce no real changes, while only one in the "helpful" group gave this response; seven of the latter felt, like Beth, that the assassination had effected some change in them.

These children had previously been rated on several dozen variables studied during the previous two years. When Alice Moriarty reviewed the material on those whose major reactions to the assassination were "helpful" she reported that they showed a broader range of emotion, seemed to experience life more richly, and were generally more open in expressing feelings, including aggression. Their frustrations appeared to be balanced by a capacity to obtain gratification, and they were able to enjoy a wide range of interests, leading to sublimation and intellectual pleasures.

The children in the "helpful" group showed higher self-esteem. They also had a capacity to withdraw constructively, showed less identity conflict, less self-restriction, affectively and motorically; their defenses were more flexible and appropriate; there was less rigidity in their thinking. They reflected less imposed restriction, and more support by their parents. They were more resilient, had a more hopeful and cheerful orientation toward the world and more trust in people. Their identity was secure and stable.

Another staff member, Marie Smith, commented that the "helpful" group seemed pleasanter, more cooperative, had more "sending power," i.e., capacity to arouse responsiveness in others or to put themselves across. Their mothers were found to be more resilient, better able to tolerate hardships and disappointments, and less self-pitying than the mothers of the "vengeful" group. Moreover, though very busy, and ill at times, their mothers were generally available, and the children also received warmth from the broader family—father, sibs, grandparents.

Sylvia Ginsparg observed that at the preschool level the "vengeful" group showed more card rejections on the Rorschach, and included largely passively aggressive children. Thus their verbal responses to the Kennedy assassination expressed aspects of adaptational style congruent or similar to those seen much earlier in their verbal responses to very different stimuli that had incomparably less reality impact.

The first analysis of responses was done without identifying the respondents. After identification, we noted some indication of sex differences in these groupings: the "helpful" group was composed entirely of girls, the "vengeful" group of seven girls and two boys.

An "intellectual" group whose reaction was that of trying *"to understand"* was composed entirely of boys. In a further exploration of the boys' responses (since they were so largely absent from the "vengeful" and "helpful" groups) it was found that five of the six children who sought help in prayer were boys. Three of the four who reported feelings of being overcome emotionally were boys, suggesting a more intense identification with Kennedy.

Influence of Previous Personal Loss

The experience of loss of the national figure of Kennedy might be expected to be strongly colored by residues from previous experiences of loss and the child's ways of dealing with these, and we noted above the relation of these to accepting the reality of bad news. We find other clear reflections of loss experience in the response of several children. The mother of the boy who wrote "Part of me died" was severely ill with incurable cancer. Another boy who expressed a strong reaction had had an early childhood shadowed by fantasies of his father, who died when the boy was an infant. A boy who lost his mother when she became severely ill was one of those who felt "sick." A girl who had recently lost her father by divorce and his subsequent remarriage wrote "I felt as if a living part of me had died." And a boy who had lost his father by divorce nearly ten years earlier was the most overwhelmed of the boys. In addition, there was Peggy's feeling, quoted at the beginning of this report: "I wanted to talk to somebody to see how they felt about it, and to see if other kids my age were as concerned about it as I was, if they realized what a horrible thing this was to the entire world." She was a girl who had reported to the psychiatrist two years earlier that, after the death of her mother when she was six years old, "a girl needs somebody to talk to."

A girl whose entire family mourned the loss of a beloved uncle who died the day after Kennedy remarked that "the Kennedy family felt sorrowful"—not differentiating between the wife and the children as did other children who had an especially close identification with their mothers. A girl who is still embarrassed because of a slight body distortion following a severe illness felt "shocked and ashamed" that this happened here.

While these and other illustrations of direct mobilization of emotions regarding loss of a love object or a part of the self fit the assumption that it is directly influenced by recent or earlier feelings of loss, because it repeats the emotions of longing and sorrow, we can also see other effects. These are visible in the patterns of defense mechanisms among some children who had suffered loss: the dry resignation of a taciturn boy who lost his mother in an accident in which he himself was severely injured. He commented (of Mrs. Kennedy and the children), "By now I think they've accepted it, and are doing regular things now." (This is the point at which many children commented on the irreparable loss Mrs. Kennedy had suffered, her "heartbroken" feelings, or their assumption that she "is still stunned.")

Concepts of Prevention

Children's thoughts about what might have prevented the tragedy were also related to previous experiences and to persistent needs, defense mechanisms, or coping orientations. Among the children who thought *better external protection* should have been provided, were:

> *Peter,* who suffered a broken leg when his older brother pulled away a ladder under a tree he was climbing.
>
> *Yvonne,* always passive and shy and wanting to be cared for.
>
> *Lori,* sturdy by contrast, but perhaps a child who pushed herself to the brink and needed external protection to help her from overexploiting her energy.
>
> *Anita,* teased by older brothers with whom even her best efforts could not cope, and neglected by an unwell mother.

We also find in this group Beverly, whose wish for police protection was related both to the recent instabilities of an alcoholic father and, more deeply, to infantile and oedipal conflicts; Marilyn, whose mother stoically tried to balance loving support with demands that the child try to take care of herself during years of rehabilitation after Marilyn's severely disabling illness.

By contrast, the view that *Kennedy should have been more careful* was held by four girls who were themselves adept at strategic self-protection.

Summary

General statements of the trends toward disbelief, shock, sadness, or anger do not do justice to the highly individual expressions and sensations of these adolescent children. They differed in their identifications with the Kennedy family, their impulses to do something, their concepts of prevention, and their predictions of effects on themselves, the nation, and the world. We have given special attention to differences between the children who responded with vengeful or retaliative impulses and those who reacted with a desire to help, and to the relationship between these reactions and previous configurations of defense and coping patterns these children developed in the process of dealing with vulnerability and/or stress. Good relationships with their mothers, and general warmth of response to people and the environment also distinguished the "helpful" group from the "vengeful" group. Defenses against previous personal losses were reflected in the various styles of defense. While many relationships between responses to this disaster and previous modes of functioning were seen, we also found that this sudden, widely shared disaster loosened inhibitions and defenses covering profound feelings of despair or hate that had not been reflected in previous examinations. The fact that the children had observed feelings being released by many other people is assumed to have made it more possible for them to express their own feelings than it had been in sessions with psychologists or a psychiatrist.

NOTES

1. This study was carried out within the current studies of Maintenance of Mental Health at Puberty, L. B. Murphy, Chief Investigator, supported by USPHS Grant M-4093, the Gustavus and Louise Pfeiffer Foundation, and the Menninger Foundation. The questionnaire here reported was prepared by A. Moriarty and S. Ginsparg, who collected the data, carried out the basic group analysis, and formulated preliminary reports. This report by L. B. Murphy integrates their work with additional analysis of individual cases. An extended discussion of the development of these children from infancy is in press: L. B. Murphy, A. Moriarty, W. Raine, *Development and Adaptation,* Atherton Press. A review of patterns of functioning is in preparation.

2. See Escalona and Heider, 1959; Murphy, 1962; Murphy, Moriarty, and Raine, cited above.

3. Nemtzow and Lesser, 1964.

LIST OF REFERENCES

Escalona, S. and G. Heider. 1959. *Prediction and Outcome.* New York: Basic Books.

Moriarty, A., L. B. Murphy, and M. Smith. 1965. "Relationships Between Mothers' and Children's Reports of Responses to the President's Death." In: Greenberg, S. Bradley and Edwin B. Parker. eds. *The Kennedy Assassination and the American Public: Social Communication in Crisis.* Stanford, Calif.: Stanford University Press.

Murphy, L. B. 1962. *The Widening World of Childhood.* New York: Basic Books.

Nemtzow, J. and S. R. Lesser. 1964. "Reactions of Children and Parents to the Death of President Kennedy." Paper presented at the American Orthopsychiatric Association Annual Meeting, March, 1964.

2

An Exploration into Some Aspects of Political Socialization: School Children's Reactions to the Death of a President[1]

ROBERTA S. SIGEL

A desire to understand how children react to or interpret a political event is not just idle curiosity. The roots of adult political attitudes and behaviors go far back into childhood. If we knew more about children's perception of the political process, it would probably help to explain a great deal about the process itself. As a rule, however, it is very hard to observe children's reactions to political phenomena. Judging from observations made of television-watching habits, spontaneous political comments during interview sessions, and from studies of school children, politics is not a topic of great salience for children. Consequently they tend not to be deeply involved with the outcome of elections, the solution of social and political problems of the day, and in fact at times seem quite unaware of political crises going on around them. Yet even though they appear oblivious to the larger political environment, they are nonetheless part of it. And it is during this time of quasi-obliviousness that they acquire the value system, attitudes and orientations on which their adult behavior will rest. If a political society is to maintain itself, it is imperative that such acquisition take place. Human beings must become socialized to all aspects of the societal life of which they want to become part. Politics is one such part of societal life, and children must therefore become politically socialized.

By general socialization we mean

the process by which the individual comes to conform to the norms of the group into which he is born and of which he becomes a fully functioning member. . . . Growing up in a group means learning to be a member of a group. It means perceiving what is considered to be correct and essential in a group, accepting these precepts as right, good, and necessary, and learning to behave in congruence with them. This process includes ways of thinking or feeling as well as ways of behaving, and it covers attitudes towards one's self as well as attitudes and behavior towards other people.[2]

From this it follows that political socialization refers to the process by which children internalize the political norms so well that their community's way of settling political problems appears to them as "right, good, and necessary." When a young person has learned not only to accept these norms but to behave in congruence with them, i.e., has accepted the obligations of citizenship demanded by his particular political community, he can be said to have matured politically. In a democracy, for example, we consider it a sign of political maturity for people to accept the verdict of an election even though they may be unhappy over it. Such maturity, like all social behavior, must be learned; it is not innate in the child. The young child, when he loses, cheats or quits the game rather than play by the rules. Among the political norms the child has to learn are: 1.) appropriate attitudes toward political authority figures and the correct way of behaving toward them; 2.) respect for the rules of the game of politics as it is practiced in a community, which would include appropriate attitudes and actions toward other people's rights, private property, etc.; and 3.) acceptance of the way in which decisions are reached and obeyed— to name a few of the most crucial.

When these norms have been learned and internalized by the body politic, the community usually has reached consensus on some of the vital operating principles of a given political system. For a long time now political scientists have agreed that such consensus is vital for the survival of a political community and that only where such agreement on broad principles (although not necessarily on details) exists can a government and nation hope for political stability.[3] It would seem then that political socialization of the young is one of the functions of political society and a country that fails in it could be courting serious political trouble.

Some authors have called the state of political socialization in which we find children and young people a state of anticipatory socialization.[4] They indicate that at an early age political socialization, like socialization in general, is still incomplete. The term also suggests that many of the values and norms that children begin to develop may not be directly and intrinsically, but only indirectly, political and hence may have great applicability to and consequences for the development of later political attitudes and preferences. For example, when a child is taught how to respond to people different from him in wealth or race or religion, the ground is laid for adult attitudes toward "out-groups." Precisely because it is "anticipatory," children's political socialization is usually difficult to study. But when a political event occurs that engages children's interest and emotional reactions, there is an unprecedented opportunity to study the political norms and values the children have acquired. Such an event was the assassination of President John F. Kennedy. From all reports it would seem that children were deeply moved and greatly shocked by this event, and were considerably less reticent than usual in expressing their opinions about it.

When, in addition, an event is of crisis or pseudo-crisis dimensions, it is a particularly propitious setting in which to study political socialization. A political crisis is by definition a situation in which existing norms or values are under attack. It thus affords an opportunity to test how firmly children share in the adult political consensus and how much they have internalized the norms of the existing political order, i.e., how politically socialized they have become.

The study we are about to report is an attempt to look at a political and national crisis—the events of the November 22, 1963, weekend—as it looked from the point of view of school children.[5] The tragic events of that weekend tested first a child's understanding of and feeling for the Presidency in general and the murdered President in particular and hence pertained to children's relation to a crucial part of American political authority. The murder of Oswald, on the other hand, tested their understanding of American norms of justice, the rights of other people, due process, etc. The complexity of the events provided clues to both children's attitudes toward authority and their comprehension of American norms and principles of political conduct, thereby testing their socialization in two different spheres (which are really two different levels): understanding of the more personalized aspects of political institutions (as symbolized in the Presidency) and understanding of the more de-personalized, conceptual aspects. Responses to these two aspects of political socialization can be used to test: 1.) the nature and stability of the child's faith in political authority, and 2.) the child's attachment to and understanding of abstract principles. Taken together the responses constitute a partial index of socialization into American political norms.

In undertaking such an investigation, one could only wish that the literature on children's political socialization was more plentiful. The value of a study undertaken in times of crisis depends in no small measure on the base lines previously established for norms in less stressful times. In this case few such base lines exist. As of the present, only two major studies have been undertaken on children's images of the Presidency. One was done at the University of Chicago under the direction of David Easton and Robert Hess; the other is the doctoral dissertation of Fred I. Greenstein. Both studies were commenced when Dwight Eisenhower was President, although the Chicago study was replicated after Kennedy had become President. Material on children's orientation toward the American value system is virtually nonexistent. Data do, however, exist on some other aspects of children's political socialization, notably party preferences and issue orientation. Most of these findings are summarized in Herbert H. Hyman's *Political Socialization*.[6]

For the purposes of this investigation the Hess-Easton[7] and Greenstein[8] findings are the most directly relevant. The outstanding impression gained from them is that children know about the President at a very early age and that what they know about him is highly idealized. The President of the United States has high visibility and is seen as a benign, honest, and highly competent person. Hess and Easton point out that children tend to see him as better than most men. This positive image of the President is not, however, a totally undifferentiated image, but is more positive on some aspects than others; "the image of the President has contour."[9] It is most positive with respect to what Hess and Easton call role-relevant aspects. The President is seen as particularly knowledgeable, hard-working, concerned with the protection of all Americans, etc. As the child gets older (Hess and Easton examined children in grades two through eight) he does not lose his admiration for the President's competence; on the contrary, the data suggest

> the President is increasingly seen as a person whose abilities are appropriate to the demands of his office—a differentiation of role functions with increasing age of respondent.[10]

Children also tend to see the President as much more of a "boss" than he really is. Both studies showed that children think it is the President who does the most to make the laws, that Congress and all other branches of the government are merely helpmates for the President. Greenstein, in addition, asserts that the child's view of our federal system is a hierarchical one with the President bossing the states and their governors, and the governors in turn bossing the cities and mayors.

Admiration for the President as a person (his personal and moral qualities) decreases somewhat with age. While Hess and Easton are impressed with the consistently positive image that children have of political authority (which included the mythical president of China), Greenstein noticed that even young children (fourth grade) are willing to make evaluations of leaders, such as the President of the United States and the mayor of New Haven, Connecticut. However, only in the seventh and eighth grade are children prepared to make *negative* evaluations. Even then the President is most often seen in positive terms, regardless of the child's social status or partisanship. Children of all social classes admire him, although some slight class differences obtain with older children (older upper-class children tend to be slightly more ready to be critical). And while children are well aware of their parents' party preferences at an early age (Greenstein found that 69 per cent knew it in fourth grade[11]), know the party affiliation of the current President (60 per cent knew it in grade two and 86 per cent in grade three in a 1960 study),[12] their liking of the President does not cease when the occupant of the White House is of a different party from the child's parents.[13]

The temptation is great to attribute such an idealized image of authority to the child's image of his own father or to the child's wish for a more ideal father. The original frame of reference for Hess and Easton's research was that the

> image of the President [is] an extension or transfer of the image of the father to other authority figures in the child's perceptual world. If this is a valid hypothesis, we would expect that the image of the father and of the President would be highly congruent.[14]

The data, however, do not show any such clear-cut congruence. In a later paper Hess then offers

> an alternative explanation [which] is that the child is not projecting onto the President the image he has of his own father but that of the ideal father of his culture.[15]

He continues:

> In the United States the highly benign, even nurturant image of the President is congruent with the image of the paternal role which, in the United States, greatly overlaps that of the mother in expressive and nurturant components.[16]

Even the alternative explanation, however, seems to us most tenuous because it assumes that political figures are a source of personal identification for individuals. Observation of the American scene does not permit such assumption. The explanation also seems untenable because it does not sufficiently consider the role of social class. If familial experience, especially with the father, determined the child's view of authority, we would expect to find great variance in the political imagery of children of different social backgrounds. One of the marked class differences in the United States is in patterns of child rearing and the degrees of authoritarianism of the father.[17] If the nature of the child-father relationship predetermined the child's image of the Presidency, the image should show variability from class to class. Yet in the studies cited no very pronounced differences were discovered. This suggests that something other than family and father must contribute heavily to the child's image of the Presidency.

An examination of the Chicago and the Greenstein data, as well as our own, indicates that the school is probably one of the important contributors to the child's image of political authority (witness the high number of children who know the President's name, can identify Presidents of history, etc.). And most school texts and children's books do not contain much about Presidents that is critical; on the contrary, they are designed to increase pride in our Presidents and our history.[18]

The wider American political culture also tends to bolster faith in our officials. Americans, in general seem neither overawed by public officials nor concerned about whether chosen officials are competent to discharge the job entrusted to them. Presidents and presidential candidates especially are usually judged to be competent to handle the job even by those who do not intend to or did not vote for them.[19]

> Whatever people may think of minor politicians, they apparently prefer to believe that the nominees for the highest office in the land are worthy men.[20]

All this plus the fact that in the United States politics has low tension and adults view government as worthy of trust,[21] may well explain why neither home nor school is apt to undermine a child's faith in his President.

The President, being far away, enjoys an added advantage over local authority figures: the child has no opportunity to check against reality the idealized image taught him by the adult world. Whereas the child may soon learn from personal experience that the policeman at the corner or the librarian in the public library are at times less friendly and helpful than their portraits on the illustrated pages of such children's books as *Our Friend the Policeman* and *Community Helpers,* few children have an opportunity to compare the real President with the one discussed in school and books. Under these circumstances we suggest that the idealized image the child has of the President is a function of: 1.) school learning and indoctrination; 2.) the absence of traumatic experiences with political authority, especially on the national level; 3.) the political culture which is generally optimistic and trusts government; and 4.) the absence of any personal observation which might indicate that the President would *not* be benign. These four alternate explanations do not deny that political orientation may also be rooted in psychological needs and/or experiences but they take the discussion out of the realm of the exclusively psychological and place it in a cultural, political, and experiential context.

A composite image of the President, as seen by school children, would probably be of a man occupying the most prestigious profession known to a child, a man who is judged to be very competent, hard-working, well informed, with a tremendous amount of power; a man who cares a great deal about people, wants to help them and to protect them. Although seen as powerful, he is not seen as punitive, particularly not by older children of upper social status.[22]

Scope of Our Study

Given the fact that a child has such an idealized image of the President and sees in him the benevolent leader who protects child and country, how would we expect the child to react to the news of his assassination? No firm hypothesis seems warranted because little systematic data exists as yet on the ways adults or children cope with death and bereavement in general.[23] Even less is known of

> the generalized massive bereavement which occurs at the death of certain public figures, such as kings, presidents or entertainment idols like Valentino. One can perhaps assume that the bereavement in these situations is qualitatively different from that experienced by close relatives, yet it is nevertheless genuine.[24]

In view of the general lack of knowledge, we shall not attempt to formulate rigorous hypotheses but rather restrict ourselves to a few assumptions, some of which we will be able to test.

Assumptions

Since the President is such an important figure to the child, and since the young child relates to government through the person of the President rather than the Congress, the court, or the law, we would expect that:

1. The child would conceive of the President's death as a threat to his own security. Because he tends to think of adult authority as steady, firm, nurturant, and nearly unassailable, the President's death would lead the child, and especially the very young child, to worry greatly about either the future of the country or his personal

safety or that of the group to which he belongs. Great worry that the country's safety depends on the "leader," we would therefore interpret as a sign of incomplete political socialization because it indicates that the child has not yet learned to separate the institutions of government (in this case the Presidency) from the persons who occupy the governmental positions.

2. The more the child identifies the President as a person who meets his needs, the more he identifies with him, the more upset and worried we would expect him to be. Thus we would expect children who identify themselves as Democrats to have been more upset than Republicans, and Negroes (irrespective of party) to have been more upset than whites.

3. Since the death was brought on by such a wanton act as assassination, the child's image of the omnipotence of personal political authority (such as the President's) would be altered—he would think of the President as somewhat less powerful.

4. Because an assassination is an assault on political authority, because it is a departure from the political norms on which they had begun to rely, we would expect children to react to it with shock, horror, and sadness, and the overt behavioral manifestations associated with such emotions, as, for example, weeping, loss of appetite and sleep, occasional headaches, etc.

5. Because of the grief, shock, and fears resulting from the experience, and because of the love and admiration that children have for the Presidency, we would expect them to portray anger, hostility, and aggressive feelings toward the person who caused the loss to the child. We would expect children at times to give vent to these feelings in wishes for revenge and punitive treatment of the perpetrator of the misdeed. This we would expect particularly among younger children, and we would predict that these feelings of anger and hostility would become most visible in their reaction to the murder of Oswald. We would predict that they would be far less concerned over the wrong done to Oswald. We base this assumption on the knowledge that notions such as due process of law, "every man is entitled to a fair trial," etc. are rather abstract notions acquired only with increasing maturity. Another reason why they would show less concern is that children recoil less than adults from the use of violence and aggression. Mastery of aggres-

sive impulses is one of the primary tasks the developing organism has to learn.

Within the confines of this chapter it will not be possible to test all of the above assumptions, or to undertake the detailed developmental comparisons such an analysis requires. We shall have to restrict ourselves here to a preliminary investigation into the nature of political socialization by performing three types of analyses:

1. A comparison of adult and children's reactions to the assassination, on the assumption that the greater the similarity between adults' and children's responses, the more children have partaken of the general political consensus. Since we operate from the premise that political socialization is a developmental process, we will compare children's reactions at different age levels to see if they do indeed change with age.

2. A partial investigation of children's attitudes toward the Presidency. Here we are particularly interested in discovering whether or not children's views of the omnipotence and/or benevolence of the President suffered as a result of the events of November 22. We entertain the possibility that children will report slightly less idealized images of the Presidency, especially in its power aspects, than they had previously. If a President can be killed that easily, children might argue, he is not all that powerful. Self-defense might then dictate that it would be wise for the child to minimize the President's importance. This analysis will also permit us to inquire once again into children's views of the Presidency. If children should turn out to have been noticeably more indifferent to the President's death than were adults, then, obviously, the President plays a less crucial role in the political world of children than had generally been assumed. His death therefore constituted no threat.

3. An exposition of children's understanding of some fundamental aspects of the American system of justice. The way children reacted to the murder of Oswald would offer us insights into the extent to which they understand such concepts as due process, justice, etc. The idea that so heinous an act as the murder of a President could be avenged by the murder of the assassin should not be uncongenial to young children, especially since they see justice of this type meted out almost daily on their favorite TV

shows. The more a child rejects the idea of Ruby's deed and the more he can conceptualize the need for due process and justice, the more he presumably has become politically socialized.

Methodology

To perform the above analysis a written questionnaire was administered to 1349 primary and secondary school children in Metropolitan Detroit within a twenty-one day period after the assassination. The urgency to move in immediately was modified only by the time required to make the necessary arrangements with school officials. While some pretesting was undertaken, ample pretesting was foregone in the interest of administering the questionnaire while the impact of the event was close to its maximum in the minds of children. A cross section of the Metropolitan Detroit school population is represented in the sample. Care was taken to have adequate representation of lower-class, working-class, middle-class, and also upper-class children and to have a sizable sample of Negro as well as white children. Three private schools were included along with ten public schools in order to get a genuinely upper-class sample. (For an exact breakdown of the sample, see Chart I, page 60.) All the 1349 children were within the normal school population; we did not use any classes with disturbed, gifted, handicapped, or otherwise exceptional children. There were approximately the same number of children for each grade, and a good representation of social class and race in each grade as well.

For grades six and up the questionnaire administrator introduced the questionnaire briefly, stating that its aim was to explore children's reactions to certain public events and that it was in no way related to their school standing. They were assured of the complete anonymity of their answers, and their teachers were not in the room while the questionnaire was given. Children were urged to answer the questions without concern about how parents or teachers might want them to answer them but rather to write down or check off how they really felt at that particular moment. The children then went ahead to answer the questions. They were helped with the reading of questions and spelling of answers if they requested such assistance.

For children in the fourth grade the introduction was the same, but the questionnaire was then read aloud to them item by item, and the children followed along answering each item as it was read. Care was taken to make sure that each child answered each question. Several graduate and advanced undergraduate student assistants were available in the room to help the children with reading and spelling.

The questionnaire consisted of 71 items, some open-ended, some check-off items, and a few matching items. Nine items came from a Hess-Easton study; 17 items from a national survey conducted by NORC (National Opinion Research Center) one week after the assassination; and an additional 45 items were constructed by us.

The items repeated from the Hess-Easton instrument dealt with the President's role relevance and his place in the American system of representative government.[25] For the most part they were concerned with the President's competence to do his job, his responsiveness to people, and his general powerfulness. In repeating the items we used the phrasing of their pilot studies[26] rather than the scalelike format of their as yet unpublished national studies which offers six multiple choices to the child on each item. Most of the six scalelike choices portrayed the President in a favorable light when compared to others. We preferred the three-item choice not merely for simplicity's sake but because the existence of so many positive choices over negative ones on the Hess-Easton instrument might pressure the child toward choosing the highly positive items and thus have the effect of exaggerating the extent to which children actually place the President above other people in their esteem. Further, the absence of any neutral items precludes any casual reaction. Yet some children may well feel casual or neutral toward the President. But when forced to decide whether a President knows more or less than most people, without being able to put him on the same level as other people, what could we expect but that the average child would place him *above* other people? To guard against this forced idealization, we preferred the format containing the more neutral item. Proof that children did not indiscriminately flock to the neutral choice can be seen in the section on results, which shows that the moderate alternative was chosen for some items but clearly not for others.

The Hess and Easton items were utilized to see: 1.) how competent the President seemed in the child's eyes (knows more, etc.); 2.) how much children thought he cared about them ("If you write the President, he cares a lot what you think," etc.); and 3.) how powerful he seemed ("Who does the most to run the country?" etc.). It is with this last item that we will most concern ourselves here. A thoughtful analysis of children's image is well beyond the scope of this paper and will be attempted at a later time. For purposes of our analysis here we interpret a marked decrease in the power image of the Presidency as a sign that the assassination weakened children's faith in the President's powerfulness.

From the NORC check lists we repeated those items that probed into: 1.) people's intellectual and emotional reactions to the news of the assassination, and 2.) people's physical sensations or psychosomatic complaints following the news. In instances where the NORC language seemed quite adult to us we simplified it slightly, but the items remained essentially unchanged.

The 45 items we constructed were designed not only to get at children's immediate reactions to the death of the President, but to gain some insight into their conception of the Presidency, their image of the relation of the President to the general governmental structure, their understanding of American concepts of justice. We also inquired into the depth or shallowness of their political knowledge of a specific President (in this case Kennedy) and into their reactions to the TV coverage. Only three of these topics will be analyzed in this paper: children's views of the Presidency; their view of his relation to government in general; and their views of the Oswald/Ruby affair.

Wherever relevant the data were analyzed on the basis of grade in school, sex, race, and social status. Children's social status was determined by the father's occupation, not the school. We divided the sample into four groups:

1. blue collar trades (U. S. Census classification 4–9)
2. white collar trades, such as service trades, clerical, and sales (U. S. Census categories 1 and 2)
3. managerial and business (U. S. Census classification 0)
4. professional (for which the U. S. Census classification also is 0)

Where no refined social class breakdowns seemed warranted,

we limited ourselves to the conventional breakdown into blue collar and white collar occupations.

Results and Discussion

1. Comparison of Children and Adult Reactions

The most interesting phenomenon is the similarity of adults and children in their emotional reactions, while at the same time they show pronounced differences in some of their political and quasi-political reactions and interpretations. Mourning and sadness encapsulated children and adults, testifying to the crucial role such a political figure plays in the lives of our children and indicating how far back into childhood the roots of political socialization reach. Table 1 clearly shows that grief, sympathy (for Mrs. Kennedy and the children), shame, and anger were the reactions most frequently given on the NORC items—given by well over two out of every three adults and children. The children's behavior was also strikingly similar to adults'. They report about the same incidence of headaches, loss of appetite, trouble going to sleep, etc. (See Table 1.) Interestingly enough, parents tended to underestimate the extent to which their children were upset. According to NORC 32 per cent thought children were "not upset at all," and only 23 per cent thought they were "very upset." The index we developed for measuring children's emotional upset showed children to be considerably more upset, as we shall demonstrate later on. This is just one example of the difficulty one encounters when trying to measure feeling. It may also be an illustration of adults' tendency to minimize the extent to which children are capable of experiencing rather adult reactions.

Only in respect to crying do children distinguish themselves from adults. Children of all ages professed to have cried less than adults (39 per cent and 53 per cent respectively). (See Table 2.) Roughly four out of ten fourth-graders and twelfth-graders denied having cried. Boys of all ages denied it almost categorically. If we were to believe the children, 81 per cent of all the crying was done by girls. We refuse to believe our children and base this refusal on teachers' and parents' reports to the contrary.

The items developed by us, especially the open-ended ones, offer further insight into children's reactions. When asked to tell in their own words how they felt when they heard the news, over half (52 per cent) said they could not believe it. Shock and disbelief usually are the first reactions of a grief-stricken person. Sheatsley and Feldman regret not having asked this question because they think "it is probable that the response of disbelief was as prevalent as those of loss, sorrow, pity, shame, and anger."[27] We tend to agree with them. Sadness was the other frequently reported emotion (30 per cent said they felt sad or bad), while anger, shame, and disgust are mentioned by only a few children. Obviously, then, disbelief (shock) was the most salient emotion. Sixty per cent of

TABLE 1

Comparison of Children's and Adults'* Reactions

Item	Adults (n = 1384)			Children (n = 1349)	
	Felt it deeply or very deeply	Crossed mind	Never occurred to me	Felt that way	Did not feel that way
Felt the loss of someone very close and dear	79%	9%	12%	71.417%	25.390%
Worried what would happen to our country	47	32	21	65.35	30.85
Worried what would happen to our relations with other countries	44	33	23	62.31	34.26
Felt so sorry for his wife and children	92	6	2	93.32	4.47
Felt worried how the U.S. would carry on without its leader	41	29	30	58.90	36.84
Felt angry that anyone should do such a terrible thing	73	14	13	81.95	14.85
Hoped the man who killed him would be shot or beat up	11	13	76	40.48	55.19
Felt ashamed that this could happen in our country	83	10	7	82.71	14.70
Was so confused and upset I didn't know what to feel	38	14	48	43.06	52.00
Felt in many ways it was the President's own fault	4	11	85	16.07	79.61
Hoped the next President would be better	—	—	—	35.55	58.76
I did not feel bad	—	—	—	13.26	80.97

* NORC Study SRS 350

the children and 53 per cent of the adults could not recall ever having felt that way before. Most of those children who did had experienced the death of a relative or friend or possibly of an animal. Unlike adults, they never mentioned a public event or the death of a public figure (a third of adults did). Death was thus related to in a very personalized fashion.

A word or two are in order here about the developmental pattern we observed in this context. Generally, we take it for granted that children behave more like adults as they increase in age. For example, Sheatsley and Feldman "presumed that teenagers would react in much the same manner as adults . . . but [they] were curious about the emotions of the four-to-twelve age groups. . . ."[28] Working from this assumption, they failed to ask parents about teen-agers' reactions. If our data are any guide, their assumption was unwarranted in this instance. Teen-agers did not prove very

TABLE 2

Behavior of Adults and Children During the Weekend

| Symptom | Behavior experienced by: | | By grade | | | | |
	Adults (n = 1384)*	Children (n = 1349) All children	4	6	8	10	12
Didn't feel like eating	43%	37%	50%	38%	33%	35%	28%
Had headaches	25	22	33	26	17	19	16
Had an upset stomach	22	18	31	23	11	12	12
Cried	53	39	39	35	39	45	41
Had trouble getting to sleep	48	45	69	48	36	39	31

* NORC Study SRS 350

similar to adults in their overt emotional reactions; instead we found that it was the younger children who behaved more like the adults. The frequency with which somaticized emotional reactions were reported decreased with age (see Table 2); in fact, for several items each increase in age brought a decrease in emotional reaction. How are we to explain this? To us it seems in keeping with the adolescent's desire to appear "tough,"[29] "cool," unemotional, uninvolved, and his horror of making a sentimental display of himself. An overt disclaimer of strong feelings may or may not be indicative of emotion experienced.

In their assessment of the political consequences and in their interpretations of the events, children were not the carbon copy of adults that they were in their emotional reactions. Both adults and children worried about the country, but children seem to have worried more than adults. Whereas on all three "worry" questions majorities of adults responded that such worry never occurred to

TABLE 3

Adults' and Children's Worry for the Nation

			By Grade				
Item	Adults*	All Children	4	6	8	10	12
Worried how the U.S. would get along without its leader. (NORC wording: "Worried how U.S. would carry on.")	41%	59%	76%	69%	59%	45%	41%
Worried what would happen to our country. (NORC wording: "Worried about future U.S. political situation.")	47	66	76	69	68	59	60
Worried what would happen to our relations with other countries. (NORC wording: "Worried about international situation.")	44	63	59	63	63	64	65

* This includes adults with the following response intensities:
1. Very deepest feelings; 2. Felt it quite deeply.
(NORC Study SRS 350)

them or at best just "crossed [their] mind but not deeply," majorities of children seem to have worried. (See Table 3.) The adult and youth figures are not quite comparable since we gave the child only two check-off choices (either he felt that way or he did not) while NORC offered four, representing different degrees of worrying. Nevertheless we doubt that the higher worry scores for children are a result of our dichotomized question wording. Worrying does not remain stable in children. It decreases sharply with increase in age (except in the realm of foreign affairs). Younger children were heavy worriers. Over three quarters worried about the country's future and how it would get along without its leaders (fourth grade 76 per cent; twelfth grade 41 per cent). Such accentuated worrying in the lower grades is in line with our prediction that young children, because of their greater dependency needs, are more upset when adult authority is shaken. In the political sphere, the most salient authority figure seems to be the President. Presumably he meets their dependency needs. It is through him that they relate to governmental authority, rather than through political institutions or principles. No wonder that the younger the child, the higher his worry score—testifying to the trauma a Presidential assassination represented.

How did children interpret the events compared to adults? Children and adults both were quite sure Oswald had killed the President (see Table 4), although 49 per cent of the children thought he might have been found innocent at a later trial. There was no consensus in either group as to why Oswald had wished to kill the President. Twice as many adults (33 per cent) as children (15 per cent) attributed it to mental illness. Also far more adults than children attributed it to Oswald's Communist leanings (16 and 6 per cent respectively). Several other items on the table indicate that more adults than children took a conspirational view of the assassination. When asked who was to blame for the President's death, children (in an open-ended question) tended to think exclusively of Oswald. Russia and Communism were mentioned by only four children. No child mentioned Castro, Cuba, or extremists of the right and left. Adults did to a fair extent (Russia and Communism 15 per cent, Castro and Cuba 37 per cent). Thus it would seem that children viewed the event with a refreshing absence of cabalism. Nor did children express much of the generalized guilt feeling to which some adults seem to have been prone. Not one child answered "we are all to blame" (8 per cent of adults did) and only 7 per cent blamed the American public (adults 25 per cent). Children seem to have seen the event in a simple and concrete way: blame must be put on the man who pulled the trigger, although many children (38 per cent) were at a total loss to explain why anyone would want to do such a thing. Such straightforwardness is perhaps an encouraging sign; children do not see any conspirational plots endangering the United States, and they are not yet given to the now fashionable stance of *mea culpa,* which assumes personal guilt for acts not of one's own doing. On the other hand, the straightforwardness may have come from their lack of sophistication. Such concepts as mental illness and collective guilt[30] are rather abstract and perhaps hard for young children or children from relatively simple backgrounds to comprehend. The children who did offer explanations in these terms not only tended to be older but consistently came from professional or upper middle-class homes.

TABLE 4

Comparison of Adults' and Children's Interpretation of the Events

Item	Adults*	Children
Felt certain Oswald killed the President	72%	75.3%
Undecided about it	28	19.1
Reasons why Oswald did it:†		
Insanity	15	14.9
Paid to do so		4.9
Communists behind it	16	5.8
Dislike for Kennedy	12	13.9
Disliked government		3.9
Bad man		.5
Too much for Negroes		1.1
Hatred	12	5.1
Publicity		2.2
Misc.	8	10.0
Don't know	15	37.9
Who is to blame for the President's death?		
Oswald	†	72.6
Security measures	22	2.0
Russia or the Communists	15	.3
God's will		.8
No one person		4.5
Hatred, bigotry, fanaticism	10	3.1
Misc.	‡	3.5
No answer	‡	4.5
The public in general	25	7.4
We are all to blame	8	
Tension and decline of morality	6	
Castro or Cuba	37	not offered
People of Dallas	15	by children
Birchers	15	
Negroes in this country	6	
Did the assassin plan it?		
Alone	24	35.4
With others	62	46.4
Don't know	14	17.7
Who do you think planned it with him?†§		
Ruby		18.5
Russia		2.7
Communists		4.1
Misc.		15.1
How do you feel about what happened to Oswald?†		
Glad	20	19.0
Now we will never know	33	24.4
Should have had trial	33	15.5
Sorry for his family		.7
Didn't care		6.1
Thought it unfair		3.6
Killing always bad	not offered	1.4
Felt a bit bad	by adults	7.1
Felt bad or unhappy		12.7
Misc.		4.2
No answer		5.3

* NORC Study SRS 350
† Answers not quite comparable because children's question open-ended
‡ Figures not broken down this way
§ Percentages less than 100 because only those listed who said he planned with others

Where children showed themselves most distinctly different from adults was in their reactions to the Oswald-Ruby aftermath. Oswald put attachment to American values of justice and due process of law to a severe test—a test many children could not pass. Few adults hoped the man who shot the President would be shot down, but 41 per cent of the children did, especially the younger children. Similarly, only 16 per cent of the children expressed regret that the murder of Oswald deprived him of a trial (for adults NORC reports 33 per cent), which is, of course, in keeping with the previously cited feelings of aggression children demonstrated toward the President's assassin. When asked how they felt about Oswald's death (open-ended question) 19 per cent (the percentage was the same for adults) spontaneously said they were "glad"; 6 per cent said they did not care; and 24 per cent expressed regret that "now we will never know" (33 per cent for adults). And yet, 85 per cent knew it was wrong of Ruby to kill Oswald even if he was the assassin. Children's reactions thus show a certain amount of ambivalence. They seem to have felt extreme hostility toward Oswald along with the awareness that what Ruby did to him was wrong.

Here again clear-cut developmental patterns can be observed. Expressions of revenge declined steadily with age. Two thirds of the fourth-graders and 53 per cent of the sixth-graders "hoped the man who killed the President would be shot or beat up." By the eighth grade this constituted minority sentiment (37 per cent). In the tenth grade, 24 per cent felt this way, and by the twelfth grade it had dropped to a mere 17 per cent. We interpreted a pro-revenge answer as indicating two things: that the child did not yet understand the inappropriateness of such a response in the setting of the American system of government, and, more importantly, that the child was coping with a frustrating or threatening event by resorting to hostility and aggression—at least in his wishes. We take this to mean that younger children have not yet been completely socialized into one important aspect of politics, namely the rejection of violence as a method of retribution. This should come as no surprise to students of child development. Yet in a political system like ours the internalization of politically nonhostile and nonaggressive norms even toward the offender is one of the crucial goals of political socialization.

Adolescents not only disapproved of what had happened to Oswald but gave adultlike responses on this item and on a variety of other questions dealing with due process and similar principles of American political life. Adolescents may show emotional reactions to a political event that differ from adults', but their political orientations apparently are similar. This is, of course, in keeping with most political socialization studies, which indicate that by adolescence a person has acquired the major political orientations that he will espouse throughout most of his adult years.

Rejection of aggression and acceptance of American concepts of justice is also related to a child's social class. Children from lower socioeconomic backgrounds at all age levels condoned aggression more readily than did upper-class children, especially those from professional families. True, the younger the child, irrespective of class, the easier he finds it to condone aggression, but even at a young age it is slightly harder for children of higher socioeconomic background, and the discrepancy between the classes increases rather than decreases with age, so that by the twelfth grade there was hardly a child of professional parents who wished to see Oswald get killed, while over a third of the working class and white collar children did (see Chart II). The impact of upper-class standing seems to be first, that it accelerates rejection of violence, and, second, that it all but obliterates acceptance of violence by adolescence. Consequently the gulf between the classes has widened by adolescence, not narrowed, or—to put it another way—while all children become more socialized with age into the rejection of violence, upper-class children are the most politically socialized to this norm. Findings such as these demonstrate the political consequences of the different child-rearing practices of the various social classes, which some scholars have observed.[31]

II. Differential Involvement and Reactions to the Event

We had predicted that even though all children love and admire the President, children who identified more with the President, for partisan or other reasons, might feel his loss most severely. This assumption was tested with respect to Negro/white children and to Republican/Democratic children.

The comparison of Negro and white reactions was undertaken on the assumption that Negroes would have particularly strong reasons for mourning the President's death. Sheatsley and Feldman comment on the fact that adult Negroes seem to have shown more pronounced grief over the President's death than did any other population group. This seems to hold even among school children. Almost without fail the Negro children were considerably more upset and worried. (See Table 5.) Many of these children wrote that they worried "how my folks will now get along." One Negro girl attending a high school in the worst part of the city poignantly wrote, "It was as though my father had died all over again."

TABLE 5

Reactions of White and Negro Children

A) NORC checklist

When I Heard the President Was Dead I:	White (n = 1006) %		Negro (n = 342) %	
	This is how I felt	I did not feel that way	This is how I felt	I did not feel that way
Felt the loss of someone very close and dear	68.6*	29.0*	80.7*	13.5*
Was so upset and mixed up, I did not know what to feel	43.5	53.1	40.1	51.2
Was mad that anyone should do such a terrible thing	81.6	16.0	83.6	10.8
I cried	39.6	56.7	39.5	51.8
Worried about what would happen to our country	63.1	34.3	74.3	19.0
Felt sorry for his wife and children	93.9	4.7	91.2	4.7
Hoped the man who killed him would be shot or beat up	35.9	60.3	53.9	39.2
I did not feel bad	10.0	85.7	22.8	67.5
I did not feel like eating	26.5	60.4	38.9	51.8
Worried what would happen to our relations with other countries	61.9	35.2	64.0	30.7
Felt in some ways it was the President's own fault	14.7	80.4	18.4	73.7
I had trouble getting to sleep	42.2	55.1	51.8	42.8
Hoped the next President would be better	29.7	66.0	54.7	35.9
Felt ashamed that this could happen in our country	85.6	12.8	75.1	19.6
I had a headache	21.0	74.9	22.9	65.5
I had an upset stomach	16.6	78.6	21.6	66.9
Worried how the U.S. would get along without its leader	55.4	41.5	69.6	23.7

* Percentages do not add up to 100% because some children failed to check each item.

TABLE 5 (continued)

B) *Answers to the open-ended question:*

"Tell us, in a few words, just how you
felt when you first heard that President
Kennedy was dead."

	White Children %	Negro Children %
I could not believe it	55.9	40.9
I felt sad	15.6	21.1
I felt very bad	10.3	18.1
I felt frightened	2.2	1.5
I felt sick	1.3	5.5
I felt ashamed	1.2	1.5
I felt mad	.9	2.6
Combination of the above answers	6.6	1.8
Misc.	5.1	4.9
No answer	.8	2.1
"Did you ever feel that way before?"		
Never	61.1	53.8
At the death of a relative	22.1	30.1
At the death of a friend	5.7	3.8
At sickness of a friend	2.8	4.1
At loss of animal	1.9	.9
At divorce of parents	.6	—
Misc.	4.3	4.1
No answer	1.2	2.9

The reactions of Negro children are interesting in many ways, but a thorough analysis would take us beyond the scope of this chapter. Here we can point out merely that they showed much more hostility toward the assassin and much more worry about how the United States would get along without its *leader*. They had far greater worries than white children about what would happen to the country domestically. Obviously in the minds of Negro children Kennedy was intimately associated with the fate of the Negro. No wonder that more of them reported trouble sleeping and loss of appetite!

It is also noteworthy that of all the groups Negro girls showed themselves the most deeply affected. While girls generally were more emotionally affected than boys, Negro girls' reactions were far more severe than white girls' and than Negro boys'. The least affected, apparently, were the white boys. These differences maintained themselves even when partisanship and socioeconomic status were taken into account.

We further predicted that children who identified with the President's party (those children who said they would vote Democratic if they were old enough to vote) would show more signs of grief and fear over the future of the country than those not so identified. Table 6 indicates that this was indeed the case, although it showed

TABLE 6

Reactions of Children Who Identify as Democrats and Republicans

NORC checklist	Democrats (n = 459) %		Republicans (n = 231) %	
When I Heard the President Was Dead I:	This is how I felt	I did not feel that way	This is how I felt	I did not feel that way
Felt the loss of someone very close and dear	79.3*	16.1*	63.3*	34.6*
Was so upset and mixed up, I did not know what to feel	38.3	54.7	47.2	48.9
Was mad that anyone should do such a terrible thing	85.6	10.5	80.5	16.0
I cried	44.4	49.9	34.2	62.3
Worried about what would happen to our country	66.7	28.1	69.3	28.6
Felt sorry for his wife and children	91.7	4.6	93.9	5.2
Hoped the man who killed him would be shot or beat up	49.9	45.5	37.7	59.7
I did not feel bad	9.6	82.8	16.9	80.1
I did not feel like eating	41.2	53.4	32.4	64.9
Worried what would happen to our relations with other countries	63.8	31.4	61.1	37.2
Felt in some ways it was the President's own fault	14.4	79.3	17.8	79.7
I had trouble getting to sleep	48.2	47.1	39.8	58.4
Hoped the next President would be better	37.7	55.1	38.5	58.0
Felt ashamed that this could happen in our country	78.4	18.1	82.3	15.2
I had a headache	21.1	72.1	22.5	74.0
I had an upset stomach	16.6	75.4	19.5	76.6
Worried how the U.S. would get along without its leader	65.8	29.8	58.4	37.7

* Percentages do not add up to 100% because some children failed to check each item.

up mainly in the area of emotional responses. Democratically inclined children reported more trouble sleeping, more loss of appetite, crying, etc. More of them identified with the President—"worried how the U.S. would get along without its leader" (Democrats 66 per cent, Republicans 58 per cent). And, not unexpectedly, more of them showed feelings of aggression toward Oswald (Democrats 50 per cent, Republicans 38 per cent). The President may have a firm niche in American children's affections and admiration, but partisanship is apparently an intervening variable, which either strengthens or loosens this bond. Even in death and tragedy children are aware of their partisanship—although not to a very marked degree.[32]

III. Comparison of Presidential Image Before and After November 22

The image our children[33] had of the Presidency was essentially positive and idealized just as Easton and Hess had reported it to be. But in one aspect of the image, the power aspect, children who were interviewed after the assassination differed from those Easton and Hess had interviewed before. As we had predicted, after the assassination the President seemed slightly less powerful. Whereas in the Easton-Hess study most children thought the President did most to run the country,[34] in our sample barely half did. His role image ("He knows more," etc.), however, remained unchanged.

Personal idealization of the President increased. In our sample somewhat more children than in the Easton-Hess group liked him very much, and hardly any disliked him. Although we were careful to tell children not to think of the late President when answering the question, but to think instead of Presidents in general, personal liking shot up.

The image of the Presidency thus remained positive and idealized among children, but their belief in his powerfulness noticeably decreased. This indicates to us that the impact of the assassination made children less sure of the President's omnipotence, perhaps brought the image closer to reality.

Another example of realism is seen in children's evaluations of American Presidents. Invited to make a guess whether

> America has had Presidents who did their job well and Presidents who did not do a good job

or

> American Presidents have almost all done their job very well

slightly over half (51 per cent) chose the more critical answer. Only five children refused to pass judgment. As was expected, the tendency to idealize *all* Presidents decreases with age, and decreases sharply (76 per cent of the fourth-graders said almost all Presidents have been good, as opposed to 16 per cent of the twelfth-graders). Most significant, however, is the fact that children were willing to admit at all that we have had Presidents who did not do a good job.

Children apparently were also able to make a distinction between the person of the President and the institution. In answer to our question

> When a President dies . . .
>
> There is no government for a while
> or
> Government goes on just the same

an overwhelming majority (84 per cent) expressed faith that government goes on just the same. It is possible, of course, that faith in the continuity of the institution of government was in part attributable to the emphasis TV coverage put on precisely this point. Thanks to television, children, shortly after learning of Kennedy's death, watched President Johnson take the oath of office aboard the Presidential plane—in the presence of the widow of the just deceased President. One may well wonder if children's faith in the stability of government would have been equally emphatic if television had not enabled them to follow with their own eyes and ears the swift and orderly succession. On this point it is interesting to note that, even so, 33 per cent of all fourth-graders thought that there is *no* government for a while. Nonetheless the answers indicate that though the assassination caused many children to worry about the future of the country, they had faith in the stability of their government.

The responses to the last two items, especially when analyzed in conjunction with the Easton-Hess items, suggest that children's highly positive image of the Presidency is not untinged by realism, and that children can apparently—in a rudimentary way—distinguish between the person of the President and the institution of the government. Their sense of political security seems to be a function of their faith in the institution of government as well as of their faith in individual Presidents.[35]

Summary

Children appear to have been greatly moved by the President's death. Their reactions were similar in many ways to those of adults.

Their socialization, however, does not yet seem complete (at least in grades four through six), for many showed feelings of revenge and slight regard for due process of law. High school students, however, seem to be nearly as politically socialized as most adults.

Negro children and children who intend to vote Democratic were noticeably more upset than white children or those who identified themselves as Republicans.

The image of the Presidency remains highly positive although a slight decrease in the power image has occurred.

All of which would lead us to believe that, probably due to the influence of home, school, peers, and mass media (especially television), even young school children quickly learned to join the adults in national mourning and in the appropriate civilized responses to the event. The optimists among us should be permitted to believe that this reaction of the young was spontaneous and a function of successful political socialization.

The fact that even young children's reaction patterns were so similar to adults' should further alert us to the fact that political socialization begins at an early stage—a fact all too often ignored.

NOTES

1. Initial assistance for the project came from Wayne State University and the Merrill-Palmer Institute but the major financial support for this investigation came from grants from the National Institute of Health (MH10112-01) and from the Society for the Psychological Study of Social Issues.

Special thanks here are due to the administrations and administrators who permitted us access to their schools within the span of a few days. These are the Boards of Education of the cities of Detroit and Dearborn, Michigan, and the headmasters of Grosse Pointe University School, Grosse Pointe, Michigan, Brookside School and Kingswood School for Girls, both of Bloomfield Hills, Michigan.

Most particularly, however, the author wishes to acknowledge the help of the following people: Judith Brent and Elinor B. Waters of the Merrill-Palmer Institute; Drs. Sandor Brent of the Department of Psychology, Wayne State University and William Kooistra, Pine Rest Christian Hospital, Grand Rapids, Michigan; and last—but certainly not least—the co-investigator, Dr. Irving E. Sigel, Chairman of Research, Merrill-Palmer Institute.

The above people need assume no responsibility for the report (since they have not seen it), but without them the study could never have taken place, as they helped in the questionnaire design, administered it, and generally saw to it that we could get to the schools before the children dispersed for Christmas vacation.

2. Hartley and Hartley, 1952, 204–6.

3. Of late political scientists have questioned just how essential such consensus is and whether it must be held by all strata of society. Cf. Prothro and Grigg, 1960.

4. Hess, 1963, 543.

5. One may, of course, argue that the event never was, strictly speaking, a crisis since no real threat to the continuity of government was ever present. If one, however, accepts the looser dictionary definition (Webster) of a crisis as a "turning point . . . a state of things in which decisive change is impending" one might well call the event a crisis.

6. Hyman, 1959.

7. Hess and Easton, 1960. Hess, 1963. Torney and Hess, 1962.

8. Greenstein, 1965.

9. Hess and Easton, 1960, p. 7.

10. *Ibid.*, p. 5.

11. Greenstein, *op. cit.*, p. 200.

12. Hess, 1962, p. 19.

13. Greenstein, however, noticed that children of Republican parents were 14 per cent more likely to rate Eisenhower as very good. *Op. cit.*, p. 196.

14. Hess and Easton, *op. cit.*, p. 640.

15. Hess, *op. cit.*, p. 14.

16. *Ibid.*, p. 24.

17. Davis and Havighurst, 1946; Miller and Swanson, 1958; Whiting, 1963; Sewell, 1961.

18. Two old, but still valid, volumes on the subject are Charles E. Merriam, *Civic Education in the United States* (New York: Scribner's, 1934) and Bessie Louise Pierce, *Citizens' Organizations and the Civic Training of Youth* (New York: Scribner's, 1933).

19. Sigel, 1964.

20. Lazarsfeld, Berelson, and Gaudet, 1948, p. 38.

21. Lane, 1962.

22. Greenstein, *op. cit.*, 104.

23. Volkart, 1957, writes, "No summary analysis of the social psychiatry of bereavement and separation can be made, since none as yet exists." P. 285.

24. Wilson, in Leighton, Clausen, and Wilson, 1957, p. 306.

25. The above terminology is not Hess and Easton's but our own. They break them down as: a.) perception of responsiveness; b.) personalized as opposed to institutionalized conceptualization of the government; c.) role

competence; d.) power index. (From a personal communication to the writer by Judith V. Torney, March 20, 1964.)

26. Hess and Easton, 1960.

27. Sheatsley and Feldman, 1964, p. 195.

28. *Ibid.,* 200–201.

29. In keeping with this toughness stance, fewer teen-agers than elementary school children reported having felt "sad," "sick," or "bad."

30. Political science literature has as yet not furnished us with any data on young children's concepts of political justice and morality. However, the work of Piaget, 1948, with respect to children's morality is of great relevance here.

31. Davis and Havighurst (1946). For a contrary view, cf. Maccoby and Gibbs (1954) as well as the Havighurst-Davis rejoinder to Maccoby and Gibbs (1955).

32. Sheatsley and Feldman also noted that supporters of the late President seemed more upset than his former opponents.

33. In part of the analysis we have eliminated the tenth and twelfth grade children in order to make our sample more comparable to the Hess and Easton one which included no children beyond the eighth grade.

34. Personal communication to the author. We are withholding exact percentage citations on this and several other items until the official publication of the Hess-Easton report.

35. We are sorry that we failed to inquire in more detail just how children perceived of this latter relationship. Such an inquiry would undoubtedly have yielded valuable insight into the role of the leader vis-à-vis the institution.

LIST OF REFERENCES

Davis, Allison and Robert J. Havighurst. 1946. "Social Class and Color Differences in Child-rearing," *American Sociological Review,* XI, 698–710.

Greenstein, Fred I. 1965. *Children and Politics.* New Haven, Conn.: Yale University Press.

Hartley, Eugene L. and Ruth E. Hartley. 1952. *Fundamentals of Social Psychology.* 1st edition. New York: Knopf.

Havighurst, Robert J. and Allison Davis. 1955. "A Comparison of the Chicago and Harvard Studies of Social Class Differences in Child Rearing," *American Sociological Review,* XX, 438–42.

Hess, Robert D. 1963. "The Socialization of Attitudes Toward Political Authority: Some Cross National Comparisons," *International Social Science Journal,* XV, 542–59.

Hess, Robert D. and David Easton. 1960. "The Child's Changing Image of the President," *Public Opinion Quarterly,* XXIV, 632–44.

Hyman, Herbert. 1959. *Political Socialization.* Glencoe, Ill.: Free Press.

Lane, Robert E. 1962. *Political Ideology: Why the American Common Man Believes What He Does.* New York: The Free Press of Glencoe.

Lazarsfeld, Paul F., Bernard Berelson, and Hazel Gaudet. 1948. *The People's Choice.* New York: Columbia University Press.

Leighton, Alexander H., John A. Clausen, and Robert N. Wilson. 1957. *Explorations in Social Psychiatry.* New York: Basic Books.

Maccoby, Eleanor E. and P. K. Gibbs. 1954. "Methods of Child Rearing in Two Social Classes." In William E. Martin, and C. B. Stendler (eds.) *Readings in Child Development.* New York: Harcourt, Brace, pp. 380–96.

Miller, Daniel R. and Guy E. Swanson. 1958. *The Changing American Parent.* New York: John Wiley & Sons.

Piaget, Jean. 1948. *The Moral Judgment of the Child.* Glencoe, Ill.: Free Press.

Prothro, James W. and Charles M. Grigg. 1960. "Fundamental Principles of Democracy: Bases of Agreement and Disagreement," *Journal of Politics,* XXII, 276–94.

Sewell, William H. 1961. "Social Class and Childhood Personality," *Sociometry,* XXIV, 340–56.

Sigel, Roberta S. 1964. "The Effect of Partisanship on the Perception of Political Candidates," *Public Opinion Quarterly,* XXVIII.

Sheatsley, Paul B. and Jacob B. Feldman. 1964. "The Assassination of President Kennedy—A Preliminary Report of Public Reactions and Behavior," *Public Opinion Quarterly,* XXVIII, 189–215.

Torney, Judith V. and Robert D. Hess. 1962. "The Child's Idealization of Authority." Paper presented at the American Psychological Association annual meeting, St. Louis, August 30, 1962.

Volkart, Edmund H. 1957. "Bereavement and Mental Health." In Alexander H. Leighton, John A. Clausen and Robert N. Wilson, *Explorations in Social Psychiatry.* New York: Basic Books.

Whiting, Beatrice R. 1963. *Six Cultures: Studies of Child Rearing.* New York: John Wiley & Sons.

CHART I

COMPOSITION OF SAMPLE

	NUMBER	PER CENT
Boys	629	47
Girls	720	53
White	1006	74
Negro	342	26
Oriental	1	—
Grade 4	264	20
6	281	21
8	339	25
10	249	19
12	216	16
Children in lower-class schools	373	28
middle-class schools	644	48
private, upper-class schools	332	25
Children with working-class fathers	580	43
Children with white collar fathers (service trades, clerical and sales help)	225	17
Children with fathers owning businesses or in managerial positions	249	19
Children with fathers in the professions	182	13
Children who don't know father's occupation	113	8

CHART II

CHILDREN WHO "HOPED THE MAN WHO KILLED PRESIDENT KENNEDY WOULD BE SHOT OR BEAT UP"

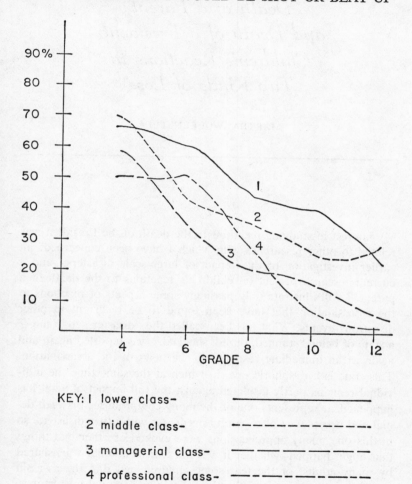

KEY: 1 lower class-

2 middle class-

3 managerial class-

4 professional class-

3

Death of a Parent and Death of a President: Children's Reactions to Two Kinds of Loss

MARTHA WOLFENSTEIN

I

My interest in studying reactions to the death of the President was related to other researches with which I have been concerned: an earlier investigation of the impact of large-scale disasters,[1] and a current research project on children's reactions to the death of a parent. I will illustrate only passingly some aspects of reactions to the assassination that have been found to be recurrent in other disastrous events. What has been called the "disaster syndrome,"[2] a state of being "stunned, dazed, shocked," was reported again and again as an immediate response to the news of the assassination. This state is a dysphoric one, in which at the same time the individual remains partly insulated against the full impact of what has happened. It represents one of the many compromises between denial and acceptance of a painful event. As with other disasters, so in this one, many apprehensions were evoked of other bad things that might happen—whether it was the fear of another war, shared by many adults, or the fear some children had that the assassin would get them next, or other large-scale or personal misfortunes. There were some expressions of people feeling closer together through sharing a moving event, which recalled the "postdisaster utopia" in which people experience temporarily a kindlier fellow-feeling. There was also the posing of the problem of evil, which recurs when something happens which is radically at variance with the belief in a benevolent order of things. The essence of this problem, which has long troubled theologians, appears in the question of a four-year-old child: "Why did they shoot him if he wasn't a bad man?" Some adolescents were led to wonder whether, if such things can happen, there is a God. Other people struggled to find some meaning in the event, or to extract some lesson from it, a common way of trying to assimilate what seem to be discrepancies in the view of the world as benevolently arranged.

The main context in which I wish to consider reactions to the death of the President is provided by the research in which we are engaged on children's reactions to the death of a parent.[3] This research is based on case material of children who have lost a parent, who are being treated in our out-patient clinic. The clinical data have been supplemented to some extent by interview material and observations of nonpatient families in which a parent has died. We have been concerned with trying to understand the ways in which children react to a major object loss at different ages. What we have found so far about children's reactions to the death of a parent provides the frame of reference in which I shall consider children's reactions to a related but different kind of loss, the death of the President. Let me add that we may distinguish two major aspects of the death of President Kennedy—that it meant the loss of a leader, and that it was a murder. For the purposes of this discussion I shall leave the aspect of crime in abeyance and concentrate on the aspect of loss.

I will deal with an age range of children in latency, prepuberty, and early adolescence. The data having to do with the death of the President on which I shall draw are the following: (1.) Case material from our out-patient clinic and from private practice (31 cases). (2.) Answers to questionnaires from child psychiatrists about their child and adolescent patients (100 responses). (3.) Intensive interviews with nonpatient subjects on their reactions to the President's death, conducted mainly within a few days of the event (23 interviews). These were supplemented in some instances by interviews with parents.[4] (4.) Essays by school children, primarily essays by junior high school pupils (ages twelve–fifteen), written at the end of January 1964, on "What I Remember about the Weekend when President Kennedy was Assassinated" (about 300 essays), but also some essays by second graders (age seven–eight), and by fifth graders (age ten–eleven), written on the first day back at school about their experiences over the weekend of the assassination. (5.) Answers to questionnaires from teachers in elementary school through high school on the reactions of their pupils.[5]

II

Let me first state, in a necessarily condensed way, our impressions about reactions to the death of a parent on the part of children in the age range which I am considering. The predominant tendency we have found is that emotional response is inhibited, and on a level slightly below the surface the reality of the loss is denied. While the child acknowledges verbally that the parent is dead, he continues to daydream that the parent will return. We observe here a splitting of the ego—what is accepted on one level is denied on another.[6] Feelings of grief are more or less interfered with; there is a great intolerance for protracted distress. Inhibition of affect and denial of the reality of the loss mutually re-enforce each other. If one does not react to an event, it is as if it had not occurred. What is most strikingly absent in children and adolescents is what Freud described, in "Mourning and Melancholia," as the "work of mourning," which commonly occurs in bereaved adults, the painful process of reality testing by means of which the lost object is gradually given up.[7]

Our observations are in accord with those of other investigators of reactions to loss in childhood. Bowlby has characterized the initial reaction to loss as one of "protest," in which a vehement demand is maintained for the return of the lost object.[8] The posture is that of the infant temporarily separated from his mother. There is a refusal to acknowledge any difference between the instance of loss by death and those less grievous times when the absent object could be recalled. In children, and also in adults who are unable to recover from a loss, there is a fixation on this first phase of reaction to an irreversible separation. Helene Deutsch, in her paper on "Absence of Grief," reported on the radical interference with affect in a young child following the death of his mother, as a consequence of which he showed a marked detachment and affectlessness in later years.[9] In the analysis of adult patients who had lost a parent in childhood or adolescence, Fleming and Altschul also observed that emotional reactions had been curtailed, a latent denial of the loss persisted, and feelings remained bound to the dead parent to the detriment of other relationships.[10]

The different ways of reacting to loss according to age often lead to conflict and misunderstandings in the family. The adult, who through maturation has become susceptible to the process of mourning, cannot understand the seeming lack of feeling on the part of the child. A mother weeping for the father who has died reproaches the child, suffering from an affective inhibition, for remaining dry-eyed.

When we started to observe children's reactions to the death of the President, what first struck us was what seemed to be a very similar discrepancy between children's and adults' reactions. This was very noticeable in the experience of the child psychiatrists in our clinic with their child patients at this time. The adults were deeply affected, even overwhelmed, while their young patients more often than not seemed oblivious or positively jaunty.[11] As we discussed this we were at first inclined to suppose that we were dealing here with the same kind of defensive maneuvers we had seen children using to ward off the impact of losses closer to home. Further analysis suggested that this was an imperfect analogy, and that the similar reactions of children in the two instances were more likely derived from rather different causes.

In great contrast to these initial observations of bland reactions of children were the essays of young adolescents about their memories of the President's death, written two months after the event. These were moving documents in which strong emotional reactions were expressed, and where we could see, even after this lapse of time, feelings of grief still contending with incredulity. These data were the most revealing and thought provoking for me. Without them I would have underestimated the intensity of emotional reaction of children in this age range. At the same time they presented a challenging paradox. In our experience, children of this age tend to show strong inhibitions of affect when someone in their own family has died. Yet they could feel and express outspoken grief for the death of the President. Both bland and intense emotional reactions thus posed problems for interpretation.

III

Let me now cite some of the observations of children in which we see reactions that are not only bland but to some extent brazen or jocose. On the afternoon of November 22, just after the death of the President had been announced, a young woman psychiatrist in our clinic had an appointment with a ten-year-old boy patient. The doctor told the patient that she would go through with the session as best she could, but that she was feeling very distressed about what had happened. The boy, who was generally a belligerent character, said, "Good! Then maybe for once you won't talk too much." When the doctor asked him how he felt about the assassination, he said, "Someone should have shot him sooner. Then we wouldn't have had to have all this physical fitness." This happened to be a clumsy, obese boy, who had suffered considerable humiliation in failing to pass the physical fitness tests in school.

A seven-year-old boy patient in his first treatment session following the assassination was asked by his therapist about his experience at the time. "Grownups were crying in the streets." "And you?" "I wasn't. I was laughing like a hyena."

A twelve-year-old girl patient whom I saw the morning after the assassination spoke scathingly about what had happened in school the preceding afternoon. "They wouldn't let us out early. Oh no! But they canceled the dance that evening." When her girl friend phoned her and said, "Isn't it terrible?" my patient answered, "Do you mean about Kennedy or about the dance?"

Such reactions were not peculiar to child patients, as material gathered from other families indicates. A mother relates that she and her husband were frequently weeping during the weekend following the assassination while their seven-year-old son remained dry-eyed. When in the course of the funeral ceremonies the television announcers spoke of the President's body, the boy remarked, "Why don't they say his 'rotting body.' It must be rotting by now."

In another family a thirteen-year-old girl reported, a few weeks after the assassination, some sick jokes which were being told by the children at school, such as, "What did you get for your birthday, Caroline?" "Jack-in-a-box." Reactions of adults to such expressions on the part of children were often of dismay or indignation.

When confronted with this kind of reaction from children, our first thought was that we were quite familiar with this kind of defense against painful emotion; this was similar to what we had observed in children's reactions to the death of a parent. As we thought further about it, we became aware of important differences in the two circumstances. The obvious but crucial question here is: how much can someone remote from their own personal lives matter to children? A child's capacity to attach feeling and meaning to persons beyond his immediate milieu depends on a number of variables. The one I would like to stress here is the developmental factor. We know that as children move into adolescence they are generally impelled to demote their parents in their scale of values and to look for other heroes and ideal figures farther from home. This is a time for the displacement of important feelings to admired personages in the world at large, whether athletes or poets, singers or scientists, emperors of past times or the President of the United States. As adults we are accustomed to devoting a certain amount of thought and feeling to outstanding persons in public life. The distress and disturbance that the sudden loss of such a person occasions in us is proportional to the amount of our emotional investment in him.[12] The difference in reaction between children and adults that I have cited may then in part be related to this: the children who were bland or jocose had probably not yet reached the stage of attaching any major feelings to personages so remote from themselves as the President.

However, I would still feel that there was a defensive quality in the reactions of these children, especially where they were a bit brazen or jocose. What were they defending themselves against if we suppose the President was too remote for them to feel his loss and to have to ward off painful feelings on this account? Here we may recall that children react to what is happening in the world mainly in terms of the reactions of their parents or other trusted adults. We know from observations on children in London during the last war, that they reacted not to the severity of the bombing to which they were exposed but to how upset or calm their mothers were.[13] On the occasion of the death of the President children were exposed to the unaccustomed sight of their parents, teachers, and other adults openly weeping. This emotional breakdown of the grownups was probably quite alarming to the children. At the same time the grownups, distracted by their own distress, became to some extent withdrawn and less available to the children. This also must have been anxiety provoking. We know that joking serves to a large extent to ward off anxiety.[14] It seems likely that the brazen or jocose expressions observed in some children in this situation were motivated largely by the need to ward off the painful impression created by the distress of the grownups around them. We may recall the little boy who said that grownups were crying in the streets, but he was laughing like a hyena.[15]

Let us turn to another kind of reaction of children to painful emotions. Where they themselves do experience such an emotion, they can endure it for only a brief space of time, after which they again ward it off by various defenses. I would call this the "short sadness span" of children. We have observed this in relation to the death of a parent in children in the age range from latency into adolescence. If they experience intense distress, they do not tolerate it for long, but quickly bring to the fore opposite thoughts and feelings. They do not seem able to sustain the process of protracted mourning that we know in adults. Similarly on the occasion of the death of President Kennedy, we had reports of children aged nine or ten who did cry when they first heard the news, but then did not understand why their parents did not want to go to the movies that night as previously planned, or became impatient when their usual television programs were not available that weekend.[16]

A very sensitive nine-year-old boy who was interviewed told us how unbearable it would be if a child could not quickly forget about a painful loss. He spoke of Mrs. Kennedy and her children, who had a lot of courage and did not weep. However, he did not know whether the children of the slain policeman would be able to be as brave. Perhaps they wouldn't be able to stand it. Then "they would cry and cry. They would cry for a month and not forget it. They could cry every night and dream about it, and the tears would roll down their eyes and they wouldn't know it. And they would be thinking about it and tears just running down their eyes at night while they were dreaming." This boy expresses with unusual articulateness how unbearable it would be for children if they could not as he puts it "forget" about a painful loss.

IV

Let us now turn to material of a different sort in which young adolescents expressed very movingly strong feelings of grief for the death of the President. This appeared in the essays of junior high school students on their memories of the weekend of the assassination, written two months later. Here are some characteristic excerpts:

> BOY, twelve: I just couldn't bear the thoughts of having someone take away the life of the heroic John Fitzgerald Kennedy. He was so living at first and then "poof" he's dead. I was grief-stricken when I heard he was shot.

> BOY, twelve: How could anyone do such a thing! I was filled with remote sadness. On the way home from school I could see people walking around in a daze. All the happiness of his family was gone in a few horrible minutes. I felt terrible.

> GIRL, thirteen: When the casket went to the church my eyes filled with tears. His burriel was simple, but my heart broke.

> GIRL, thirteen: [When it was announced at school] everybody started to cry. When I got home I put on my radio . . . when I heard about our wonderful President my tears started coming out of my eyes.

> GIRL, thirteen: The weekend that followed that tragic Friday was to be the worst one in my life. . . . Things that I usually enjoy doing just weren't fun for me that weekend. . . . The whole world seemed upset and disorganized.

> BOY, thirteen: This turmoil of sadness went on for a weekend on the television and for the people of the world, all their lives.

> GIRL, fourteen: I remember that tears came in my eyes and that I just couldn't control myself. "Oh!" you may say that a fourteen year old girl doesn't know to much about things like this. Well, may be not. I really don't know why I cried. I didn't know President Kennedy very well. President Kennedy wasn't my father. I just can't answer the question, "why?"

> GIRL, fourteen: When I heard the news of his death, I broke out in tears, uncontrollable tears. . . . Even now, people who are reading this, I am almost crying.

One circumstance that I think facilitated the expression of these strong feelings was that they were communicated in writing. The children seemed to welcome the opportunity to confide in this way to some unknown but interested reader feelings that were evidently still very vivid in their minds.[17] In contrast, a child or adolescent face-to-face with an adult therapist or interviewer would be apt to show more reserve or inhibition about expressing his feelings.

There is also the developmental factor mentioned before: we have here an age group in which there is beginning to be an important displacement of interest and feelings to personages in the larger world, outside the home environment. Younger children may have vague and perfunctory ideas that the President is an important man, that he does good things for the country. A thirteen-year-old boy can tell us of very precise and personal images that he had of President Kennedy. Speaking of the Saturday after the assassination:

". . . while watching his aides and friends file in I first realized that he wouldn't make another speech like he made in West Berlin or wouldn't be back to his family in Ireland every ten years as he promised nor would he address us in a television speech as Dear Fellow Americans." Such concrete images testify to a real attachment and also to the mental pain entailed in having to say good-by to someone so regarded.

We recognize, then, that with advancing age children could attach more feeling to the President, that he became more of a real person to them. This would seem to account for the fact that, as we move into adolescence, we find children reacting with such strong emotion to the President's death. However, I should like to come back again at this point to what we have observed about children's reactions to the death of a parent. Within this same age range of early adolescence we have found great inhibitions against grief in response to a more personal loss.[18] Let me describe briefly the reaction of a fifteen-year-old girl patient to the sudden death of her mother. She was, to begin with, sad and tearful, though constrained by an aversion against showing emotion in the presence of other family members. Within a few days feelings of frozenness and emptiness replaced those of grief. She thought it was ironical when people praised her for being brave, since she was exercising no voluntary control but suffering from an inhibition. A glass wall, as she put it, seemed to have descended between her and what was going on. She felt intensely uneasy about her affectlessness and sought reassurance from others so as not to blame herself too much for it. Many other instances could be cited, of both patients and nonpatients, in which we have observed a similar interference with affect in like circumstances. If our observations are correct, we are confronted with a paradox: that at a time in life when children usually are inhibited in their response to the death of a parent, they could give way so much more freely to grief for the death of a President.

It would seem that there may be circumstances that make it easier to grieve for someone far away than for someone close to home. I should like to call this phenomenon "mourning at a distance." A well-known instance of it occurs in Freud's case of the Wolf Man.[19] This has to do with an experience the patient recalled from when he was in his early twenties. His only sister, to whom he was much attached, died. He felt no grief, but only a rather brazen satisfaction that now he was the sole heir to the family fortune. A few months later, he happened to visit the grave of Pushkin, where he was overcome by bitter weeping for the premature death of the poet, who had died more than two generations before. Freud tells us that this was displaced mourning for the sister. There was a connection between the sister and Pushkin, as the father had praised the verses of the precocious girl, comparing them to those of the famous poet. Freud explains the inhibition of grief for the sister as related to childhood rivalry and frustrated incestuous impulses. The blocked emotions sought outlet in relation to a remote but associated object.

I should like to relate a similar instance of mourning at a distance, occurring in childhood. The boy of whom I speak was ten when his mother died. He was unable to cry, although he showed other upset reactions in the time immediately following. Some time later, after reading through the several volumes about the three musketeers, with whom he became intensely involved, he reached the end when they all died. He cried profusely over this loss, saying, "My three favorite characters died today." Other instances of this phenomenon could be cited. Let me only call attention passingly to how this relates to feelings evoked by stories, plays, films, etc., which provide occasion for releasing, on behalf of characters remote from our own lives, feelings that are often otherwise blocked.

We may now ask: why is it sometimes easier to express grief about a remote object than about one closer to home? Here it is important to distinguish two aspects of reaction to loss. One is release of sad feelings, the other, giving up of the lost object. Inhibited feelings press for outlet in one direction or another. At the same time there is a strong objection against admitting that someone urgently needed is lost beyond recall. If one begins to weep for the lost person it is a step toward acknowledging the reality of the loss. If one weeps by substitution for a remote object, one finds release for pent-up feelings, and at the same time one can go on covertly denying the loss of the person whom one cannot bear to give up. There is also another factor here, which Freud mentioned in connection with the Wolf Man, namely, that conflicting feelings toward the lost object may interfere with a grief reaction. We do not know what the Wolf Man's image of Pushkin was, apart from the association with his sister's writing verses. But we may suppose that he had a very ideal image of this romantic personage and great poet of his native land. I would suggest that one of the reasons why he could weep more readily for Pushkin was that his feelings for the poet were more purely ideal, less fraught with ambivalence, than those he had for his sister. Also, by releasing his feelings toward this substitute object, he could still put off admitting the reality of his sister's death. The same analysis would apply to the boy who wept over the death of the three musketeers. He could react to their death with more evident emotion than to his mother's, because, though he loved them, he was more able to bear saying good-by to them forever. Also, they were more purely ideal objects, toward whom his feelings were less complicated by ambivalence and guilt than those he had for his mother.

Let us return to the point from which we digressed about the intense emotional reactions of young adolescents to the death of the President, which so contrasted with what we consider to be the usual inhibition of affect in this age group in response to a death closer to home. The developmental phase with which we are dealing here, adolescence, is one in which a major life task is that of giving up the parents as primary love objects.[20] This withdrawal from the parents is a long-drawn-out process, in which there is a great deal of vacillation over the years. There is apt to be much ir-ritability toward the parents. At the same time depressed moods express the loss of earlier childhood feelings for them. There is not only regret and conflict, there are many regressions in this difficult process, as children become yet again very clinging toward their parents. How the individual masters this phase of development is, in my opinion, decisive for how he will face losses of loved persons later in life. A certain degree of renunciation of the parents in adolescence is, I think, the necessary precondition for the ability to mourn as we know it in adult life, to endure the kind of mourn-ing as the result of which one can eventually part from the lost object and be ready again to form new attachments. In adolescence this capacity has not yet been established, since the work of parting with the first love objects, the parents, is still in progress.

I have tried to indicate this emotional context in order to show why the death of a parent and the death of a substitute ideal object could have very different impacts at this time in life. The death of a parent would find the young adolescent still far from ready to give him up. At the same time conflicting feelings toward the parent would further interfere with pure regret and sadness. What we have observed instead is inhibition of emotion with a covert obsti-nate denial of the reality of the loss. We may suppose that the sen-timents of these young adolescents toward the President contrasted with feelings toward their parents in several ways. For those who had been able to displace important feelings to the President he was a more ideal person, corresponding to the way in which the parents used to be regarded in earlier childhood. Feelings toward this ideal person could be more pure, less conflict ridden—like the feelings of the Wolf Man for Pushkin, or of the young boy toward the three musketeers. The greater purity of feelings toward this ideal object facilitated the expression of sadness and regret. Their grief for the lost President corresponded to their more diffuse feelings for the loss of the ideal image of their parents of earlier childhood. At the same time the attachment of these young people to the President was of more recent date, their involvement with him was much slighter; he was more dispensable than their par-ents. Their ability to experience grief for his loss was related to the fact that, although painful, it was not that intolerable to think of giving him up as it would be in the case of a parent.

The process of giving up the parents in adolescence is long-drawn-out, inconclusive, characterized by recurrent unpleasant feelings of varying intensity. For young people in this phase of development the death of the President had an effect of bringing these feelings to an unusually dramatic climax. Here was a substitute parent figure, seen in a relatively ideal light, an object of some genuine attachment, but still much more dispensable than their parents. The sudden death of the President provided the occasion for experiencing in an exceptionally dramatic and concentrated way some of the feelings of loss, and having to give up the elders to whom they have been attached, that more usually go on and on in a diffuse, muddled, chronic, and episodic way over many years. One might say that it was a variation on the theme of their time in life, an episode of intense feeling with a dramatic focus, in a context of diffuse emotional difficulties, the sources of which are often obscure on the conscious level. Some of the grief for the gradual loss of their parents in growing up could be expressed toward this ideal and remote personage. At the same time the giving up of the primary love objects, the parents, could still be postponed. This is what I mean by calling the grief of young adolescents for the death of the President an instance of mourning at a distance. Feelings related to the loss or required renunciation of familial objects could be released for the loss of an ideal, remote person. There was an outlet here for otherwise inhibited feelings, or feelings more usually experienced in a less intense and noble, more nagging and mediocre way. At the same time, since these feelings of grief were experienced in relation to a remote object, the giving up of the indispensable familial objects could still be postponed.

Let us now consider feelings of disbelief in reaction to the President's death. We know that generally for persons of any age a sudden catastrophe evokes the initial reaction: "I can't believe it." Partly we are ready, at least temporarily, to sacrifice our commitment to reality when it is too painful. Partly the inner reorganization of our mental economy in response to a major change in our world takes time.

In children's reactions to the death of the President we found repeated expressions of incredulity. It is interesting to note that this feeling frequently occurred in combination with weeping and sadness over what had happened. In those cases where child psychiatrists (responding to our questionnaire) stated that a child or adolescent was sad and cried it was very usual to say that the patient also expressed disbelief.[21] Our junior high school informants show this same combination and also something else that is noteworthy. They not only emphasize very strongly their incredulity at the time of hearing the news, but the persistence of this feeling two months later. "We girls were all crying, and the boys had to hold themselves back [at the time of hearing the news in school]. . . . I still couldn't believe what had happened [on Sunday]. . . . [Watching the funeral] I was seeing what was going on, but I still couldn't understand it. Even now, after it's all over with, it's still hard to believe and understand." (Fourteen-year-old girl, ninth grade.) "At the moment I just couldn't believe it. Things like that don't happen in this day and age and in this country. A few girls started crying. I couldn't. I was really dumbfounded. When I got home, I cryed. I couldn't hold it in anymore. The whole weekend was a nightmare. . . . Even after two months, I still can't believe those events did happen but we must believe them. . . ." (Fourteen-year-old girl, ninth grade.)[22]

When it comes to denying or accepting the reality of a painful event we have to do with many intermediate positions. Logically something is either so or not so. But we know that this law of contradiction does not prevail in the emotional life. In reaction to an exceedingly painful fact, such as the death of a loved person, there are many intermediate stages between disbelief and acceptance. An emotional response of grief is only a partial acknowledgment of the loss. There is also the work of mourning, the protracted process of reality testing, in which memories are painfully renounced, recollection is separated from hope, and the lost person is little by little given up. It is this process that, I think, becomes possible only after adolescence. What our teen-age informants tell us seems to be in conformity with this view: they were able to react with sadness and tears, but the work of reality testing remained incomplete. It seems likely that the emphasis they put on the feeling of disbelief and on its persistence after a considerable time would be more characteristic of this age group than of adults.

V

I should like to summarize the range of affective reactions which I have tried to interpret to some extent: (a.) Bland, brazen, or jocose reactions, which I related mainly to a relatively slight involvement with a remote object, and the children's need to ward off the impact of the unaccustomed grief of their parents, teachers, and other adults. (b.) The short sadness span, which is usual in children. (c.) The phenomenon of mourning at a distance, which may account for the occurrence of more outspoken grief at the death of the President among young adolescents than we would expect in this age group in reaction to the death of a parent. (d.) The combination of sadness and disbelief, and apparent persistence of disbelief in this same age group, indicating the incompleteness of reality testing, which is in accord with our impression that at this age the capacity for the work of mourning is incompletely developed.

Any of these phenomena could, of course, occur on a wide range of age levels. The bland, jocose reactions, of which I have cited instances from latency and prepuberty, also appeared in a number of adolescents. On the other hand, some children in latency and prepuberty showed strong reactions, though they tended to recover relatively quickly. No doubt in addition to developmental variations there were individual differences, differences related to social background, and to other variables, which I have not attempted to deal with here. Also there was a range and complication of reactions beyond what I have concentrated on in this discussion.

The following hypothesis may be advanced as to how feelings of loss evoked by the President's death tended to vary (a) in intensity, (b) in duration, according to age, from the beginning of latency into adulthood. Intensity of reaction seemed to increase from latency to prepuberty to adolescence, with probably a sharp rise between the latter two phases. A point of high intensity was reached in early adolescence (age thirteen to fifteen) and was maintained from there on into later adolescence and adulthood.[23] The variable of duration of grief shows, I think, a different curve. While it first rises in the same way as we move from earlier childhood into adolescence, it then declines as we proceed into adulthood. The persisting disbelief of both younger and older adolescents does not, I think, find a counterpart in adults. The major research study on adults' reactions to the assassination showed intense distress over a few days, with quick subsidence thereafter.[24] It would seem that adults became more readily reconciled to the loss and able to accept it as a *fait accompli*. For adolescents, the feeling of loss tended to persist; they had difficulty working it through. The problem of giving up a loved and admired leader coincided with the basic unresolved task of their time in life, that of giving up their childhood attachment to their parents. It will be of great psychological interest to observe how this national tragedy will eventually be assimilated by these young people.

NOTES

1. Wolfenstein, 1957.

2. Wallace, 1956.

3. A research project on children's reactions to the death of a parent has been in progress for the past four years in the Child Psychiatry Division of Albert Einstein College of Medicine. I should like to acknowledge the collaboration of Dr. and Mrs. Gilbert Kliman, and of Drs. Peter Bokat, Richard Evans, Karl Fossum, Paul Gabriel, Leonard Hollander, Saul Kapel, Sally Kove, Manuel Martinez, Eli Messinger, Judy Roheim, Edward Sperling, Eva Sperling, and Miss Betty Buchsbaum.

4. These interviews were conducted by Dr. and Mrs. Kliman.

5. The schools from which we obtained children's essays and teachers' reports were public schools in middle-class neighborhoods in the New York area. The questionnaire used to obtain information from teachers was devised by Dr. Kliman.

6. Freud, 1938.

7. Freud, 1917.

8. Bowlby, 1963.

9. Deutsch, 1937.

10. Fleming and Altschul, 1963.

11. Similarly, Sheatsley and Feldman (1964) report, from a large scale questionnaire study, that "the nation's children . . . seem to have been considerably less upset than their parents."

12. This should be qualified in relation to President Kennedy's death, in that the shocking manner in which it occurred tended to rouse deep feelings of oedipal malaise in addition to whatever feelings there were for the man

himself. Our students in child psychiatry kept saying after the assassination, "We never knew we cared so much about him." My impression was that they never had cared that much about him before. Alive, he had his individual qualities, but murdered he assumed the aura, evoking horror and guilt, of all murdered leaders.

13. Janis, 1951.

14. Wolfenstein, 1954.

15. I should add that anxiety was no doubt also stimulated by the children's being confronted vividly with crimes of violence. This aspect of the assassination impressed many younger children to whom the President had not yet become a sufficiently real person to evoke feelings of loss. An essay of a second-grade school child sums up the events of the assassination weekend in this way: "President Kennedy was killed by Oswald and Oswald was killed by Mr. Rubbe and Mr. Rubbe is in jail now." Cf. Augusta Alpert's analysis, in this volume, of reactions of boy patients between the ages of five and seven, in whom the assassination apparently evoked alarm that their own aggressive impulses might get out of control. Such reactions were also observed among older children.

16. The essays of fifth grade children, written on the first day back at school after the assassination weekend, repeatedly spoke of having recovered from whatever distress they had felt. The following excerpt is typical. "On Friday afternoon . . . I did not bealive it. . . . When I saw the news that night it was again hard to beleave. . . . On Saturday I still said it was hard to believe. But the shock was wearing off. . . . This morning [Tuesday] I did not say any thing at breakfast about Kennedy. The shock had worn off almost completely." (Fifth grade boy.) Contrast the young adolescents who repeatedly expressed the feeling after the passage of two months that they still could not believe it.

17. The essays were submitted anonymously. The students were told that they would be read by some people who were studying how children of different ages felt about the assassination. See Appendix II.

18. These inhibitions also appear in children in latency and prepuberty.

19. Freud, 1918.

20. Cf. Jacobson, 1961.

21. Junior high school and high school teachers, replying to our questionnaire on their pupils' reactions on the afternoon of the assassination, very frequently reported both weeping and disbelief.

22. Cf. Pratt and Lane, in this volume, on a similar persistence of disbelief in college undergraduates. In January a majority of their subjects still said they sometimes found it hard to believe that President Kennedy was really dead.

23. In addition to the findings already cited I should like to mention the following which support this generalization. The reports of teachers (obtained by questionnaires) on children from the beginning of elementary

school through high school showed a marked increase in emotional reactions with beginning adolescence. Greenstein's study, in this volume, based on interviews with college undergraduates, gives evidence of strong reactions among these older adolescents. Sheatsley and Feldman (1964) indicated the high frequency of marked emotional distress in adults. The latter study also stated that, in the age range from earlier childhood into adolescence, intensity of reaction tended to increase with age.

24. According to Sheatsley and Feldman (*op. cit.*) a majority of adults said they had wept, and felt nervous, tense, and also dazed in the period between the assassination and the funeral. Nearly half acknowledged difficulty in sleeping and loss of appetite. At the time these subjects were interviewed, two to five days after the funeral, "a prompt and marked recovery had clearly occurred."

LIST OF REFERENCES

Bowlby, J. 1963. "Pathological Mourning and Childhood Mourning," *Journal of the American Psychoanalytic Association*, XI, 451–73.

Fleming, J. and S. Altschul. 1963. "Activation of Mourning and Growth in Psychoanalysis," *International Journal of Psychoanalysis*, XLIV, 419–31.

Freud, S. 1917. "Mourning and Melancholia." In *Standard Edition*, XIV, 237–58. London: Hogarth Press.

———— 1918. "From the History of an Infantile Neurosis." In *Standard Edition*, XVII, 7–122.

———— 1938. "Splitting of the Ego in the Defensive Process." In *Collected Papers*, V, 372–75. London: Hogarth Press.

Jacobson, E. 1961. "Adolescent Moods and the Remodeling of Psychic Structures in Adolescence." In *The Psychoanalytic Study of the Child*, XVI, 164–83. New York: International Universities Press.

Janis, I. 1951. *Air War and Emotional Stress: Psychological Studies of Bombing and Civilian Defense.* New York: McGraw-Hill.

Sheatsley, P. B. and J. J. Feldman. 1964. "The Assassination of President Kennedy: A Preliminary Report on Public Reactions and Behavior," *Public Opinion Quarterly*, XXVIII, 189–215.

Wallace, A. F. C. 1956. *Tornado in Worcester: An Exploratory Study of Individual and Community Behavior in an Extreme Situation.* Washington: National Academy of Sciences–National Research Council.

Wolfenstein, M. 1954. *Children's Humor: A Psychological Analysis.* Glencoe: The Free Press.

———— 1957. *Disaster: A Psychological Essay.* Glencoe: The Free Press.

4

The Diagnostic and Therapeutic Utilization of Children's Reactions to the President's Death

OTHILDA KRUG and CYNTHIA FOX DEMBER

Several aspects of the clinical, teaching, and research activities of Child Guidance Home[1] determined the nature of this study on children's reactions to the death of the President. It evolved from the basic clinical program of comprehensive diagnosis and treatment for emotionally disturbed children in this inpatient psychiatric center. Routinely the residential procedures include the observation and recording of everyday activities, especially the responses of the children to both ordinary and extraordinary events. In this setting the staff is attuned to and particularly interested in dealing with the patients' reactions to life events that have emotional impact, whether apparently trivial or crucial. These have included a wide range of human experience, often relatively insignificant daily events but also situations such as recurrent, temporary separations from parents, the repetitive separations from some staff members that inevitably occur in a training center, the admission of new patients, the births of siblings in the patients' families, occasionally a patient's acute outburst of destructiveness, and the deaths of relatives and staff.

Thus, in one sense, it was the universality of its impact that distinguished the death of the President from the crises we ordinarily encounter. Therefore, our routine procedures were automatically geared to the kinds of observations and to the collaborative process that constitute a major portion of this research.

In addition to the staff's shared orientation and collaboration, the individual skills of the different staff members contributed an important multidisciplinary approach to our observations and formulations. This study reflects the intense involvement and the coordinated efforts of the entire staff,[2] which are essential in this kind of clinical research.

Further, as part of a university center our clinical activities also constitute the foundation for both teaching and research.[3] It was the underlying orientation toward expanding the body of knowledge in this field that subsequently led to the institution of some special observations and follow-up procedures as a means of supplementing our usual clinical data.

The child psychiatry inpatient treatment service of the Department of Psychiatry, University of Cincinnati, at the Child Guidance Home provided a unique challenge for staff to study and cope with the immediate and ongoing reactions of emotionally disturbed children to an unusual crisis of universal impact. This comprehensive psychiatric treatment program for fifteen children from five to twelve years of age includes intensive individual child psychotherapy at least three times weekly, the collaborative treatment of the parents, a therapeutic milieu or a round-the-clock corrective living experiences in residence, and special or remedial education. Hence, it was possible to study these children individually and in groups in several treatment areas in relation to various staff members of several professional disciplines. In addition, the parents' active participation in regular weekly treatment and their frequent contacts with the child-care staff, as they called for their children and returned them from weekend visits home, enabled the staff to learn about the parents' reactions to the assassination and about their ways of handling this crisis with their children.

On November 22, 1963, shortly before two o'clock, in stunned and quiet disbelief staff members gathered gradually in the staff communications room as they learned of the Dallas shooting. During this time, most children were in the school area downstairs, having just left the early afternoon general assembly for individual tutoring or small group sessions with their teachers. When the principal, a man, first learned the news, he immediately checked the several school activities, quietly informed the three staff teachers, and discussed with each in turn the timing and procedures for telling the children of the attack on the President. Soon each teacher in her own way told her students that something very serious and sad had happened to the President. The children expressed interest in listening to the radio in their own schoolrooms; and after awhile, as they asked more and more questions and began to express some of their feelings, they gathered with their teachers in front of the television set used in the school area. Thus, the entire school group was brought together to share this experience. The immediate reaction was predominantly one of great concern and distress. Initially, there were many anxious questions: "Is he dead?" "Is he still alive?" "What's happening now?" "Who did it?" Periods of such questions by the children and explanations by teachers were interspersed with periods of stunned silence. As tension increased, the children showed some restlessness and hyperactivity and occasionally some mild impulsive aggressiveness, but for the most part the prevailing tone was that of quiet, controlled distress and some weeping which was shared by the children and staff during their discussions together.

In the staff room upstairs shock and disbelief were all pervasive. Periods of heavy silence were punctuated by questions about the welfare of the President, the Vice President, and the governor of Texas, soon with great concern for Mrs. Kennedy and her children, and gradually by speculations about possible assassination plots and the future of the country. As seminars were forgotten and appointments canceled, the communications room became crowded with staff, consultants, and trainees who, fixed at the television, joined in the shocked immobilization of the group. This was eventually relieved in part as many shared the weeping of one of the staff psychiatrists in her reactivated grief and mourning about the death almost three years previously of her husband, who had been assistant director of this program.

At frequent intervals various staff members inquired about or visited the children in the school area. The chief liaison between the children and the clinical staff was the principal, who reported that the initial reactions of two of the children seemed quite different from those of the others. These two children gave no obvious evidence of any immediate concern and were apparently unmoved as they quietly proceeded with their schoolwork.

One was twelve-year-old Barbara, who only rarely spoke of her father, who had died before her birth. Her mother, feeling strong and brave in denying all her own feelings, had never grieved or mourned her husband's death until just recently, during her own treatment. However, as will be pointed out later in some detail, this girl's marked underlying reaction to the President's death was utilized as a crucial experience in her ongoing treatment. Within the hour following the assassination her psychiatrist took her and another patient from the group to the principal's office for some discussion of the event. Her apparent lack of response gave way to her insistence on locating Dallas on the wall map and to cries for protection as the other patient, Albert, became excited and began to push her around.

The second child who showed no immediate assassination reaction was a nine-year-old psychotic boy, Jim, who had serious defects in reality testing and much compulsive ritualistic behavior. He continued apparently unperturbed with his regular schoolwork, but gradually he began to cut out long rectangular pieces of paper. He finally identified these slips as ballots which he distributed to the other children, announcing that they were now going to have an election to elect a new President. The significance of this seemingly strange behavior became quite clear as the staff realized that this boy's name was similar to that of the successor to the Presidency. The report of this child's dramatic response helped in part to focus the staff's attention on the individual as well as on the group reactions of the children.

It was apparent even this early that, although there was an overall response of sadness and grief, each child also responded in his own unique style, which reflected his particular anxiety, defenses, and life history. It should be pointed out that only a few hours after the assassination the children were picked up for the weekend by their parents, as is usual on Fridays; that at least one parent of each child was inevitably involved in some conversation with staff members; and that therefore the tragedy readily became a shared experience among children, staff, and parents. On Monday, after living through in detail, and in relative isolation, the events of those two intervening days, staff and children (and parents again in their brief encounters with staff) were reunited in sharing this stress and its culmination in the funeral proceedings. Actually many parents had telephoned to inquire about their children returning Monday since public schools were closed. Some parents preferred to keep their children home; some children insisted on staying home, and in all probability at least two of these children wished to avoid the encouragement to face their feelings, which they would have encountered at Child Guidance Home.

For the nine children who returned, a relatively unstructured program was planned. The entire staff of child-care workers and teachers (as well as some clinical staff at various periods) made a point of being even more than ordinarily available for participating with the children as they watched TV or listened to the radio or engaged in craft or musical activities. For some children it was important to have staff support and explanations as they watched the funeral proceedings; for others it was equally important that they have staff help in disengaging themselves temporarily from the funereal atmosphere. For example, at one point one child remarked that they were so tired of all this funeral music (there had been nothing else all weekend), couldn't they please have something cheerful. The children seemed relieved when their teacher played a light classical recording which was part of the classroom collection. Later these same children joined the others at the television set to watch the graveside ceremonies.

As the staff participated in these activities, there was ample opportunity to observe the children's individual and group responses. Staff members were specifically asked to record their observations of each child and of the group interactions. In the weeks and months that followed, special note was made in school, in residence, and in therapy sessions of any comments or incidents that seemed related to Kennedy's death.

Finally, a special projective procedure was devised and administered almost three and one half months later to assess further the children's attitudes toward and ways of handling the Kennedy assassination. This consisted of three parts. The first was a word association test, heavily loaded with more or less directly relevant words. Secondly, there was a series of three pictures, one of the late President, one of Mrs. Kennedy, and one of the Kennedy children. These were shown one at a time, and in connection with each picture the following questions were asked: First, "Who is this?" and after the identification had been made, "Tell me about him." The last part of the projective study was the Thematic Apperception Test Card 15, the graveyard scene, shown with the usual TAT instructions to "Make up a story around this picture telling what happened before," etc. All responses were recorded verbatim. One teacher,[4] who has a close tutorial relationship with most of the children, administered these tests individually to each child. The children were scheduled consecutively throughout one day, and that day's program was carefully arranged to avoid any opportunity for a youngster to hear about the tests before he took them. After each child finished, he was escorted to the children's lounge in the residential area to join others who had taken the test. Staff was prepared to note any discussion by or reactions of the children to what might well have represented a fairly heavy bombardment with Kennedy-relevant stimuli. Furthermore, each child was interviewed by his therapist within the next day or so, specifically around the youngster's thoughts about the projective procedures.

In reviewing all these immediate and ongoing observations and the projective results at the end of three and a half months, it became evident that there were several different ways of categorizing the children's responses. For example, there were some definite differences in the immediate and subsequent reactions of the three girls compared to the eleven boys. (Actually there were four girls in residence at the time, but one very immature six-year-old autistic girl gave no indication whatsoever of any knowledge of these events.) Each of the three girls was immediately concerned about Mrs. Kennedy and the Kennedy children rather than the President, whereas initially no boy even mentioned the President's family. The boys were consistently most preoccupied with the manner in which the President was killed and the details of where and how he was wounded and how much he bled and hurt. Although one might expect that girls in general would show greater interest than boys in the women and children of a family, it may be that these girls had a particular reason for their interest and sympathy in the surviving family members. None had ever known her natural father—two were adopted and one was born after her father died. Following the assassination these girls for the first time began to play together with a particular set of paper dolls of Jackie and the

Kennedy children, which had been available but completely ignored for the entire preceding year.

There are many aspects of the children's immediate responses that one might examine. One is the extent to which they were able or compelled to acquire information about the assassination. Depending on their own personalities, the children demonstrated wide variations of interest ranging from almost total repression to an avid seeking of information and constant preoccupation with the many details of the assassination and the Kennedy family. Similarly, they varied considerably in the degree and quality of emotional response. Further, there were substantial differences in their capacities to integrate their intellectual understanding and affective responses.

As indicated above, one girl seemed totally oblivious, intellectually and emotionally, to these unusual circumstances. Tim, an autistic boy of twelve, who typically asked repetitive questions about the minute and trivial details of almost anything, knew all the facts of the situation the day after the funeral but did not seem to comprehend. Although restless and tense, he seemed to be responding more to the anxiety of others around him than to an appreciation of what had occurred. He responded to the projective tests as though the assassination had never occurred, although once when directly questioned he mentioned Kennedy's death. Most noteworthy is the contrast of his TAT card response with those of most other children. He responded with typical themes of physical defect and the loss of a loved one—the kind of response he might have given a year before—whereas most other children showed definite indications in their stories of the impact of the Kennedy material to which they had just been exposed.

Keith, an eleven-year-old, very inhibited boy of at least average intelligence, ordinarily avoided any recognition of his own and others' feelings. Throughout these difficult days he was completely engrossed in reading and playing games and seemed to be struggling to avoid hearing any news or reading any accounts of the assassination. He was the only child who refused to discuss the President's death; in his treatment sessions he dealt largely with themes of planets exploding and everything being bombed and destroyed. Usually remaining very isolated, this child found any closeness extremely frightening. His mother had recurrent depressions and frequent hospitalizations; in fact, at the time of the assassination she had been hospitalized for some time. It was especially intolerable for him to face the idea of the loss of a parent figure. His treatment material, behavior in residence, and the projective studies indicated that three months later he was still unable to acknowledge even the facts of the assassination. On his word association test he, also unlike most of the children, gave no response which referred in any way to the assassination. To the stimulus word "Dallas" he said, "I don't even know what that is," and to "Oswald" he said with some puzzlement, "Was that a movie star?" When shown Kennedy's picture he guessed "Kennedy?" uncertainly, and then commented, "It sure don't look like him." When pressed to amplify he finally declared, "I don't know, all I remember is when he got assassinated." To the picture of Mrs. Kennedy and also to the TAT card he again replied, "I don't know anything," and to the picture of the children, "They are his *boys,* I don't know anything about them."

In contrast to this boy who used the defense of denial so blatantly, twelve-year-old Earl, who presented a pseudo-adult façade of superiority and self-sufficiency, knew the facts of the assassination and made realistic comments. Although initially he expressed a sense of personal loss as well as concern about what the President's death would mean to the national scene, these feelings seemed mainly superficial and isolated from the major currents of his life. The studies three months later substantiated this superficiality, in that they pointed up both his anxiety and his defenses of denial and silly humor.

Dave, another twelve-year-old boy, responded in a relatively mature manner with serious concern about the future of the country, but his anxiety was evident in his regression to his preoccupation with numbers, in which he emphasized that numbers do not die. In the follow-up study in response to the pictures, Dave reviewed the life history of the President and all the events of the assassination weekend, stressing quantities, dates, ages, the numbers of people, etc. He made many errors of names and family relationships; for example, he referred to Kennedy as "the children's President, no, their father . . . ," and seemed unable to integrate in one person the roles of President, father, and husband. His TAT response illustrated the children's tendency to tell stories after the Kennedy stimuli that were more disturbed in both form and content than the stories they told under usual testing circumstances. In the Kennedy projective study Dave's story to the TAT card of the graveyard scene was as follows:

> "Well, before he looks down at the grave and remembers before—when his wife died. This was about four years ago. He still looks at his—at the death place of his wife. Sorrowfully, he folds his hands and looks down. Then presently he is in sorrow because of his sadness. Even though it has been about 3 or 4 years ago, he still remembers her. His children, about 14 and 12, will pretty soon be going out to college and getting married. Still he is very sorrow because of his wife. He really does look sad."

In October, just one month before the assassination, Dave had presented the following response to the same TAT card:

> "The man went to cemetery and saw . . . and saw all the graves and decided to go and see more graves beyond. While he was there he decided see his, his, the dead people in his family . . . so . . . and he put a flower by the grave. That's all." ("Who?") "His mother, his father, his grandfather; his grandmother is living."

The degree of disorganization following the Kennedy material and in response to a stimulus that this boy previously handled in a more orderly way suggests that the impact of the Kennedy material was sufficiently disturbing to interfere temporarily with his ego functioning. The marked anxiety apparently aroused by the assassination is understandable in view of his frequently expressed concern about the influence of his grandfather's death on his own father's current attitudes toward him and about the effect on him if his own father were to die. In addition, Dave was disturbed by the teasing of other children, especially seven-year-old Bobby, who had become quite hyperactive and whose only reference to the assassination was to yell at Dave, "You're shot in the head, shot in the head."

An important part of the response of all the boys was that of anxiety, often very obviously about the dangers of being an active assertive man in a position of leadership or responsibility. This certainly was evident with Jim, who insisted on having an election because he could not tolerate being identified with the new President. Jim is typically grandiose in his manner and behavior and often compulsively wants to learn all the details of any event. Yet on the day of the funeral he tried to ignore the TV, glancing at it only out of the corner of his eye. At lunchtime when the tables had been slightly rearranged to permit everyone to watch TV, he was described as "having a tantrum and falling apart because people were not in their customary seats." Subsequently, he frequently had disturbing dreams. In treatment sessions he made many motorcades which contained only sergeants and privates and never any captains, Presidents, or other leaders. This stood in marked contrast to his usual preoccupation with high-ranking officers. In the follow-up projectives, his anxiety was manifested by delayed reaction times to Kennedy-relevant words and by bland replies such as "President-person," "Kennedy-name," "head-things," "Dallascity," "widow-lady," etc. In response to the word "Johnson" he said, after an extended pause; "Got me in a trap that time, all I can say is that it's sorta like my name." His TAT response was a restitution fantasy of getting everyone out of the graveyard and restored to a second life.

Don (age eleven) was another boy for whom this event highlighted the dangers of being a man. As a reaction formation to marked dependency wishes, he always appeared very independent and self-sufficient. When he arrived at the Home, over two years before, he had serious learning problems and could not control aggression; in fact, his destructive outbursts prevented his remaining in his small classroom except for very brief periods. Both initially and subsequently Don was very distressed about the President's death and anxiously and repetitively insisted, "This could happen to anybody, I always thought I'd grow up to be a President, but I'm not so sure about it now; maybe I don't even want to." Interestingly, Don's father in his own treatment interview immediately after the assassination never mentioned the disaster but spoke at great length of how he always wanted to be president of his own company.

In the projective studies Don gave consistently relevant, orderly responses, which were not anxiety laden even though they evidenced full awareness of the situation and its implications. His TAT response illustrates this:

> "The guy doesn't look familiar. Is he supposed to be any particular man?" (Examiner: "No, just make up a story.") "I'll bet he's visiting

Kennedy's grave . . . to pay respects 'cause of that dreadful thing that happened. Now President Johnson is President; he probably thinks that . . . he hopes there aren't any wars in the future."

It was particularly striking that this boy who was able to express so openly his distress and anxiety at the time of the assassination was able subsequently to integrate the experience effectively. His capacity to cope with this crisis was consistent with his clinical progress as evidenced in his new-found ability to learn and to attend public school during the previous few months.

Ten-year-old Mac, ordinarily anxious about all destructive impulses yet fascinated by violence, did not talk about the assassination immediately, but his underlying anxiety was manifested by the recurrence of arm and facial tics that had not been apparent for many months. His first verbal expression of anxiety occurred when he asked his psychiatrist, who had been in Dallas two weeks before the assassination, "You went to Dallas, what if something had happened to you?" In January at a table conversation, he calmly described the details of the shooting, explained how the second bullet had been the fatal one, and demonstrated just where the bullets entered and left the body. In March he responded to the stimulus word "funeral" with, "I don't know," and to "Dallas" with, "What is Dallas?" In the subsequent treatment session his tics were again prominent.

A major component of the response to the assassination of a small group of children included concern about retribution and explicit approval of and pleasure in Oswald's murder. These children were aggressive and provocative and had marked problems of impulse control. Their parents seemed to discuss the assassination in their own interviews more than other parents and independently seemed to show similar pleasure in the fate of Oswald.

The most extreme example was Mal (age twelve), a very narcissistic boy preoccupied with violent, weird, and macabre fantasies. Initially he was excited by the news of the shooting, but as soon as the President's death was confirmed, he lost interest and became absorbed in demonstrating yo-yo tricks. He could not understand why he could not involve others in his performance. Mal's immediate interest in the violence of the deed and his subsequent blandness paralleled his father's expectations and casual attitude when he called for Mal and learned about Oswald that

Friday afternoon. When a staff member told Mal's father that Oswald had just been arrested, he immediately and matter-of-factly commented, "Well, of course, they've killed him, haven't they?" Mal's father, who had just come from his own interview where previously made plans had been discussed about Mal's referral to a school in Texas, commented rather wryly, "You might lose someone who goes to Texas." The apparent indifference was probably maintained at home during the weekend when the parents did not discuss the assassination or turn on the TV, ostensibly because Mal seemed upset.

On Monday, Mal still showed no grief, loudly denied any sense of loss, angrily protested the absence of the usual TV programs, and was generally provocative with the other children. In his psychiatric interview, he described the planes that flew over the cemetery at the burial services, exclaimed with delight, "Oh, that really was neat," and speculated, "What if they had dropped bombs on all those important people."

Another provocative boy, Albert (age nine), who ordinarily invites attack, tattles on others, and seeks the protection of adults, was at first very frightened, crying out, "He really isn't dead, is he? God can bring him back if he wants to, God can do anything." But soon he gave up this magical thinking, and then became hyperactive and angry, telling his therapist that he would hang the guy who did it or chop off his head. On Monday he was quiet and genuinely sad and tearful as he sporadically watched TV. Later he said he was glad Oswald had been killed, but he seemed to understand a staff member's explanation of the injustice of taking the law into one's own hands. When his therapist encouraged him to discuss the disaster, he expressed concern about a father being killed. In his own treatment session his father talked at length and with great interest about the tricky weapons that had been used, emphasizing that Oswald certainly knew what he was doing. Like Don, Albert was able to express sadness and anxiety during the initial three days, and three and a half months later on the projective tests he showed consistently relevant responses with excellent recall and integration of the experience. He emphasized the protective role of policemen, the mutual helpfulness of the President and others, and the theme of restoration of the dead.

The group of children with problems in control of aggression included Patty (age nine), who, in addition to her major concern about Mrs. Kennedy and the children, was also pleased that Oswald was killed. Immediately on learning the news, she commented how serious this was, alternately turned toward the TV and then away from it, and finally sought out the punching bag which she hit 50 times. Then, after banging on the piano briefly, she commented, "It's not nice to kill people." She inquired about when the Pope had died, wondered if her mother and father had heard the news, proceeded to turn the TV off and on several times, and eventually announced that it was time to go upstairs to get away from all this. On Monday after the weekend at home, she commented that she was really glad that Oswald was killed. Again she vacillated between watching TV and provoking other children, with only abortive attempts at other activities. Her parents talked at length about the assassination in their own treatment sessions, the mother emphasizing the tragedy in view of the President's being such a handsome, appealing man, the father being concerned about the political implications.

In response to the picture of Kennedy, Patty focused on a description of the funeral, but immediately asked if the next picture would be that of Oswald. On the word association test, she employed her usual pattern of defensive ignorance and was unable to identify many Kennedy-relevant words such as "Caroline," which she had known when playing with the paper dolls. She seemed to repress those words relating to family and loss. She retained, however, the relatively more esoteric word "Oswald," responding, "Bad . . . kill, is that wrong [to say]?" Subsequently, she was able to discuss with her therapist her uncertainty and bewilderment about feelings of sadness—about how and when one expresses sorrow and really cries. She persisted in proclaiming that she was glad that Oswald was killed, but seemed to be inviting reassurance that there might be more desirable ways of dealing with acts of violence.

Patty's concern with violence served to emphasize that the reaction of the children was not only to the death of the President but also, and perhaps to an even greater extent, to the nature of the President's death; that is, to the violence of the assassination. Those children whose behavior was the most impulsive talked more frequently of Oswald than did the others and expressed some pleasure in his death. Indeed, the responses to the word "Oswald" on the word association test could almost be taken as an index of the children's freedom to express aggressive impulses. For example, Mal, who had said that he was glad Oswald was killed, responded to "Oswald" with the word "lunatic." Albert's response was "killer" and Patty's was "bad . . . kill, is that wrong?" All these children presented severe problems in impulse control. Don's response of "assassin" to the stimulus "Oswald" seemed to reflect not only destructive content but also some control of impulses by intellectualization. This response seemed to be in accord with Don's behavioral changes during treatment—from early frequent aggressive outbursts to later emphasis on rigid control.

Abbie, whose occasional impulsive outbursts tended to be less overtly destructive, identified Oswald in a somewhat more tentative, cautious manner: "Is he the one who killed President Kennedy?" Dave, who often handled anxieties about impulsive behavior by compulsively enumerating a series of events or numbers, responded with "Ruby" to the name "Oswald." This seemed consistent with his pattern of establishing ongoing progressions and sequences.

Another group of children, all of whom were less overt in their expressions of aggression, responded to the name "Oswald" in ways that gave no indication that Oswald had committed an act of violence. Some identified him by name but without apparent affect, whereas others repressed his identity. For example, Earl responded merely with the name "Lee," and Barbara with "Lee Harvey." These two children, in thus further identifying Oswald correctly, displayed their intellectual mastery of the event without revealing any affective components. Two children not only gave emotionally neutral replies, their responses were also completely nonidentifying of Oswald or his behavior. John responded to the word "Oswald" with "a name" and Lennie offered the word "man." If these children were aware of Oswald's identity, they clearly preferred not to talk about it. The most extreme examples of total inability to face the feelings associated with "Oswald" took the form of naïve questions implying complete ignorance. Tim asked, "Who was that?" and Keith, who was mentioned previously as relying heavily on the mechanism of denial, queried, "Was that a movie star?" Thus, none of these less overtly aggressive children even referred to violence in their spontaneous associations to Oswald. However, the gradations in the specificity and relevance of their responses represented variations in intellectual efficiency, which may reflect different degrees of impairment of intellectual functioning by emotional factors.

The most bizarre response to the word "Oswald" was given by active seven-year-old Bobby, who replied, "Hiccup." At the time of the assassination, Bobby's only observable response was hyperactivity, and three and a half months later on the projective studies he gave a series of seemingly bizarre responses to Kennedy-relevant words, all representing some kind of hyperactivity such as jumping, hopping, running about, etc. This seemed to confirm the impression that much of Bobby's hyperactivity was his way of dealing with his anxiety about aggressive impulses.

The most outstanding example of the therapeutic use of a child's reaction to the President's death was that of Barbara (age twelve), a physically and emotionally immature girl who initially appeared quite disorganized in her thinking and behavior. She was the girl whose father died of a heart attack before her birth and whose mother had never grieved until she began her own treatment. After the initial shock and apparent lack of response, Barbara became quite distressed. She was heard muttering something about a mother having a baby to take the father's place, as she believed she had done in her own family. After spending the weekend at home weeping in front of the television set, she brought to the residential setting for the first time pictures of her father, which she showed repeatedly to staff members, proudly pointing out that one had been taken in Washington. On the day of the funeral she remained glued to the TV set, often in tears, so that one staff member was moved to comment that she seemed to bury her father that day.

For several weeks Barbara spoke almost constantly and interchangeably of the President and her father. After that she talked frequently and freely of her father, in marked contrast to her reluctance to do so before the assassination. She spent many hours in subsequent weeks making a scrapbook of President Kennedy and his family, and during this process she acquired a great deal of well-integrated information about Washington, politics, the restoration of the White House, etc. Like Barbara, her mother was greatly concerned about Mrs. Kennedy and the children, emphasizing that only she could fully comprehend Mrs. Kennedy's intense sorrow. Moreover, she thought her own suffering was even greater and more genuine since she felt Mrs. Kennedy's was "so dramatic and somewhat insincere."

Earlier Barbara had identified with the child in family relationships, but gradually she shifted her identification, becoming less preoccupied with the theme of the child losing a father and more concerned with teen-age activities, courtship, marriage, and the fate of women, especially with respect to the potential loss of a husband. She frequently compared Mrs. Kennedy to her mother in regard to the suffering and hardship of being a widow. Although interested in her sister's approaching marriage, she insisted that she herself would find it fun to be a teen-ager and a bridesmaid who might some day accept a fraternity pin but never an engagement ring. She identified with Maria of *West Side Story* as she wept over her dead lover. She became concerned about whether her therapist would be at the center next year, about whether he was the same age as her father at the time of his death, and about whether both she and her therapist would soon die of heart attacks. As Barbara continued to deal effectively with these problems, she showed much progress in learning and in her relationships with others.

For Barbara the projective procedures constituted a pleasurable experience of mastery. She was able to display with confidence and enthusiasm her thorough knowledge as well as her emotional appreciation of all the nuances of the assassination. This was particularly striking in a girl who had earlier used the mechanism of denial so pervasively and could not talk of anything remotely unpleasant. The maturity of her response was only one indication of the extent to which she had synthesized this experience and the way in which she utilized it to further her own growth and development. It was fortuitous that the nature of the event served so readily to highlight her own and her mother's psychodynamics, that they were ready to utilize the experience constructively, and that there was effective collaboration on the several aspects of treatment.

In general, those children who most readily expressed affect, feelings of loss and sadness, anger and anxiety—and who might

have appeared most disturbed by the event—seemed in the follow-up study to have best assimilated and integrated the experience. In part, this was evident in the mature and informed manner
with which they discussed the assassination. In contrast were those
children who at the time of the assassination knew the facts but
dealt with their feelings by denial and avoidance. These children
three and a half months later had only meager knowledge about
this important historical event and seemed to have lost much of the
information they had possessed earlier. This is consistent with our
view of the importance of the interrelationship of intellectual and
emotional factors in the learning process.

The reactions of the children after the projective studies merit
some consideration. As each finished, he joined the staff and the
previously tested children in the lounge where table games and
other quiet activities were available. The most positive comment
was that of Barbara, who said with pleasurable excitement, "This
is a special day." The only other comments about the projective
sessions indicated some dissatisfaction with the interruption of the
regular school routine. Similar changes in the past for other purposes had not elicited such complaints. The children seemed to be
voicing indirectly their wish to continue the regular business of the
day and not to be reminded of the past turmoil. At the lunch table
and later there were no direct references to the Kennedy material
or to the projective procedures. However, the children became
absorbed in looking at old picture albums, talked about "other
kids who had been here," and asked questions such as, "Would
their pictures be kept here after they left?" "How and where was
the building built?" and "Which staff members were here longest?"
etc. This interest was initiated largely by Don, who knew he was
to be discharged at the end of the school year. However, these
concerns about separation and about continuity, history, and tradi-
tion might also have been stimulated by the recall of the Kennedy
assassination that morning.

With at least one patient the assassination provided a nuclear
experience for working through both the emotional and intellectual aspects of a central theme that had blocked her development
for many years, so that she was able to move significantly from a
predominantly pregenital emphasis to an involvement with het-
erosexual interests at both oedipal and adolescent levels. In

several instances the tragedy seemed to serve as a catalyst in re-activating earlier experiences and affects, which could then be dealt with more directly in treatment.

In summary, there were wide variations in the children's reactions to the President's death which related in manifold ways to their central problems and developmental histories. The specific reactions served to confirm and enhance our understanding of each child's current position in the ongoing therapeutic process.

NOTES

1. A joint activity of the Jewish Hospital, the Community Chest and Council of the Cincinnati Area, and the Department of Psychiatry, College of Medicine, University of Cincinnati, with the support of the Division of Mental Hygiene, state of Ohio.

2. We are grateful to C. Caroline Maas, R.N., M.S.W., director of residence and her staff of psychiatric nurses, group workers, and recreational workers; to Edward Requardt, M.A., school principal and the staff of teachers of special education; and to the psychiatric case-work staff, the staff child psychiatrists, and child psychiatry Fellows-in-training for their excellent teamwork and valuable contributions to this study. Special appreciation is extended to Wesley Allinsmith, Ph.D., Professor of Psychology, University of Cincinnati, and Consultant in Research Methodology to this program who has contributed significantly to our increased activities in more organized research; and to Margaret Mead, Ph.D., Visiting Professor of Anthropology to the University's Department of Psychiatry, whose continued interest in our over-all clinical and research programs as well as her special interest in the reactions to the President's death has further stimulated our thinking and the development of this study.

3. Cf. Krug, 1952, 1953, 1958; Krug, Hayward, and Crumpacker, 1952; Krug and Lenz-Stuart, 1956; Newman and Krug, 1964; Sutton, Maas, and Krug, 1962; and Wise, Krug, Hayward, Crumpacker, and Graham, 1953.

4. Miss Peggy Glenn, B.S., merits special recognition for her sensitive administration of the projective materials.

LIST OF REFERENCES

Krug, Othilda. 1952. "The Application of Principles of Child Psychotherapy in Residential Treatment," *American Journal of Psychiatry,* Vol. 108, pp. 695–700.

_____ and Helen Hayward and Bernice Crumpacker. 1952. "Intensive Residential Treatment of a Nine-Year-Old Girl with an Aggressive Behavior Disorder, Petit Mal Epilepsy and Enuresis," *American Journal of Orthopsychiatry*, XXII, 405–27.

_____ 1953. "A Concept of Education in the Residential Treatment of Emotionally Disturbed Children," *American Journal of Orthopsychiatry*, XXIII, 691–96.

_____ and Barbara Lentz-Stuart. 1956. "The Collaborative Treatment of a Mother and a Five and a Half Year Old Boy with Fecal Retention, Soiling, and a School Phobia." In *Case Studies in Childhood Emotional Disabilities*, II, 1–28. New York, American Orthopsychiatric Association.

_____ 1958. "Child Guidance Home–1958," *Cincinnati Journal of Medicine*, Vol. 39, pp. 568–74.

Newman, C., Janet and Othilda Krug, 1964. "Problems in Learning Arithmetic in Emotionally Disabled Children," *Journal of the American Academy of Child Psychiatry*, Vol. 3, pp. 413–29.

Sutton, Helen, Charlotte C. Maas, and Othilda Krug. 1962. "Child Psychiatric Nursing in the Comprehensive Residential Treatment of Emotionally Disturbed Children," *American Journal of Orthopsychiatry*, XXXII, 800–807.

Wise, Louis J., Othilda Krug, Helen Hayward, Bernice Crumpacker, and Virginia T. Graham. 1953. "Residential Treatment of a Ten-Year-Old Boy; Problems in the Differential Diagnosis and Treatment of Marked Destructive Behavior." In *Case Studies in Childhood Emotional Disabilities*, Vol. 1, pp. 331–68. New York: American Orthopsychiatric Association.

5

Choice of Defenses Used by Prelatency Children in Reaction to the Assassination

AUGUSTA ALPERT

These notes are based on excerpts from therapeutic sessions as reported in supervision, and cover one boy of four and a half, two twin boys of five and a half, and another boy of six and a half.[1] On the basis of age one would expect at least three of these boys to be in the oedipal phase and one in early latency, but their psychosexual development shows them to be at various substages in the phallic-oedipal phase.

The double tragedy of the killing of President Kennedy, the "father of his country," and of his assassin was a concrete and dramatic demonstration of the law of talion, which characterizes the superego of this developmental stage. We would expect, therefore, that the anxiety and guilt of these boys would be heavily reinforced by this event. On the other hand, the fact that they became aware of the event, with one exception, in their home and in the presence of mother (and father), would tend to have an attenuating effect on their anxiety. The parents of the exception, the four and a half-year-old, were out of town attending a wedding. A further fact to keep in mind is that the first therapeutic sessions with these children were held after a long weekend of viewing, in the midst of the family, the full pageantry of the event, with ample time in which to assimilate, elaborate, and repress what they had seen and heard. Notwithstanding all this, the marked shift in defenses seen in the therapeutic sessions leaves no doubt as to the anxiety-arousing effect of the event.

Freddy, four and a half, is deeply attached to his father and ambivalent toward his mother. Before the assassination, in analysis and out, he was obsessed with games of "get the enemy." But this externalization of his aggressive feelings was coupled with a turning of the aggression against himself in the form of accident proneness and depression. He is the little boy whose parents were out of town during the weekend of the assassination.

When he came to his first therapeutic hour, the therapist[2] says

> Freddy did not mention Kennedy's death. However, there was a change in his behavior. Whereas he had been playing shooting games, he now was subdued and depressed. He requested we have a party and began to drink from the doll bottle, something he had never done in previous periods of depression. For the next two weeks there were no shooting games. Instead, he began to impersonate a bull, confined in a fenced-off area. He developed a ticlike clearing of the throat, which proved to be "angry noises" of the otherwise gentle bull.

His defense shifted from identification with the aggressor, which never adequately bound his anxiety, to *avoidance,* a primitive protection against pain, and *regression,* i.e., drinking from the bottle. The latter may also represent a regressive attempt to repair the damage of his early relationship with his mother and to establish a more positive, less ambivalent one (in transference). A further attempt was made to control his aggression by identifying with a gentle, confined bull, i.e., by restriction of his own aggression as expressed previously in the shooting games. The ticlike throat clearing is an interesting symptom, condensing a reaction against the self-imposed restraint with aggression in miniature.

Though this is not strictly on the subject of defenses, another example of condensation in Freddy's analytic hours, following the assassination, suggests that a climate of anxiety is favorable to such distortion of the thought process. He described Kennedy as having been "the most important man" and referred to Mrs. Kennedy's putting the wedding ring on his finger; and then talked of his (Freddy's) father, who was the "best man" and had the ring at the wedding. Thus the two fathers lent themselves readily to fusion of image and some confusion as to who the dead hero was, especially in the absence of his father. One can speculate on the accretions which such a condensation would acquire over the years and its implication for analytic work.

Saul, a five-and-a-half-year-old twin, was the first born of the two boys. Typically, he was from the beginning taken over as the mother's boy, whereas the second twin, Roy, was related to the father, as his boy. This continued over the years and of necessity placed an indelible stamp on their personality development.[3] Saul is the passive member of the twinship, with an already clearly masochistic orientation. Both in therapy and in the nursery, his libidinal development at the time preceding the event was that of a barely phallic boy, with a rich phantasy life dealing mainly with sado-masochistic themes. These were often interrupted by welling up of anxiety for which projection, turning aggression against self, and regression were his main defenses. The therapeutic period immediately preceding Kennedy's assassination was full of overdetermined fire play, with better-sustained phallic behavior in the nursery and at home. He started his first therapy session after the event by jumping into his therapist's[4] lap and kissing her on both cheeks, taking her by surprise. His mood was euphoric and his first words on meeting the therapist were, "I wasn't sure you would come today." Still in a euphoric mood, and out of context, with a note of uncertainty he said, "My mother loves me—she really loves me." He showed very little interest in the fire games and was furtive in what lukewarm approaches he made. He made no reference to President Kennedy until the therapist made some comment on the long weekend, to which Saul replied in a flat voice, "Kennedy was shot." "For the rest of the hour," says Miss Tejesay, "he tried to be a terribly good boy, carefully cleaning up what messes he made. When I said he was trying to be so good, his answer was, 'It isn't fair that you should have to clean it up.'"

In terms of defenses, this boy's behavior seems to say: it is safest to be mommy's and the therapist's good little boy, i.e., via regression and identification with her, away from hostile phantasies and phallic mastery, which he had only so recently permitted himself with the help of the therapist. The accompanying mood of euphoria is appropriate for the reunion with the primary love obect, i.e., mother, as it is for the renunciation of hostile, rivalrous feelings toward father (and twin), a triumph of the barely nascent superego. It also represents a reversal of the affect of sadness. The euphoria disappeared soon enough, and in the next sessions he remained regressed: wanting to be picked up, passive, enuretic, sickish, sleepy, in fact, just as he had appeared before therapy.

In the nursery, his teachers'[5] diary notes state that Saul, looking at the picture of Mrs. Kennedy, said, "She's a widow now. I have some good advice for her and she'd better listen: she should marry President Kennedy's brother and make some more babies." It is consistent with this boy's feminine identification that his chief interest should be with the widowed wife-mother. It also confirmed what we have already glimpsed in therapy, i.e., that Saul's oedipal phantasies are fused with his twin rivalry. Thus the surviving brother, he, will marry the wife of his dead brother, Roy.

Roy, the second twin, was forced into an early identification with his father, who is given to emphatic statements of how much *he* resembles his son. It is not surprising that Roy's most available defense before therapy and in therapy has been identification with the aggressor. This took the form of phallic rivalry with his father, whom he vastly admired and envied. Dressed in his defensive armor, he was something of a caricature, what with his bombast and managerial manner. But barely beneath the surface lurked the hopelessly frustrated and anxious little boy. He was a one-defense boy.

In his first therapeutic session after the event, he came down sucking his thumb, by no means typical for him.

According to his therapist,[6] on the way down, he asked, "Did you hear the President was killed? There is a new President Johnson. The man who killed the President was shot by a man named Ruby, who is now in the county jail . . . I feel sad." In the room he drew a picture of a donkey and three tails and said he was going to play Pin-the-Tail-on-the-Donkey. He peeked in order to pin the tail precisely. [He had not played this game over the weekend, or before in therapy.] Roy then played briefly with puppets: the boy-puppet says, "I'm so angry, I could bust," then he strikes the other boy-puppet who complains to mother who calls the doctor. He then lines up some plastic policemen, blows them over, saying; "I'm like a bad giant and they are good." He cuts off the hands and head of one policeman and then decapitates another. He interrupts this and then selects a book to be read to: about a little girl who grows bigger and bigger and can do many things, again sucking his thumb while listening; asks to leave because he'd like to tell his brother what he did to the policemen.

Regression is seen in the thumb sucking. This is followed by an attempt at mastery by a detailed verbal account. Then comes the undoing of castration-death by means of the donkey game, which incidentally fits in with the dismemberment phantasies, shared with his twin brother, only to be followed by a frank expression of his hostile phantasies vented on his twin brother (puppet) and the policemen. It is after this breakthrough that he regresses again in the choice of story, "The Little Girl Who Grew Bigger," as well as in the passive receptive attitude, so untypical of him. But apparently his defensive shifts have failed to subdue his guilt-laden anxiety and he asks to leave so he can tell his brother what he did to the policemen, presumably to share the guilt.

By Christmas, Roy recovered and returned to his old defense. The teachers report that he came to the nursery after the holidays announcing that he was President Lyndon Johnson and insisted on being called Lyndon. In the sessions, his most reliable defense, identification with the aggressor, appeared less protective. As late as January 23, 1964, he interrupted the reading of "Bunny Book" at the point when Bunny becomes the mayor, with, "Oh no, there may be a shot!"

The family is a closely knit unit, which often behaves in a *folie-à-quatre* style, which does not help these boys to differentiate between phantasy and reality. Thus during the recovery period, the father was elected president of his professional organization, but the parents decided to keep these happy tidings from the boys lest they worry that their father might be shot. I was reminded by Roy's teacher, Mrs. Cuffaro, that in October both twins had received from their parents miniature pistols of the type used in the assassination of Lincoln, and had acted out for the group the shooting of Lincoln (Roy) by his brother, Saul. The father's name is very like Abraham. Thus the twins' oedipal phantasy is intimately associated with the fate of Presidents! The group play in the nursery, following the assassination, as reported by the teachers, indicates the typical defense of mastery through play, and consists of re-enacting the funeral pageantry, and of undoing of the assassination: A "funny play" was put on about killing the President who then gets up and makes funny faces (ha, ha—he's not really dead!).[7] One child, not in my report, looked at the picture of

Kennedy and passionately called him "stupid," thus expressing his contempt and anger at the father who dies. The outburst was followed by a kiss of undoing.

Martin, six and a half years old, now in first grade in public school, is chronologically in latency, but in his psychosexual development he is deeply involved in his phallic-oedipal conflict. He came into therapy about one and a half years ago with severe narcissistic anxiety against which he defended himself with strong omnipotent phantasies, and when these failed, with deep regression into immobility. But these ego weaknesses in reality testing and in identity were in process of being compensated for in therapy by the time of this report. Denial of painful reality and identification with the aggressor against castration anxiety became the established defenses. The central conflict was between rivalry with his father over size, power, omnipotence, and a preoedipal longing for handling and fondling by his mother overlaid with a passive orientation to his father. In the course of therapy, this shifted to a phallic orientation toward his father and therapist, and he was moving toward a more normal oedipal conflict in the period preceding the assassination.

In the session on Friday, before the event, his therapist[8] reports that Martin was concerned with the absence of his father, elaborating phantasies of his death in the midst of catastrophes. His mother reported that he watched TV with his family (the father returned) over the fateful weekend, and saw Oswald shot. He did not seem overly disturbed but protested whenever the President's death was discussed. In the first session (Tuesday) after the event, he talked of the assassination in a relatively realistic fashion. By Friday there was a resurgence of his phallic competitiveness with the therapist, which had been in the foreground before the event. Monday, Martin's mother phoned to report that Martin had behaved in a frightened and violent manner over the weekend: he prowled around and made stabbing gestures with a pencil at his younger sister, with an alternation of roles; he would throw himself on the floor in an exuberant manner, roll around, and get up, and continue doing this over and over.

In his Monday session, he reported two dreams over the weekend. In the first dream, "a funny dream, my glasses needed to be fixed, so you came to school and gave me new glasses." In the second dream an elephant was chasing him and he cut the elephant's trunk off. He then turned his attention to some play money, which in the past he had greatly coveted, especially if the therapist held it. Now he said, as he was lying on the floor, "I'm better, I don't want it any more. I hardly even want your tie pin!" The rest of the session was spent drawing two happy faces representing himself and his sister "because we both have appointments." For the next few sessions, according to Dr. Frankel, he was a "model boy", i.e., compliant and more communicative, accepting interpretation and undemanding of direct gratification, in contrast to the past.

In terms of defenses, Martin started out trying to avoid the painful topic when it came up at home. In his first therapeutic session, when questioned, he gave a detailed, factual account, with repression of affect. This was followed by a quiescent period, and by Friday there was an upsurge in the phallic competitiveness with his therapist, in the foreground before the event. The mother's report on Monday indicates that avoidance and denial failed to accomplish their defensive work. What we saw was an attempt at active mastery of anxiety through the repetitive game of stabbing and falling. In this game he characteristically identified with the victim and the aggressor. His identification with the killer, Oswald, brought the inevitable punishment of death, by his own hand, accompanied by exuberance, indicative of the return of his earlier masochistic position, as a defense against castration from outside. His dream of the glasses, reported in the Monday session, expressed a strong positive reliance on the therapist as the fixer of his defective eyes (strabismus), which contributed to his damaged narcissism. In his next dream, he did to the charging elephant exactly what he expected from the elephant (father), i.e., he cut off his trunk. In other words, he identified with the aggressor under the influence of his positive alliance with the therapist. Under the pressure of oedipal guilt and anxiety and to ensure the alliance of his therapist, he made a remarkable renunciation of phallic *envy,* disclaiming any interest in his money, his tie pin, or other possessions. He was only grateful for his appointments and was too ready to be a compliant patient, incidentally demonstrating that a positive transference can be a source of serious resistance to treatment!

In summary, all four little boys reacted to the assassination of President Kennedy as though they felt implicated and were out to prove their innocence. They all renounced their phallic strivings, and each in his own way moved back to earlier libidinal positions. It is an interesting developmental confirmation of the structural hypothesis that the only child to show clear signs of superego anxiety (guilt) is the oldest boy, Martin, six and a half years of age, and incidentally also the sickest of the boys.

NOTES

1. These children attend the nursery and are in individual treatment at the Child Development Center, New York City.

2. Mrs. Charlotte Kearney.

3. This is based on my observations of a goodly number of twins treated over the years at the Child Development Center. The mother reacts to the first twin as the expected child. The second one is either an extra "gift" or more often an extra burden. The extent to which the second twin is rejected or neglected or overprotected varies with the mother's health or pathology. Similarly the role of the father in the emotional vacuum between the mother and the second twin also varies in accordance with observable variables. But the broad pattern I speak of here, i.e., mother–first twin and father–second twin, is a verifiable phenomenon, which has been insufficiently studied in its effect on the personality development of twins.

4. Miss Charlotte Tejesay.

5. Mrs. Harriet Cuffaro. Miss Paige Epps.

6. Mrs. Harriet Berchenko.

7. Author's parenthesis.

8. Dr. Norman Frankel.

6

Oedipal Themes in Children's Reactions to the Assassination[1]

GILBERT KLIMAN, M.D.

Before entering the murky arena of fantasies and related conflicts indicated by the title, it should be kept in mind that the material drawn upon is deliberately circumscribed and selected. It deals with part of the data sought and found by our research team. At the time of the assassination our already existing team had been investigating children's reactions to the death of a parent.[2] One of my own immediate responses to the assassination was to take careful notes following all therapeutic sessions. In this essay I will use principally those notes concerning twelve children, three of whom were in analysis and nine in various degrees of analytically oriented psychotherapy. Additional data were derived from intensive individual interviews conducted separately with a total of twenty-three presumably well children ranging from three through nineteen years.[3] These interviews began twenty-four hours to one week after the assassination and were tape-recorded. They averaged forty-five minutes.[4]

One forceful segment of childhood reactions to the Kennedy assassination will be considered here, somewhat in isolation from others. That segment is the expression of oedipal themes by children. Such an endeavor is necessarily stark, an artificially incomplete statement of psychological functioning even within a single individual at a single moment. It is undertaken in order to explore a few lines of psychoanalytic thinking under special circumstances: stimulation of children by the murder of an extremely important leader.

My deliberately simplified approach depends on the assumption that the President served as the partial object of feelings human beings ordinarily direct mainly toward their fathers. Fairbairn described in analytic detail the reaction of his patients to the death of King George V.[5] Several had particularly strong oral-sadistic trends in their prior emotional lives. These analysands were especially disturbed by King George's death. In their dreams, the three orally sadistic patients readily linked the death of the king to the death of their fathers. De Grazia, describing the responses of 30 analysands to the death of Franklin D. Roosevelt, states: "All made explicit linkages of the President with the father figure."[6]

Certainly, no man can serve the same function for all children or all adults. Kennedy was perceived at different times and by different people as an adult, a peer, a boy, an older brother, an ego ideal, or even a mother image providing civil bounty. It is the purpose of this essay to deal only with the theme of his significance as a father image toward whom some portion of oedipal strivings could be directed. Defenses are regularly brought into operation against such strivings, especially when the competition with the father for mother's affection takes place in a child who also loves his father. Kennedy's death could therefore become a source of painful conflict as well as a source of pure sadness because of personal loss.

There is a body of psychoanalytic thinking to the effect that at times certain primitive tribes and young children have much in common concerning taboos.[7] Both are said to defend against father-murdering and incestuous impulses with taboos against such actions, and are said to find such impulses to be major burdens. A sudden, unexpected murder such as Kennedy's would add to the burdens of children dealing with such urges.[8] The patricide might stimulate by example or contagion the frank emergence of the child's own patricidal impulses. It could at the same time stimulate defenses against such impulses. Various returns to earlier modes of dealing with such urges might be observed, modes not appropriate to the child's ordinary, current ways of thinking, acting, and feeling.

Some feelings of triumph over the dead authority might arise in a few children. Rarely, some disguised idea concerning ingesting the dead leader could appear, perhaps with a suggestion of magically assuming his ingested powers. To carry this simplistic, exploratory thinking further, the murdered father-President might try vengefully to wreak havoc from within. Primitive defensive modes might be noticed, such as prolonged denial of the event, protective avoidance of mentioning it by name, attempts to restitute the dead leader via fantasy, dream, or legend-making. Fears of his vengeful ghost might occur. Then, according to certain primitive notions concerning the mysterious power (mana) of leaders, the power of the violated leader would become transmitted to the assassin. By violating the taboo against patricide, the assassin would become an object of dread as well as indignation. The tribe, or the children, wishing to capture and punish the violator, would at the same time be intensely fearful of him.

Of course, extreme confirmations of such propositions seem quite unlikely. In order to inspect the possibility that Kennedy's murder led to an increase or outbreak of such thoughts among children, a great deal needs to be known that is unknown. The question in fact reveals a gap in knowledge of base-lines in childhood mental life. It is not known how regularly and in what form ideas of father-murder, leader-murder, and retribution for the violation of related taboos are present in children's expressions at various ages and under various circumstances. A special sample can be used for a crude, admittedly unrepresentative but nevertheless informative and expedient approach. That is the base-line occurrence of such oedipal and patricidal processes among children in psychoanalysis before the assassination. Data will therefore be presented from the child analyses and therapies I was conducting before the assassination, the afternoon of the assassination, and the following weeks.

In three analytic cases rather detailed daily notes had been kept before the assassination as well as after, and these will be drawn upon.[9] Less regular but still helpful notes from analytically oriented child therapies will also be used, as well as material from the post-assassination interviews with nonpatients.

With some exceptions, the nonpatient material provides little opportunity to assess the base-line of related preassassination themes. Further methodologic handicaps are apparent: the non-patient interviews were conducted with an openly stated research purpose, to which the children were generally cooperative. Unlike patients who came for help, nonpatients came to help the investigators and came for the specific purpose of talking about Kennedy's death and their feelings about it. No comparable agreement was made with any patient. There is no clear indication of how unrepresentative of children in general are our psychoanalytic patients (not to mention the often more profoundly disturbed patients in therapy of other kinds). In the case of a shared loss—the death of the President—the therapist or investigator may all too readily assume that a particular theme or response of the child is related to the death, whereas an entirely different source may be at work.

Problems in Assessing the Assassination's Impact on Children

Data from the psychoanalysis of children is especially rich in illuminating methodologic difficulties. Each of the three children[10] I had in analysis at the time of President Kennedy's death reacted with characteristic defenses as if against a death wish toward the same-sex parent. Each child also drew upon prior and ongoing life experiences to construct fantasies about the assassination or its consequences. In each case there were current life circumstances that reinforced the child's response to the national tragedy.

Scrutiny of information concerning Charles is chosen here to represent several features also found in the two other analysands. Charles was six and a half and had been in analysis for three sessions a week since early 1963. His presenting symptoms were a mixture of aggressive and destructive behavior. He often threw rocks at other children, made holes in doors and furniture, flooded the sinks and rugs of his house, poured sugar over his sibling, and threw eggs out of windows. Charles' fury was often directed against his mother. He once threatened to kill her with a steak knife, and often threatened to beat her up. After his mother suffered a serious neck injury Charles feared that someone would cut off his mother's head. He sucked his thumb, curled up with a blanket, and suffered dissociated states in the middle of the night during which he sometimes roamed the apartment. Once he tried to climb into the oven. Despite these symptoms and ongoing environmental disorder, Charles behaved well in school and was a rather good student.

His response to the death of a paternal uncle in 1962 included the development of a phobia about the basement of that uncle's house. Charles was heavily laden with castration anxiety long before Kennedy's death. Ridden with oedipal strivings, he lived in a family where the marriage was rocky. He often bathed nude with his mother, and frequently exposed his penis or buttocks to her provocatively. He gave her many passionate embraces and made pelvic thrusts against her body.

There was not much trouble discerning the apparent immediate reaction Charles had to the President's assassination, provided one took advantage of his mother's reports. Information from the mother then necessarily influenced the analyst's comprehension of the immediate post-assassination sessions.

Charles' reaction to the death of Kennedy included much evident sadness. According to his mother's account (given on November 23) Charles came home from school on Friday and sat down with his head on his arms. "Nothing" was the matter he said, "but did you hear the terrible news? Kennedy was shot." Mother: "He died." Charles: "No, he didn't. Oh, where did he get shot? In his chest?" (At this point his eyes filled with tears for a moment.) A little later he said, "How will I remember him?" He had asked the same question when his uncle died. Upon being told that Kennedy would be written about in history books, he went on to ask, "What will happen now? Who will be President?" He then lay down with a blanket and his thumb in his mouth. This was a regression to chronic thumb-sucking, which had ceased only three or four months before. The next day he was very demanding that his father buy him a certain toy. When the toy was obtained, he didn't want it. In fact, he "didn't know what he wanted" except that he wanted something from his father. From that time there were no more tears for Kennedy. According to his mother his maximum shedding of tears had been less than a minute on several occasions during Friday afternoon. Saturday was mainly a day of questioning and badgering. He directed most of his questions to his father rather than his mother, asking, "What does a President do?" When told that the President was a leader, he insisted wryly, "No, the President isn't. The lions are leaders. Do the fish have a leader? Do they vote? Oh yes, they do. They all bring worms and that's how they vote." His jocose attitude did not extend to his concern over remembering the President. On the way home from a drive that Sunday, he held his head out of the window and shouted to passers-by, "Don't forget President Kennedy! Don't forget President Kennedy," over and over, at first in a low voice, later in a louder and louder voice.

During his first session after Kennedy's death, the morning of Saturday, November 23, Charles spied a naked boy doll in the first moments. "It stinks. Pu what a terrible doll." In the last moments of the session he came back to the same theme and had a sister doll demand of the boy, "Put your clothes on. I don't want to see your penis and tushie!" The doll was made to put on his clothes, coming back in a Halloween costume. Then Charles pretended that the boy doll was growing much larger. Charles had many wishes in that session—to bring in a table, to work with play dough, paper, Scotch tape, pencil, wood, wire. I pointed out to him that he had so many wishes at once that the wishes were fighting with each other and couldn't all win. He seemed amused and a bit relaxed by this comment, which came in the opening moments of the session. He then talked about moving away, which was a fantasy. Then he would not be able to see me. He was going to move and would be very busy cleaning his room and visiting his grandmother in another city. He soon began stabbing a can of play dough rather dangerously with his jackknife. Then a false finger of play dough was constructed, making his own finger look very long. He held his hand so only the big finger showed over the table. Then he said it had been cut off, but couldn't talk about how the hand felt or how it had happened that the big finger was cut off.

His play during this first session apparently included a concern over exhibitionistic impulses—defended against with resultant disgust. This conflict is clearly revealed in the exhortation that the boy doll must put his clothes on. Conspicuous erection of his penis was apparently represented by the boy doll suddenly becoming larger after the naked exhibit. These themes are by no means unusual for Charles. Separation themes and castration themes were also evident. The largeness of the false finger and capacity to take charge of the castration were important and characteristically active, mastering responses, which Charles had in the past made to many threats.

At the point where he discussed moving, I asked if he had thought about whether the Kennedy children would be moving. This led him to ask in turn if I would tell him how old they were. When I said that Caroline was about six, he assured me that she was five. He knew this for sure, and that the baby is one year old for sure. He had heard a lot on radio and TV about Kennedy's death, he told me, first hearing it in school from his classmate. One of the boys in the class who lies a great deal told him. Charles couldn't be sure whether the boy was lying or not. Nobody believed it was true, but then the teacher said it was.

Castration and disappearing themes continued in particularly clear expression on November 27. During that session Charles "accidentally" cut off the bottom of a paper Christmas tree, which led him to become very agitated. He then drew an immense candy cane and a building in which 10,000 people could live. He next played a disappearing trick with a piece of crayon, concealing it in the palm of his hand and then in a hunk of plasticine. His agitation seemed more intense than usual, yet the theme was not unusual. What neither his mother nor I knew at this point was that the school had discovered an abdominal mass in Charles, prior to the assassination. The school physician had set in motion a letter to his mother informing her of the fact. The letter had not yet arrived. Charles' castration concerns may have had a large component of true somatic threat underlying them. He had been concerned about the bulge near his groin, of which the mother and I did not learn until December 4. The child's concealment of his physical problem was partly a consequence of having been recently threatened by a neighbor. Caught masturbating, he was warned, "If you do that, you will need an operation." Thus the play session concerning a long finger which was cut off should be considered in the light of bodily anxiety heightened by a new, real, somatic threat. Similarly his general agitation on the morning of November 23, when he had so many wishes at once that he hardly knew what to do, can best be understood as more than a response to the recent murder of Kennedy. Kennedy's murder occurred at a time when Charles was anxious about his own possible death. His heightened conflict over exhibitionistic impulses resulted in part from a need to reassure himself about his bodily integrity. On November 25 Charles spread his buttocks, pointing his anus at his mother, saying, "Look at me." He also did a somersault backward, exposing his anus to her. He went into a public room of his apartment house and walked around with his pants off and penis exposed. This extreme exhibitionism might well have been attributed to castration anxiety over the assassination. However, a slightly less intense but generally similar episode had occurred two weeks before. At that earlier time Charles was probably first becoming aware of his abdominal bulge.

Only the *timing and intensification* of Charles' oedipal turmoil can be attributed to the assassination. His material serves as a cautionary note against the use of *post hoc, ergo propter hoc* reasoning. A mistake could easily be made by focusing exclusively on the assassination as follows:

1. Charles knows Kennedy has been murdered and he links Kennedy with his father.
2. Charles, because he has often wanted his father out of the way, now has increased anxiety concerning oedipal strivings.

Hypothetical examples of easily misreading Charles' expressions can be seen from the following table. A deliberate selection has been made of items from session and history notes taken before the assassination. The selected items could readily be attributed to the assassination had they occurred contemporaneously with it. The remarks in the right-hand column are entirely *erroneous* constructions such as might have been made if the observations had occurred shortly after Kennedy's death.

Material from analytic session or history	*Erroneous interpretation, as if the observation was made following Kennedy's assassination*
ACTUAL DATE: *History, from fall, 1961*	
"Did you know my father is dead and my mother went to Europe?"	Charles heard current rumor that following the assassination Mrs. Kennedy was considering going to live in Europe.

ACTUAL DATE: *Session of May 20, 1963*

"I'm the toughest kid in the world. All the other children are afraid of me. I cut them. I make them bleed, beat them up. Nobody else can go into the sand pile besides me."

Identification with the assassin.

ACTUAL DATE: *Session of Nov. 19, 1963*

The patient brings the body of a dead squirrel to the session. He carries it in a box, stating that he intends to clean the dead squirrel and mount it for his bedroom. "Maybe the squirrel will come back to life. I'll wear rubber gloves and clean it off . . ." "You know, boys killed it with dirt and stones. I feel very sorry for it . . . [later in the session] a wolf might come and try to eat the squirrel."

Experiencing guilt over his identification with the assassin, Charles has begun a restitutive effort. He wants to bring Kennedy back to life, expressing this idea through bringing the squirrel back to life. The cannibalistic overtones of his attitude toward the dead President are expressed by the wolf.

ACTUAL DATE: *Session of Nov. 13, 1963*

Charles is having a great deal of trouble at night. He is more disturbed than his mother has ever seen him before. Two nights ago he came into his parents' bedroom saying he was seeing something terrible whenever he closed his eyes. During the subsequent session he was unable to respond verbally to my interest in his frightening night experiences. However, as an apparent response he made a skeleton out of small plastic pieces.

Charles is occupied with thoughts of the President's body and particularly his skeleton in the grave.

None of the above should be taken to indicate an either-or quality to an assessment of Charles' responses. For example, there is no question that he temporarily regressed to several modes of earlier behavior. He clung to his mother more than usual. He wanted his blanket and sucked his thumb, activities beyond which he had recently progressed. There is also no question that Charles was strongly reminded by the President's death of his uncle's death. When the flag was at half-mast, he wondered why the flag had not been at half-mast when his uncle died. One of his first thoughts was whether his widowed aunt knew of the assassination. His questioning about how he could remember the President was related to his problem of how he could remember his uncle. There is no doubt that Charles was saddened. There is also no doubt that Charles' castration anxiety was heightened. One of his questions about the President's body was whether the entire body would be transported from Texas or whether parts would be cut off and transported. This was partly due to a semantic problem concerning the word "body." Charles had the notion that there is a head and a body, the body being a headless portion. However, the persistence of this notion at age six and a half must be attributed in part to his anxiety over bodily integrity. Charles at one point manifested an identification with the cadaver by lying down with his arms above his head and asking if the President was lying in the coffin just like that.

The scientific problem is complex indeed. On the one hand there are clear and apparently indisputable observations. Yet Charles' mother and I were oblivious of his body-integrity threat, due to the abdominal bulge. Therefore the increment of castration anxiety could all too easily be attributed entirely to his distress over the President. Further discredit is cast upon the reliability of point-for-point correlations to an external event when one sees that on November 13 the child was occupied with a skeleton. A particularly clear death and resurrection fantasy was expressed only three days before the assassination, which would readily have been attributed to a wishful thought about Kennedy being revived.

The month of January, however, left little doubt in my mind that Kennedy occupied the boy profoundly. On January 6 he asked me to draw a picture of President Kennedy next to an American flag. He then told me he had in mind a picture of President Kennedy wearing a black suit and a black tie. This request occurred in a context of making unfavorable contrasts between me and his father, whom at that time Charles was idealizing as a person of boundless generosity and helpfulness. This idealization ran parallel to his feelings about Kennedy. Charles engaged in a bitter quarrel with his mother over the purchase of a Kennedy photograph. She had bought a toy for him, which he allowed her to do.

No sooner did he leave the store than he chided, "You should have bought me that picture and not the toy. What is more important, anyway, the money or President Kennedy?" This boy, who had formerly wanted to be "a playboy" along the lines of the popular magazine of that name, had now changed his ambitions and wanted to become a great builder of bridges; at the same time he had an idealized notion of Kennedy as a man of superhuman accomplishments. Kennedy was now the most wonderful man in the world. He also made a slip during a session in January that suggested a thought about Kennedy. While constructing a lighthouse he called it a "White House." Since that time (through August, 1964) Charles has been occupied with other matters and scarcely a single reference has been made to Kennedy, although themes that could readily be related to the assassination certainly abound. These include occupations with graves, killings, and underground events.

Turning from analytic patients to the larger though less well-studied group of nine psychotherapy patients and our presumably well sample of twenty-three nonpatients permits a broader view. For convenience nine overlapping categories of response can be considered, all of which will be documented to varying extents, although each cannot be thoroughly documented. These by no means exhaustive categories are: expressions of death wishes toward the same-sex parent and the President, identification with the assassin, incestuous fantasies, rescue themes, fearfulness, identification with the victim, fantasies of an assassinatory female, special features of girls' responses, and immediate constructive responses. The use of a selective viewing approach gives an impression that the assassination heightened the problems of children already specially burdened with murderous and incestuous urges. Several variants of my patients' and nonpatients' oedipal predicaments were visible with what seemed to be special clarity. Once more, caution is necessary in reaching any conclusions concerning the significance of the observed data. The number of cases is small and reliable quantitation of the processes involved was not feasible. It is also valuable to keep clearly in mind the sectorial nature of my current report. There is a glaring omission, for example, of information concerning the effect of parental and peer grief upon the responses of the children to whom reference will now be made.

Expression of Death Wishes Toward the Same-Sex Parent and the President

A six-year-old boy who began treatment with me at age four provides us with another cautionary note when interpreting belligerent responses to the assassination. Kenneth had numerous problems, and they often took on an assassinatory, belligerent, and violent character. He suffered many anal preoccupations, and during the first year of treatment expressed considerable confusion in his thought processes. This extended to reversing the pronouns "you" and "I". He had been through a period of physical closeness with his mother at age three, which had stopped rather abruptly. Base-line data include the fact that Kenneth told me in 1962, "When I grow up I want to be a grave digger." This was said following the death of a neighbor. A few months later, during 1962, while in a very good humor, he produced material I might have easily attributed to the Kennedy assassination. He was shooting fireballs and cannon balls from an imaginary cannon. He shot one right through my house and "right through your *head*, Dr. Kliman." At the same time he was imagining himself to be the boss of the world. "See, I am the king of the world, the dictator. I'm beating you up, I'm drowning you." His dictator and world-boss fantasies were very active at the time of the assassination, often accompanied by self-destructive behavior. When Kennedy died, Kenneth made no reference to the event during his session that afternoon until after half an hour I could not refrain from asking if he had heard the news. After I brought up the subject, the child became agitated. In a bellicose fashion he affirmed his previous desires to become the dictator of the world, also saying, "Sure, I know about it. What do you think will happen with all that money? Kennedy left $255,000,000." Kenneth set up the doll house and began to rob Mrs. Kennedy of her money. Four weeks of world dictator, large-scale piracy, and related themes followed. There was some increased agitation at home, from which a good recovery was made during that period. He identified quite plainly with Oswald, whom he said he would like to resemble. For three months he remained convinced that Oswald had committed the murder in order to become President. During late February he had a serious argument with a friend on this subject. Only during March did some more tender attitudes toward Kennedy appear. At that time Kenneth pretended to be Superman, who was catching the bullet which was aimed at Kennedy. Kenneth had, in fact, many tender feelings toward his own father, and his agitation following Kennedy's death apparently expressed a true conflict. He was not simply a boy who wished Kennedy or his father out of the way, but rather a boy deeply distressed by the event of a father-murder. In his subsequent treatment, much advantage has been taken of this episode, with parallel clinical progress.

There are unusual burdens in response to the assassination for children when a parent has already died. Of interest in regard to the stirring up of conflict over death wishes is the case of a twelve-year-old nonpatient boy.[11] He had been paternally bereaved fourteen months before the assassination. He displayed a wide spectrum of reactions to Kennedy's death. The President's death reminded him consciously of his father's death and funeral. He made comparisons, noting that, unlike his father, Kennedy had a closed casket. After his father's death from a painful chronic illness, Donald stated that he had wished his father to die. "If he was going to go through pain and agony, there was just no use sitting in bed." Regarding Kennedy's death, he evinced no such attitude of a possible benefit. Yet his responses indicate an underlying mixture of attitudes. For example, he was unduly critical of details of the funeral. The carriage was not clean enough. Mrs. Kennedy also came in for Donald's criticism: "She was out at twelve midnight, and that is no time to be out even for a visit to the coffin." There is some evidence to suggest that Donald's carping was a defense against an assassinatory wish—as revealed by the following dream, which occurred on November 22, 1963. In that dream Donald became the President at first. Then he changed identity and dreamt about "what possessed Oswald. I dreamed I was Oswald and why I did it. I was thinking what I would have done to get away. Actually I wouldn't do it." Through this dream, Donald not only revealed an identification with the assassin, but also revived some features of his reaction to his own father's death. He had wishes for his father's death but also identified with his father. He suffered abdominal, chest, and arm pains quite startlingly like those of his father. The primitiveness with which Donald manifested both death wishes and physical identity with the dead person is interesting in the light of our preliminary thoughts about the notions of savages and children confronted with death. It is reasonable to suspect that Donald's attention to form, cleanliness, and propriety was in proportion to the intensity of his conflict concerning death wishes toward his father and incestuous wishes toward his mother, who became more available through his father's illness and ultimate death.

Identifications with the Assassin

Evidence for the identifications of Kenneth and Donald with Oswald have already been noted. The responses of an unusually creative and sensitive seventeen-year-old patient are noteworthy in regard to his rapidly developing identification with both John Wilkes Booth and Harvey Lee Oswald. His initial reaction to hearing the news of Kennedy's shooting was one of strong disbelief. He ridiculed the possibility of the report being true, and made some jokes, which he could no longer remember by the next day, having been deeply distressed to learn of the grim reality a few moments after joking. That night Thomas dreamt of "one of the worst punishments" he could experience. His girl friend was unfaithful to him in the dream, flirting and having dates with two handsome boys. This he regarded as retribution for his own unfaithful thoughts. Thomas realized in the session of November 23 that he had been feeling guilty not only about joking but also about a pleasurable feeling of excitement following the news of Kennedy's shooting. Then he also recalled a feeling of doubt concerning historical facts. This appeared in a displaced form late in the afternoon of November 22 when he engaged one of his friends in a discussion of whether a certain event in the friend's childhood had ever actually occurred. He hoped it wasn't true and was unreasonably relieved when he learned that it had never really occurred and had been only a rumor. The notion of a rumor had appeared in his mind when he first heard of Kennedy being shot, and became his excuse for joking when others criticized him.

During the first weekend (November 23 and 24) a partially

conscious identification with Oswald began to crystallize in Thomas. He became interested in details of Oswald's life while driving home from his session of November 23. He felt particularly sympathetic when he learned of certain similarities in his own and Oswald's childhood. Oswald was a cranky, sick boy at age thirteen. Thomas remembered needing psychiatric help himself at that age. By age seventeen hardly any of his friends were talking to him, and that was just what had happened to Oswald. Oswald was too close to his mother, as Thomas also was. Oswald's lack of a father reminded Thomas of his difficulty in being close to his father. Thomas began affecting a cool, composed cruelty to his peers in the next few days. He deliberately rammed his elbow into the face of one boy, and cruelly twisted the arm of another. He developed a homicidal intention toward his mother, with whom he had a severe argument. In an unusual burst of affect Thomas told me, "Oh, I could just *kill* her. I really want to kill her. If I could get away with it I would. I can understand how people want to kill. I've really got it in me." Homicidal impulses toward both his mother and father, with bitter criticism of them, continued for several days. In his dreams he suffered greatly. Once he dreamt that his left arm bone was broken and pushing up through the skin like a tent. Awaking from this dream he made a point of telling his father that he felt as if all the bones in his body had been broken. Tormenting thoughts about the loss of his girl friend continued, and he began to recall how often he had made himself suffer as a little boy. (Then he used to inject some frightening blasphemy into his prayers so that he would be unable to rest.) After two weeks his identification with Oswald was fully conscious and he began to admire John Wilkes Booth:

> There was a man with style. He didn't make the mistake Oswald made of refusing to admit what he had done. He was proud of his assassination. I keep thinking how someday I can grow up and be an assassinator. Wouldn't that be cool? Boy, is this ever sick! But I can't help enjoying the feeling of power and masculinity it gives me. That's why I'm so hard to treat. But, can you imagine Wilkes jumping up on the stage and saying *"Sic semper tyrannis!"* Man that was really cool. Oswald didn't quite have that style.

The following months he had a homicidal wish toward a girl friend's relative and dreamt another punishment dream in which he was on trial and placed inside a large coffinlike box in which he would be crushed by an enormous force. Fantasies of assassinating various school authorities were quite evident at this point, but were no longer being expressed in action such as he had taken against his mother and friends earlier. Clinical progress was moderately uphill for the next six months. His hero worship of Booth was revived during that time by a brief and incompletely felt sadness concerning the death of a friend's wife.

Thomas had a predisposition toward identification with aggressors. Noted as a gifted mimic, he would often conduct elaborate imitations of people who had imposed themselves unpleasantly upon him. He was fond of ridiculing his father through mimicry. A few years prior to the assassination, Thomas was severely beaten by more powerful boys. Thomas could never understand the reason for the older children's attacks. Among his responses was to fantasy becoming very tough. While walking through the streets of New York City he had fantasies of powerfully asserting his physical superiority to all other pedestrians.

Responses Closely Related to Incestuous Impulses

Two of my own twelve patients had marked sexual responses. A seventeen-year-old bereaved girl responded to Kennedy's death with revival of her response to her mother's death a year before. When her mother died, the patient had a "rolling around" feeling in her stomach and a sensation of "deadness." A few weeks later she began to have sexual curiosity about her father. She then went on to feel similarly about a number of other married men. When Kennedy died her stomach again "rolled around" and she felt "dead." A few weeks later she began to imagine it would have been very pleasant if President Kennedy had lain on top of her while he was alive, kissing her. She began to seek out pictures of the handsome young President, although ashamed of her sexual interest in him. Thus she recapitulated her sexual fantasies concerning her father. Her plight seems to be an exaggeration of that suffered by less burdened children. College boys close to her own age were apparently experiencing a defensive reaction against sexual attraction to Mrs. Kennedy. Greenstein reports they spoke of the impossibility of Mrs. Kennedy's ever marrying again.[12] In addition to real considerations of Mrs. Kennedy's plight, such a thought has other uses. It helps prevent her from becoming a fantasied object to the boys themselves.

On November 22 a seven-and-a-half-year-old nonpatient, Edgar, had a dream which is probably related to the theme of Mrs. Kennedy's new and tragic availability. He dreamt of going to India with a beautiful brunet lady friend of Mrs. Kennedy. Edgar was a man in this dream. The lady was six feet tall. They had a wonderful time in India, where the lady had been previously on a trip with Mrs. Kennedy. The tall lady was very attractive. Edgar described her clothing in detail. He stated, "It was a very pleasant dream. You know, it's terrible when you have dreams so pleasant like this and you wake up. It's terrible." His feeling of waking up to a terrible reality probably refers to this bright and sensitive boy's horror at the death of the President, as well as his reluctance to give up the pleasant companionship. The lady whose identity relationship with Mrs. Kennedy is openly stated also bears a strong resemblance to Edgar's mother.

A painful and clear outbreak of an undeniable impulse to have intercourse with Mrs. Kennedy occurred in another boy, who was in analytically oriented psychotherapy with me because of sexual identity confusion. Deeply distressed, this thirteen-year-old faced his thoughts with the courage gained from three years of therapeutic work. He could now dare to feel and overcome such disturbing wishes, and had already told me of similar thoughts about my wife. Kennedy's assassination occurred two years after the transference fantasy developed. At first, when I saw him on the afternoon of November 22, he stuck fast to realistic facts about the assassination. These seemed to be useful for avoidance of painful feelings. Toward the last half of the session he described a sequence of inner events. "I couldn't think of anything for about fifteen seconds. I felt absolutely dumb and numb." (This has happened to him many times before, particularly when a girl has been seductive to him or an older woman has been angry at him.) "But then I got an erection and it lasted for a couple of minutes. Then I felt just like a corpse." Here he began a remarkable identification with Kennedy. Forty-eight hours later he had a daydream that President Kennedy was naked on the stage having intercourse with Mrs. Kennedy, watched by many people. This partly restitutive fantasy was followed by one in which he himself got up on the stage and had intercourse with Mrs. Kennedy. He told me this fantasy with deep shame and a feeling that he just had to get it out because he knew it was terribly important.

Rescue Themes

In his "Supplement to Freud's Analysis of the Oedipus Legend," Karl Abraham points out the importance of father-rescue themes in the fantasy of neurotics.[13] In these fantasies "a neurotic sometimes rescues his father, at other times his mother, from danger of death . . . the tendency to rescue the father is chiefly the expression of an impulsive defiance on the son's part . . . the son generally rescues some representative of the father, for instance a king or any other highly placed person, from an impending danger to life." Among our nonpatients, the latency and preadolescent boys who were interviewed during the first week demonstrated much ingenuity regarding means of rescuing President Kennedy. (Such ingenious mechanical occupations are widespread at all times among this age group.) One boy dreamt of a time machine that allowed him to warn the President in time to avoid Oswald's bullet, and another had a daytime fantasy of similar content. Another youngster constructed a bulletproof vest for the President in a waking fantasy.

We have several reports of the President coming alive in dreams. A particularly interesting example concerns a boy who had long-standing needs to bring back lost love objects:

> An eleven-year-old under achieving boy with few male friends, often suffered nightmares. He had been raised by foster parents since age two because of his own parents' alcoholism. Both natural parents have had very little contact with him. On November 25th the boy dreamt the following. "I was standing next to Mrs. Kennedy watching the caisson with the coffin on it go past. When it was even with us, it stopped. Suddenly the coffin rose upright and the body fell out. It almost landed on my foot and hurt me. The President woke up. Pushing with one hand, he looked around and said 'Where am I? What happened?'" This boy then proceeded to recapitulate his dislike of his own father who had totally deserted him. He also berated the undependability of his alcoholic and psychotic mother. She had visited him only twice in nine years, he had pointed out to the therapist. She had become drunk on those two occasions, and had broken promises for other visits.[14]

Fearfulness as a Response

Feelings of panic and ideas of personal impending disaster were most common and most transparently irrational among latency and preadolescent boys. Only two girls among our subjects and patients had such manifestations.

Among the nonpatient boys reporting fears, an interesting example was told November 23 by seven-year-old Edgar, whose pleasant dream of that night has already been reported:

> It was silly, but Jack and I, when it got real dark—you know it gets dark about five o'clock—I went over to Jack's house and I was so scared when I opened the electric garage door . . . I heard a screech from the door when it opened . . . like a lion was in back of me or a tiger and I ran. . . . Later in my own garage I heard some voices so far away I couldn't understand what they were saying. It was like an echo. It might have been a mile away or a passing car, but I didn't know what it was . . . I just ran. Boy, I got so scared that I ran faster than a train or something over to Jack's house!

A similar fear of Oswald was expressed by the nine-year-old son of a corporation president:

> I still feel very angry right now [Nov. 23] from the very first minute he was shot and when someone told me he was dead I was so mad that I stomped all over the place. . . . I sort of had a fear when I went to bed because I would look out the window and sometimes think that I would see a man here and that it was the assassinator and if it was I said to myself, "Well, stay in there." I felt I would rush into my closet and get a baseball bat and hit him over the head. . . . I walked upstairs and I was thinking, "Any minute now the assassinator is going to jump out of any one of the doors there in the hall . . ." It took me an awful lot of time to fall asleep. I know that because I kept on hearing things. It was just I guess my ears were probably playing tricks on me I guess, and I was trying to go to sleep . . . well, I heard people say—I thought it probably meant my father was turning around the stairs or something like that . . . I was pretty scared. I went to sleep and dreamed I got out of bed and heard the assassinator and went downstairs. I got my baseball bat and I saw the man. And I just hit him over the head and went upstairs.

A suggestion of the castration anxiety aroused was expressed by six-year-old Quentin in the early afternoon of November 23:

I usually have different fears, but last night I got scared the most. I started shaking all around . . . I got to thinking that my fingernails are going to break. They sort of felt dry last night. When they are dry and I hear that squeak I try to get my fingernails wet so they won't break.

Identification with President Kennedy

At first, extreme fearfulness developed in a seventeen-year-old patient who had been concerned his father would die of overwork. This young man called me the night of the assassination to tell me he was very frightened. Perhaps the country would be unable to have a regular government, and a war might occur immediately. Although rather ashamed, he also recognized a selfish concern about whether his out-of-town girl friend could join him if the country was in a state of chaos. Within two weeks he was constructively identifying with Kennedy, with parallel diminution of anxiety. An intermediate phase was spontaneously to deny that Kennedy was like a father in his own thinking—although adding that "everybody thought of Kennedy as a kind of father, a young father, and they grieved his loss like the loss of a father." He felt Kennedy was more like an older brother or a young married man whose situation in life had only a few years before been one that he would like for himself.

Since the second post-assassination week, this patient has manifested a persistent and scholastically useful interest in material related to the Kennedy Administration. He has gradually idealized Kennedy and is leaning seriously toward a political career, beginning with appropriate college studies. He regularly reports to the therapist new bits of information he has acquired about Kennedy's life and work.

A pathological and abrupt form of identification with Kennedy already has been described in the case of the thirteen-year-old boy who imagined replacing the President and having intercourse with Mrs. Kennedy. Several reports concerning nonpatients reveal that there was an immediate feeling of wanting to die, which may involve identification with Kennedy. One ten-year-old nonpatient boy told me on November 23 that he immediately felt like killing himself. He imagined a pair of bullets going through his brains.

It is my impression that very little can be said with certainty about the mechanism of identification with President Kennedy at this point. I believe social and political studies may be more fruitful in this respect. His death may have had considerable influence on the acceptability of Kennedy's known ideologic goals.

Fantasies of an Assassinatory Female

Several schoolteachers reported that a few youngsters put the blame on Madame Nhu.[15] Among the patients at Jacobi Clinic, fifteen-year-old Harvey[16] had a similar thought. In his first post-assassinatory session he described this belief in the initial moments following Kennedy's death with the words, "Mrs. Nhu might be behind it all." His therapist had considerable understanding of the individual nature of this response. It was not simply a politically determined one. Harvey had repeatedly supposed there was a woman behind anything bad that happened. When his therapist pointed out the relevance of his current thinking to his past trend, he went on to consider whether there might be a woman behind everything. "Perhaps there is a woman behind Khrushchev and perhaps a woman behind the murder of Lincoln. There is usually a woman behind every great man, telling him he is wrong." He proceeded to tell a story about a mother who interfered between a father and son.

A powerful determinant of this boy's disposition to blame women was that his father had died an alcoholic death after years of absence from the home. In the months preceding Kennedy's death, Harvey had been inclined to blame his father's absence on his mother's treatment of the father. It is of interest that Harvey spoke of his fear of his father's ghost and of hearing a voice calling him at night, both for the first time in the session following Kennedy's death. The phenomenon of hearing a voice occurred among several latency boys in our nonpatient group as well.

Special Features of Girls' Responses

It has already been noted that girls were more tearful than boys. The most prolongedly tearful and depressed youngster I saw was a nineteen-year-old girl, who was among our twenty-three non-patient subjects. Interviewed on Thanksgiving Day, she said she did not "know what was wrong." She was "taking it terribly hard," more so than anyone else in her family. The girl had wept intermittently for hours each day, was glued to television, and could think of nothing but the sad fate of the President and his family. I had known her before and had never observed her to be depressed. She considered her condition extremely unlike herself. She was, however, specially predisposed because of a remarkable death fantasy she had spun ten years before concerning her natural mother. Abandoned, in her view, by her natural mother, the child invented a story that her mother was dead. She spread the story among her friends and neighbors, some of whom came to accept it as true. The profundity of her response to the assassination becomes more understandable in the light of her prior loss and chronic, conflicted protest over it. It is significant that no conscious death wishes toward the President or her mother were elicited by the assassination, but rather a markedly depressed mood. The nearest she came to expressing a death wish was an unprecedented fear for the safety of her father. Despite his moderately dangerous occupation, the child had not been anxious about him in the past.

Oedipal implications for girls are necessarily more complex than if a woman had died. Yet several cases indicate Kennedy's death could serve as a stimulus for anxiety concerning maternal death. Conflicts associated with a matricidal wish were mobilized. A four-and-a-half-year-old nonpatient, Olga, condensed thoughts about her mother and Kennedy.[17] Her mother had an appendectomy at the time Kennedy was assassinated. Olga considered the possibility that Kennedy might have had the same operation. She was frightened and tried to reassure herself about whether people could be shot in her own city. Nobody could be shot in her own city, she concluded. Also, her mother could not die. Thus condensation of ideas occurred in regard not only to the surgery but also to the shooting. Only later did she begin to link Kennedy with her father. By February she commented that her father's hair looked very much like Kennedy's.

Our female nonpatients in general demonstrated more linkage between Kennedy and their fathers than their mothers. A six-year-and-eleven-month-old nonpatient, Sara, had intense fear over her father's well-being. She sobbed uncontrollably when her father had to take a plane trip one week after the shooting. "Something could happen to Daddy." A few hours after the assassination she said, "I'm so glad my daddy isn't President." This is very parallel to words used by boys her age. We heard of two corporation presidents' sons, both in latency, who feared that their fathers' lives were in special danger. One of these latency boys required a psychiatric consultation, precipitated by his extreme reluctance to let his father out of his sight.

Progressive and Constructive Responses

With the emphasis we have deliberately given to primitive oedipal themes, it has been necessary to exclude many observations. It seems fitting to add that many of the same youngsters described here had quite constructive responses. For example, the seventeen-year-old maternally bereaved girl who had fantasies of intercourse with Kennedy also had a rather immediate helpful response while in school. She comforted many of the students around her, feeling quite strong because of her prior experience with death. She apparently succeeded in conveying the message that one could face such a situation after all.

A fifteen-year-old girl patient whose father had been dying of a chronic illness frequently tormented her mother with threats to reveal to the father the truly hopeless nature of his condition. She had much difficulty in restraining hostile impulses with both her mother and her dying father, and was burdened by guilty responses to these impulses. Immediately after the news of Kennedy's death this child began and maintained a successful constructive attitude toward her father in his terminal illness, from which she did not waver for the next six months. The improvement was in great part a result of hard therapeutic work. The timing was related to the assassination, but there had been occasional comparable periods of smooth father-daughter relationships.

Eighteen-and-a-half-year-old Michael, a nonpatient, experienced a wave of disbelief in the reality of the President's death followed by the fear "that it was a foreign nation and we were in for a big war. I was very scared." He was grief-stricken and even numb at moments. Although momentarily dissociated so that "words seemed like it's a play or it's unreal," his next reaction was distinctly constructive. "Then I thought that after all I was working at the college radio station and I should get right down to it because they might need help down there. There was a big turmoil down there. I was assigned to watch the teletype and tear news off and bring it right into the radio room. I kept watching for news . . . I just couldn't think at this time. I just knew that I had to get the news into the radio room. . . ." This same boy showed considerable grief, shedding a few tears and crying a great deal "inside." He experienced a revival of the grief feelings he had had a year before, when a young uncle of his died unexpectedly.

Summary and Conclusions

I have presented findings concerning twelve children in treatment and twenty-three nonpatients, together with reports from other therapists. Those children about whom the most was known in advance provide the most reason for caution when interpreting details concerning the effect of President Kennedy's assassination upon any one child. Data cited from analysis of three children show extreme difficulty in correctly attributing a child's specific behavior, play, or verbal communication to his feelings about the President's death. There is a temptation for adult investigators, like mourners, to read into the behavior of children the feelings of adults. Examples of misleading inferences and *post hoc, ergo propter hoc* reasoning have been given in some detail. They serve as a caution applicable in other studies of childhood stress and tragedy.

Microscopic study of single children, as in psychoanalytic treatment, does not exclude from view the fact that (however enigmatic were the causes and meanings of a given child's behavior) the children studied had marked emotional distress and intensely charged fantasy. It is my clinical judgment that at any given point in 1963 prior to November 22, the thirty-five children involved in my report would not have been so disturbed or occupied with the material described. Unfortunately there is no reliable measure of the nonpatient group's oedipal preoccupations in the prior months. Where clinical cases are used, there is much evidence for similar pre-existing themes. My judgment of the twelve patients is that as a group they were not *usually* so occupied with readily accessible oedipal themes. This is a matter of degree, and not one to which a true quantity can be ascribed. According to concepts of nonparametric statistics,[18] the likelihood of intensification and increased overtness of oedipal material occurring simply through chance and simultaneously in most of the patients is low. The accessibility of similar themes among presumably well children is a phenomenon that requires much further study. I am inclined to conclude cautiously that if my observations have any general validity, President Kennedy's assassination was followed by a transient outbreak of familiar but highly personalized oedipal themes among many children.

Although the twelve patients and twenty-three nonpatients received the President's murder in markedly individual ways, several general features do emerge. The event seems to have been a threat of a complicated sort. It strained defenses erected against the children's death wishes toward their own parents. The stimulus of the assassin's example was followed by statements of savage notions among several patients and nonpatients studied shortly thereafter. The primitive idea of the President being replaced by the assassin himself was briefly and rarely entertained. Sexual aims toward Mrs. Kennedy or the late President rarely developed in clear form, and again only among incestuously predisposed children. Latency boys viewed the power of the assassin as enormously frightening. He appeared everywhere, invading in their imaginations the very homes of some seven- to ten-year-old children. The anxiety of children about the assassin resembled in outline what might have been predicted from Freud's thinking about the transfer of dangerous influences from a violated leader to the violator. Various forms of castration dreads appeared, presumably because of fears that the unconsciously wished-for patricide would be revenged. Oedipal and latency-age children sometimes expected the President's ghost to appear. Girls as well as boys found themselves responding with oedipal themes. Apparently the assassination served as a tragic screen onto which each child projected his own emotional style and thought content, not only of murder and violence but also concerning the guilty competition for love within his own family.

NOTES

1. Presented at the Albert Einstein College of Medicine Conference on Children's Reactions to the Assassination of President Kennedy, April 4, 1964. A fuller publication of the material outlined in this chapter is planned.

2. Research on children's reactions to the death of a parent has been in progress since 1958 in the Child Psychiatry Division of Albert Einstein College of Medicine. Directing the clinical aspects of this study is Dr. Martha Wolfenstein, Associate Professor of Psychiatry. Dr. Wolfenstein has conducted a continuous case seminar on the theme of childhood bereavement since 1960. Mrs. Ann Kliman and I have concentrated on bereavement phenomena among presumably well children. In addition, a pilot project for preventive intervention following death of a parent is now beginning.

3. See Appendix III of this volume for specimen interviews.

4. Conducted by Mrs. Ann Kliman and myself.

5. Fairbairn, 1936.

6. De Grazia, 1945.

7. Freud, Sigmund, 1913.

8. *Ibid.,* p. 32: "Anyone who has violated a taboo becomes taboo himself because he possesses the dangerous quality of tempting others to follow his example: why should *he* be allowed to do what is forbidden to others? . . ." P. 35: "Disobedience to prohibitions spreads like a contagion. . . ." According to this line of reasoning the action of Ruby in killing Oswald can be understood partly as a defense against further spread of father-murders.

9. My thanks to Drs. Marianne Kris and Grace Abbate, who supervised and encouraged me in the endeavor to keep close track of these three analyses before the assassination made an application of my notes evident. They studied the analytic data with me as it unfolded, but should not be considered responsible for the views stated.

10. In addition to Charles, described below, two other children were a girl, age six and a half, and a boy, age seven. Alpert, 1964, describes the impact of President Kennedy's death on three boy analysands. Each boy showed regressive response, which was less evident in my set of three. Charles had the most distinct regressive movement in my series.

11. Interviewed by Mrs. Ann Kliman.

12. Greenstein, 1965.

13. Abraham, 1922.

14. Reported by Dr. Leon Yorburg. This was one of 100 responses to the author's questionnaire which was distributed to 500 qualified child psychiatrists in January 1964. A complete account of that material is beyond the scope of this essay.

15. These were among reports by 100 teachers in suburban New York schools, in response to the author's questionnaire. This particular idea was noted on the afternoon of the assassination, having been expressed by children who heard the news and were still in school.

16. Reported by Dr. Sally Kove.

17. Reported by Dr. Peter Bokat. Fusion of President Kennedy's image with that of a parent is also reported by Alpert in this volume. The existence of such data is clear support for the hypothesis that a leader is frequently invested with parental attributes. In the reported instances, the investment apparently occurs at a level of mental functioning where ideas and energies are readily displaceable and coalescent, characteristic of early childhood as well as of "primary" processes throughout adult life.

18. Siegel, 1956. The significance of my findings concerning the distress of my patients after the assassination could conceivably be tested by nonparametric statistics. Considering the two weeks prior to November 22 and the following two weeks, none of my patients were less distressed than usual, eleven were more distressed, one was unchanged. If one takes such ratings by a therapist as reliable and valid, then the significance is very high: according to the Chi Square Test, P = .001.

As for the accessibility of oedipal themes in my patients during those same two-week periods, a similar pattern emerges from my own ratings. No patient was less accessible in these matters, three were unchanged, and nine were more accessible in the two weeks after November 22: according to the Chi Square Test, P = .01.

Serious difficulties stand in the way of such an approach. Techniques for evaluating judgmental reliability are arduous. The use of other raters to judge the data is desirable, and a method should be used by which pre- and post-assassination data are not identified as such when the rater is scrutinizing them.

LIST OF REFERENCES

Abraham, Karl. 1922. "Father-Murder and Father-Rescue In The Fantasies of Neurotics," first published in *Internationale Zeitschrift fur Psychoanalyse,* VIII, 71. Also in Fliess, Robert, 1950. *The Psychoanalytic Reader.*

Alpert, Augusta, 1965. This volume.

De Grazia, Sebastian, 1945. "A Note On The Psychological Position Of The Chief Executive." In *Psychiatry,* Vol. 8, pp. 267–72.

Fairbairn, W. Ronald D. 1936. "The Effect of the King's Death upon Patients undergoing Analysis." *International Journal of Psychoanalysis,* XVII, 278–84.

Freud, Sigmund, 1913. "Totem and Taboo." In *Standard Edition,* Vol. XIII. London: Hogarth Press, Ltd.

Greenstein, Fred, 1965. This volume.

Orlansky, Harold, 1947. "Reactions To The Death of President Roosevelt," *Journal of Social Psychology,* Vol. 26, pp. 235–66.

Siegel, Sidney. 1956. *Nonparametric Statistics for the Behavioral Sciences.* New York: McGraw-Hill.

7

The Impact of the Assassination
of President Kennedy
on Child Psychiatric Patients[1]

I. Introduction

Self-evident though it may be, one of the most interesting aspects of the impact of President Kennedy's death was the fact that a singular and relatively similar tragic stimulus affected very different individuals living under widely different conditions. Thus, by observing the reactions of the range of children and their parents, we were able to study the different ways in which this common event was the focus for a variety of adaptive maneuvers. Nationwide grief and mourning were strikingly apparent, particularly in adults. There were occasional reminders of children, but with little or no reference to their mourning or grief reactions. Photographs of John-John and Caroline appeared, and a brief report of a classroom in Texas where the reactions to the first report of "threats to the President's life" reportedly produced childish cheers. Some of us who are concerned about and work directly with children began to wonder about certain questions: How are children actually reacting? What about the different age groups? Are disturbed children reacting more or less severely? How was the situation seen through the special perspective of a treatment situation?

After the initial shock and mourning, and possibly as part of our own "working through," we turned to these questions and became increasingly concerned with the necessity for gathering some of the immediate material on children before it disappeared.[2] This report covers only the material on child psychiatric patients. The material on a large school population will be reported in a later publication.[3] In this report I will present: 1.) some ideas and research areas that have influenced this study and some definitions of relevant basic terms, such as depression and mourning; 2.) a clinical description of reactions to the assassination and the death of President Kennedy of children in treatment at the time; and, 3.) the reactions of some of the parents of these children, fathers as well as mothers.

II. Basic Definitions and Some Research Considerations

The death of the nation's leader is, of course, an experience of loss leading to reactions of mourning, depression, bereavement, and grief.

Mourning was defined in Freud's classical paper "Mourning and Melancholia":[4]

> Mourning is regularly the reaction to loss of a loved person, or to the loss of some abstraction which has taken the place of one, such as one's country, liberty, an ideal, and so on.

"Depression" is used here as described by Greenacre:[5]

> Depression, as a symptom, is as ubiquitous as life itself and, in a mild degree, appears "naturally" as a reaction to loss which no life escapes. Its occurrence under these conditions is so regularly present as to be accepted as an accompaniment or sequel to loss which need hardly be questioned. It is, however, a positive, forceful, affective state, though in a negative direction, as in contrast to apathy or indifference which it may superficially simulate, and it implies inherently some degree of identification of the subject with the object lost. It is certainly the intensity, the excessive duration and the domination of the organism by the affect, rather than its occurrence, which is pathological.

Bibring's paper[6] extended our understanding of depression in terms of the newer insights of ego psychology in ways particularly relevant to the present study. He emphasized that

> basic depression represents a state of the ego whose main characteristics are a decrease of self-esteem, a more or less intense state of helplessness, a more or less intensive and extensive inhibition of functions, and a more or less intensely felt particular emotion; in other words, de-

pression represents an affective state, which indicates a state of the ego in terms of helplessness and inhibition of functions.

These and other major contributions, including those of Abraham[7] and Lindemann,[8] are based primarily on observations and work with adults. Lindemann's classic work, "The Symptomatology and Management of Acute Grief," studied specifically the reactions to actual loss of 101 adults. He commented, "Grief reactions are just *one* form of separation reactions. Separation by death is characterized by its irreversibility and finality." He described normal and morbid grief reactions in the observed adults, providing us with important clinical material which amplified and extended Freud's original description.

Separation reactions are phenomena that have been studied in children, but the specific course of normal and morbid grief, as just mentioned, has not been extensively discussed. The classical studies of children dealing with reactions to early loss include the work of Spitz,[9] Bowlby,[10] A. Freud,[11] Rank,[12] and Mahler.[13] Rochlin,[14] in his paper, "The Dread of Abandonment," reminds us of the long history of concern with matters of death, loss, grief, etc., reaching back to prehistoric times. In another paper, "The Loss Complex,"[15] he states that depression, as seen in adults, does not occur in a child's reaction to loss, and that mourning is not common. Another author, Mahler,[16] has commented, however, that

> we know that systematized affective disorders are unknown in childhood. It has been conclusively established that the immature personality structure of the infant or older child is not capable of producing a state of depression such as that seen in the adult (Zetzel 1953, 1960). *But grief as a basic ego reaction does prevail.* This implies that as soon as the ego emerges from the undifferentiated phase, the mimetic, gestural, and physiological signs of grief do appear, albeit in rudimentary form. The child's grief is remarkably short-lived because his ego cannot sustain itself without taking prompt defensive actions against object loss . . . Mechanisms other than bereavement, such as substitution, denial, and repression, soon take over in various combinations. Children recover from transient reactions of mourning, accordingly, with lesser or greater scar formation.

And another author, Shambaugh,[17] in the same series of papers in a volume of *The Psychoanalytic Study of the Child* dealing with loss reactions in children, commented in a summary way that three factors, at least, separate a young child subject to an important loss from a bereaved adult; his real state of dependency on adults, his not yet fully incorporated super-ego, and his relatively undeveloped ego.

These three factors obviously undergo progressive changes in the course of chronological and psychological development of the child, and would thus differentially influence loss reactions. The data we have collected fortunately cover the age span of five to seventeen.

Studies of children can concentrate on the child himself, on the parent-child constellation, or on the child in the larger world of family and community. A paper by Rochlin[18] exemplifies the first type of study dealing with the inner functioning of the child and he comments that

> this paper has emphasized the central role of the mother but has not concerned itself with her (the mother's) character or her conflicts. Clearly her personality is a force that affects the child's disorder and the course of her treatment is important. We have too often tended to think of the child's disorder as merely reflecting the mother's conflicts—unquestionably, it often does reflect them—but we must not overlook the fact that the child has an *autonomous psychic life* of his own.

The familiar work of Szurek and Johnson[19] illustrates the second category, parent-child study, and particularly the interrelationship of their conflicts. Their theoretical formulation and clinical investigations have emphasized how the parent's forbidden impulses are acted out vicariously by delinquent children and that "this very acting out, in a way so foreign to the conscious wishes of the parent, served often as a channel for hostile, destructive impulses that the parent felt toward the child." This approach appears to have had considerable influence. In the early phase of our study, as we attempted to collect data, we repeatedly were told, "You'll get back from the children what they've heard from their parents." This was the common attitude among professionals. The report of some observations in the parent-child area will clarify the limitations of this view.

A very brief mention of the third area, the child in the larger community, reveals both some of the complexities and the importance of these considerations. This study of children can possibly extend our knowledge of the wider ramifications of reactions to loss in the context of a special situation—one of national crisis.

There is a recent and growing body of literature on crisis reactions and crisis theory. The work by Lindemann[20] describing grief reactions was done in the aftermath of a crisis, the Coconut Grove Fire, and was a first attempt to analyze and systematize the reactions of people to an acute situational crisis. This and other works by Lindemann, Caplan, and co-workers have focused on acute, short-term crises resulting from external and sudden unexpected events such as the reactions to the crisis of entering school, of premature birth,[21] or of geographical displacement.[22] The developmental schema of Erikson[23] includes crisis as a part of normal psychological development. Normal maturational crises have been studied, for example, in the pregnancy studies of Dr. G. Bibring, et al.[24] In an article, "Crisis in Chronic Problem Families,"[25] an attempt was made to organize some of the growing material on crises and their effects on families. The details of this classification of crises are not relevant, but it is necessary to note that the material to be reported here is on children and reactions to loss in the context of a national crisis. This is another acute, externally initiated situational crisis and thus is similar to the crisis reported and studied by Lindemann, only our study concerns mainly children, not adults, and the effect of a national loss rather than a local personal, or individual loss. Crisis as a general phenomenon may be covered by a universal definition. However, as increasing knowledge accumulates, the specific characteristics of particular kinds of crises emerge. This material is on a national crisis and can be compared to and differentiated from reactions to an individual crisis, family crisis, or group crisis as in some of the literature just mentioned.

III. Reactions of Children

In these data, the first therapeutic interview following the assassination of President Kennedy was described by child therapists.[26] This material will be reported in age groups: 1.) the youngest children, four to five; 2.) eight to ten; 3.) ten to twelve; and 4.) thirteen to seventeen years.

(1) *The youngest children,* ages four to five. There were only two children in this group.

The five-year-old's reaction: Carl, an active little boy, immediately began to play with some blocks. He shortly switched to a game of Uncle Wiggily, and from knowledge gained in previous sessions the therapist commented that he "chooses Uncle Wiggily when he is upset." The boy said he liked to win. The therapist, continuing with the idea of upset, asked generally about the weekend. Carl responded immediately, "Kennedy died—they put him in the ground with dirt over him—that's all—I watched TV." Then he said, with emphasis, "People *oughtn't* to do things like that—it's terrible." The therapist wondered why, and the patient became restless. The remainder of the hour was spent in play with the doll house in which the family was kept physically close together.

Carl's moral "oughtn't" response was striking and clear. At the age of five the consolidation of the superego with the subsequent development of morality and its strict "ought's" and "oughtn't's" is a major concern. We can see how this event of national concern was viewed by this child in relation to his major internal work of the moment, a superego "ought not."

In other situations involving this young age, such as a nursery school, a strong tendency was observed for the teachers and other workers to feel that these young children were *not* involved with national events. After appropriate probing, however, Carl indicated a clear and reactive response. In another group setting of four- to five-year-olds[27] an adult observer noticed one boy standing apart from the group's activity. Asked if he was making anything, he replied that he felt "tired." The observer commented that he, too, felt "sad" because of President Kennedy's death. The boy looked very surprised and said, "How did you know?" and went on to describe his mother's reaction of crying. In large group situations where probing was not usual, lack of spontaneous material does not indicate lack of inner response. Carl's response raises the question of psychological susceptibility to certain kinds of external events, national or local, at certain ages and stages of development. Carl made it clear that this national event impinged upon his superego concerns. What long-range effect this had cannot be answered. But the lack of spontaneous material in young children cannot be used as evidence of lack of concern with an issue. This clinical fragment in a time of national crisis, which results in stronger responses, opens some larger issues in the area of preventive psychiatry and mental health work. What effect do national crises have on very young children and have we passed these by in our concerns? Children, particularly the very young and possibly the most susceptible, do not usually inform us of their reactions unless asked in ways that are appropriate to their age, stage of development, and preferred modes of expression.

(2) *The next group,* eight to ten years old. There were eighteen children in this group. Two individual reactions will be described and then some general descriptions given of this age group.

(a) EDWARD, age eight years and three months talked first about his younger brother moving into his room (a baby had been born recently). Edward mentioned that his brother had been falling out of his new bed. He did not hurt himself, his mother did not come in, and Edward helped him. After greedily drinking Coke and eating candy, Edward responded to the therapist's general question about the weekend by looking anxiously at the box of soldiers. The therapist continued, saying, "It was a sad weekend—it was sad about the President." Edward responded, "My grandmother said, 'The whole world might be blown up.'" To further query by the therapist he looked puzzled and increasingly anxious. After some reassurance by the therapist that the world would not be blown up, he said, "I don't think anything like that will happen either." Edward had requested some new soldiers for the war games he often played and spent the remainder of the hour in such games. This included references to the national events in the form of killed kings being replaced by the next in line and captured spies who must be made to suffer.

The idea that the world may blow up as a result of President Kennedy's death was clearly an important and affect-laden one and of special concern to this boy. We turn to his history for some help in understanding this.

Edward is the first son of parents of European origin. The grandparents migrated to the United States, and since that time the family has experienced considerable improvement in circumstances, education, and general status. However, Edward's parents were still poor (actually poverty-stricken) when they married, and they lived with the paternal grandparents. Edward's mother describes these years as full of terrible tension and distress. The paternal grandmother adored Edward and argued continually with the mother about his upbringing and rearing, involving any other available paternal family member in these disputes and getting them to side with her against the mother. The mother described walking out of the house impulsively on Edward's first birthday, and then returning shortly afterward. The tension continued, the familial situation worsened. The grandmother kept the boy from playing with other children because of the dangers of the outside world. When he was a little older she interfered with his attendance at nursery school and kindergarten because of the "dangers." Recently the mother insisted that Edward's father decide whether he was "to be husband or only his mother's son." They moved away from the paternal grandparents, and Edward strongly missed his grandmother.

In the Kennedy crisis situation, the boy's expression, "The world might be blown up," came from his grandmother's world picture. He had undergone a recent experience of loss in his relationship with her; their close day-to-day relationship had been disrupted after his family moved. This grandmother-colored material becomes even more striking when we observe how his parents handled the death of Kennedy (described in a later section). Under ordinary circumstances, ideas of world destruction are encountered more frequently in psychotic conditions. Edward was an anxious, constricted, neurotic child, somewhat estranged from his peers and with mild learning difficulties. Here again we can see the importance of actually studying crisis reactions. Such ideas were not uncommonly expressed by children, and in this example were due to the combination of Edward's particular experiences and his age. The familiar cowboy and Indian games played by children at this age, with their multiple killings, and even more the modern space games, include many varieties of violence and destruction as part of the child's normal development and vicissitudes of aggression. Violence and other forms of aggression are played out by children within familiar family settings and also outside in the exciting world of the Wild West or outer space. Thus some very violent and world-destructive ideas are not psychotic but part of a developmental process in children.

(b) JOHN, age eight: John began the interview by complaining about his sore throat, fearing that if he went to a doctor for care it would immediately result in a tonsillectomy. He then discussed an emergency appendectomy and described his ideas: "Water went into the appendix—it got chapped—swelled up," and that caused the appendicitis.

Toward the end of the hour he brought out a picture of his dog and reported that this dog had been housebroken but was now soiling the floor again. In response to a query by the therapist as to what might be the cause of this, John replied, "He's like Oswald. Oswald was trained once when he was in the Coast Guard; he got untrained and shot the President. That's just like my dog; he was trained not to soil and he got untrained and started to soil." The patient thus explained in his own way that training meant control. "That's right. Oswald lost control and killed the President, and my dog probably doesn't know what he's doing either." While formulated in different terms than Edward's, John's response showed the similar issue of control in contrast to the more rudimentary superego formulation of the five-year-old.

John is the only son in a comfortable middle-class family. He was referred for treatment when his parents and the school got into a wrangle; the school said John couldn't read and therefore needed help. The parents became furious, insisting that at home he certainly could read! John's mother, after marriage, had remained very close to both her mother, who was a chronic invalid, and to her older brother, who was crippled. Most days of John's early years were spent in "running" with his mother to the home of his maternal grandmother and maternal uncle while his mother cared for them. When the maternal grandmother died, the boy was not told that she was dead but rather that soon she would send a special present from heaven. Similarly, when the boy was brought to the clinic his mother, taking the initiative in the lobby, said to John, "This is a teacher," and winked at the therapist. Other material indicated clearly that this mother had great difficulty in allowing any expression of John's aggression and growth of independent identity. Her descriptions of him emphasized only his being thoughtful and sensitive. Her only response to an incident in which some schoolmates outside his house were overheard ganging up on John and talking about beating him up, was to comment on his "wanting to give candy to the neighborhood children." This mother also depended upon John for affection and other important feelings. She described as a daily event lying in the den and waiting until John brought a blanket and covered her, and then, "If the dog jumps on me, John will too, and I giggle in my extremely humorous, happy home." The night of the assassination she slept with John, and his father slept in the den. This she described as a specific reaction to the crisis and said it had happened only once before when John was two years old. Seeing an actual shooting was clearly extremely anxiety-provoking to this boy for whom expression of aggression was prohibited.

These two boys represent only a portion of the kind of responses encountered in this age group. Here are brief representative descriptions of some of the other kinds of responses in this age group, without the background clinical material given in the first two case examples.

One boy, age eight and a half, described where the President got shot, pointing with exactness to head, chin, etc. He added, "The man who shot him was his friend." The boy felt "sad." "People on TV were crying." And he added, "I did cry at first." He also reported that his "grandmother and grandfather had their hearts set on Kennedy," but could not say what this meant. His mother, he reported, "forgot" about her appointment at the clinic because of the news of President Kennedy's death. Feeling "sad" and "bad" was a frequent response in this age group.

Some children initially commented by noting activities important to them. Sandra (and others) said, "Kennedy's death just meant I was off from school." Later, however, she described watching the funeral and crying. She described her "mother crying all the time—all weekend when TV was on." She noted, as did other children, that she cried for a shorter period of time than her mother. Frequent references to parental reactions do not necessarily indicate the dominance of parental behavior on the child's view of the situation. Rather we may expect that the occurrence of such extreme parental reactions is unusual and, in its own right, a factor that had an impact on the children.

It is well known that children in the age group (seven to ten) experience a rapidly expanding world of activities, peer-group associations, and social involvements of a motoric nature. Affect can thus often be more easily approached via actions rather than through verbalization. It seems clear, though, that a strong affective reaction took place in most of the latency-age children in this study. There were many activities surrounding TV and very complex and subtle affective reactions could thus be summarily reported as "I cried when I watched the funeral."

(3) *The in-betweeners,* ten to twelve. There were nineteen children in this group.

A dramatic reaction occurred during one interview that took place at 3 P.M. on November 22. Charles, age eleven, immediately said that he had heard that President Kennedy was shot. He felt "bad." He heard, he said, that "a kid" shot him. The therapist wondered about a kid getting mad enough to kill and asked if Charles ever got very mad. "No," he replied, but he did hit other boys. Charles then described badly beating up another boy; he said he "felt like killing him." He then wanted to play some games. Suddenly he said, "I spilled the beans." He explained that he took (or stole) a coat hanger from another boy's coat at school the previous day. "God is angry at me for this, and it is my fault that the boy killed President Kennedy." He continued by saying that "sometimes God talks in my ear." He has "a devil and an angel" and has had them since being an accomplice to the theft of a boat approximately two years ago. He had not mentioned either the devil, the angel, or other such primitive material in any previous interviews. He feels that he is "bad" sometimes because of his devil and paints a picture of a "devil owl" (a big, red, primitive owl with yellow eyes).

This boy's presenting problem was described by his therapist as minor delinquency with passive-aggressive behavior. He had been in treatment for two months before this interview. This was the first time this kind of magical, bizarre thought process had been evident. (We will have to leave open the interesting question of how much of this psychotic thinking was a crisis-caused or precipitated reaction. Regardless of this, however, the potential for such severely regressive conceptions is itself a point of marked diagnostic importance.)

Another boy, age twelve, who had been in Washington over the weekend, described much of his visit with pleasure and relish. But when asked more specifically about the death, he said seriously that he felt "bad" but that "you can only feel so for three or four days, then poof! You can only feel bad for so long."

Another kind of reaction was encountered in this age group. One boy reported laughing when the announcement of Kennedy's death was made in school. His schoolmates ganged up on him and the rest of the weekend was spent in a series of fights, arguments, etc., with these boys and their parents. This boy was aware of feeling "awful—awful, and I could hardly keep from crying." It is interesting that during this weekend the many intrafamilial fights that characterized his family dispersed into altercations with neighbors and their children over their actions toward the boy who had laughed.

Again in this age group there was clear evidence of marked reactions of sadness in many children. There were many more specifically aggressive references than in the younger children—particularly wanting to kill Oswald before his being shot and considerable confusion after he was shot. Some of the ten- to twelve-year-old children were quite direct in asking the therapists what they thought, felt, and did during those days. The impact of so massive and widely significant an event that obviously occurred outside the transference is unusual, and there were no readily available therapeutic rules. This will be considered further in the later discussion of crisis work and its implications.

(4) *The adolescents* (thirteen to seventeen). There were thirteen boys and fifteen girls in this group.

Among the adolescent girls there were many reports of initial dramatic reactions. Screams, shock, and disbelief were frequent. After reporting strong initial reactions and sequences of thoughts about Kennedy, Oswald, Ruby, etc., the adolescent girls frequently told of a fight with their parents concerning their affective reactions and subsequent behavior. The parents, according to many of the girls, thought they ought to be more upset or did not approve of their resumption of normal activities following the more direct grief and mourning. For example, one thirteen-year-old girl said she had become "sick and tired of that stuff by Monday" and decided to go to the "Y." Her father became furious, and in the course of a protracted fight with him she threatened to hang herself. Another girl reported fighting with her grandmother just after she wandered from the TV room. Her grandmother wanted her to remain on the scene and the girl "had had it."

These adolescents' direct responses lasted a shorter time than their parents'. The girls were quite expressive in their own characteristic adolescent way, and then were through with crying and watching. Their parents were not, and often could not tolerate the teen-age method of coping with crisis. Whether these girls were denying their affect or not is in some respects less significant than the fact that, after an initial, intense affective reaction, they had to turn to more usual social and motor involvements.

More agitated states accompanied by some somatic reactions also appear in this age group. For example, Nancy, seventeen years old, came in saying that she felt awful, had been having trouble sleeping, and was anxious. She reported getting along very badly with her mother, who had recently undergone a radical mastectomy and now had a lump in the other breast. The patient insisted that this was not the difficulty; it was the death of Kennedy that had upset her. She described weeping the entire weekend. She emphasized seeing a funeral for the first time and also seeing a man shot down. She described an increase in phobic behavior, being afraid to sleep alone and that someone would shoot her. Eventually she talked of her anger at the Kennedy family and described discord in the Kennedy family. After the therapist commented on how the events of the weekend had stirred her fears of injury, this led to her family and her anger at her brother. She threw a glass at him on this weekend when she wanted to kill him. Her belief that her anger was killing her mother occupied the remainder of the hour. Under the intense impact of the various events of the weekend—the assassination and associations to the Kennedy family—the more persistent material concerning her feelings toward her brother and mother became available for discussion and expression in her therapy hour.

Another girl, Mary, sixteen years old, was clearly agitated and depressed but unable to understand why. She had remained glued to the TV set during the weekend and during the therapy hour showed the therapist a picture of herself taken by her mother's grave. She could not see any direct connection with her own feelings, stating only that she felt sorry for Mrs. Kennedy. In this patient some early material was stirred and rose to the surface but did not become available for work as it had with Nancy.

Adolescent boys also reported initial dramatic reactions. One of these was directly observed in the lobby after an interview when the news came over the radio. This boy screamed at his therapist, "Kennedy's dead, and now I'll see you buried!" During the previous hour the boy had been dealing with material stimulated by the original announcement of Kennedy's being shot. Shortly before the end of the hour he had talked of the things he and his father had never done together and had identified himself with Benedict Arnold, who had both good and bad qualities.

Only four of the thirteen boys discussed their reactions, in comparison to thirteen of the fifteen girls. There are many more specific references in the boys' sessions to plans, school, work, and occupational choice. In addition to the general differences in adolescence in terms of role differences of boys and girls, one may also conjecture that for the boys the loss of a national figure—a father figure—provoked far greater guilt, stirring up old parricidal impulses, than among the girls. In fact, in three of the four boys who did discuss the assassination, there is evidence of guilt and in two of the four it is extremely marked. Issues of guilt are not so prominent among the girls.

IV. Parent-Child Material

The relationship between the material from parents and the material from their children can be examined from several vantage points. First, to investigate the frequently stated impression that children's reactions reflect their parents' orientations let us see how much correspondence there is between the level of affective expressiveness on the part of the children and their mothers and fathers.

Fifteen parent-child interviews were rated according to degree of expressiveness.[28] There was certainly no direct correspondence between parental and child ratings. All of the possible combinations of expressiveness-inexpressiveness between parents and children occur, and the twelve cases for whom this material is available are equally divided among the four types. Conclusive interpretations from this analysis would require more cases with both parental and child ratings. These ratings are mentioned only to dispel some of the prevailing notions about the parallelism of parent-child reactions to such crises, hopefully provoking investigation to replace *a priori* and inadequately founded assumptions. Aspects of affect expression other than over-all expressiveness also need to be investigated, and subsequent work will focus on these issues. For example, which affects were expressed by both parents and their children, and, a more complex question, what is the relationship between the parent's and child's expressed emotion? Another interesting area involves the question of which defensive or adaptive maneuvers were predominantly used in dealing with the crisis and crisis reactions. As with the affect expressiveness, there has been a tendency to think that choice of predominant defense mechanism is "transmitted" from parent to child; for example, denial in the parent leading to the predominant use of denial by the child. This also deserves further investigation.

We may note some clinical observations in this very interesting area of comparison between parent and child:

(a) EDWARD and his parents. Edward is the eight-year-old boy described in an earlier section whose sole reaction was, "My grandmother said the whole world may be blown up." As mentioned, his parents had lived unhappily with his paternal grandparents until he was six years old. He had had a very close relationship with his grandmother, who adored him and kept him very close to her in his early years. Edward's mother, in her interview, spontaneously, tearfully, and fully discussed her reaction to the assassination and death of Kennedy. She commented on Mrs. Kennedy's composure, wondering if she was unable to show feeling. She discussed the death of her husband's father a year before, when she had not taken Edward to the wake. She added that in the present crisis Edward refused to watch TV and assumed that "he didn't care." She described her husband's emotions over the weekend and also the year before at the time of his father's death. Very briefly and incidentally she mentioned that her mother-in-law had visited them during the weekend. Toward the end of the hour she discussed how easily she expressed anger in contrast with her difficulty in expressing sadness. She cried again and left.

In the father's interview, he described being very upset and unable to work. He discussed the death of his father and the re-action of his mother. He reported in detail how she had repeated a sequence of crying all day and then getting sick at the time of his father's death and again on the weekend of the death of the President.

Both Edward's parents were "appropriately" expressive and seemed able to deal with death and their losses. And yet, these issues are strikingly larger and unresolved for the boy. The paths of transmission are not so simple. In this case the ideas and fan-tasies of the paternal grandmother are particularly important; one can see how the boy incorporated them so that they emerged in the crisis situation. However, even with respect to this other cen-tral figure, his grandmother, Edward's reaction was similar but far from identical. His central concern of overwhelming danger was strongly influenced by his grandmother, yet her use of the weekend to cry and grieve did not also emerge in the boy.

(b) JOHN, the second boy, represents a different kind of parent-child combination (perhaps more familiar). This was the boy who said that his dog had become untrained and was like Oswald, who became untrained and shot the President.

In the mother's hour she emphasized how John had immediately looked at her with concern when she became upset at the news of the Kennedy assassination. She talked of how good and kind and considerate John was in his feelings about Caroline and John-John. She was unable to see any fright or upset in the child, only his "good, kind spirit." She talked of him as "an angel on earth," reporting other experiences of being upset, John's noticing it, and her saying to him, "I'm not upset," and then pinching him, patting him, and begging for kisses. Her mechanism of denial of the reality of her affect is apparent.

In his hour, John reported his concern about shooting, training, and control. Could he have wondered, on seeing his mother's re-action, whether similar feelings and anxieties had been stirred up in her? A marked component of compliance with maternal ex-pectations is very clear in this boy, but it is only one feature of his total reaction. The crisis, in fact, seems to differentiate the boy and his mother more strikingly than daily events. At the same time, we must remember that on the night of the assassination the boy and his mother slept in bed together while the father slept in the den.

Only one of the mechanisms in this mother-child interaction has been described, i.e., the repeated experience of denial of reality of affect on the mother's part and the effect of the crisis in partially counteracting this in the boy. In this rich material there are other important mechanisms that can be discovered and discussed. Obviously there are many facets and complexities in the parent-child relationship and in testing the idea of "transmission," particularly in the face of crises, one must take into account the many complications and opportunities to alter (or to intensify) patterned conformity or unconscious acquiescence.

V. Crisis and Crisis Work

The definition of crisis as "a state of things in which a decisive change one way or the other is impending"[29] implies that in any crisis there is a disruptive potential on the one hand, and an adaptive one on the other. The nationwide crisis situation of the assassination of Kennedy affected the children, parents, and their therapists. More usual crises in the course of therapeutic contact affect the child and his family, leaving the therapist an observant outsider.

The formulation that any crisis is a disruptive experience, which can lead to increased difficulties or to increased adaptational potentials, obviously has to be understood in terms of its various parts—the crisis itself and the outcome. As mentioned in the first section of this paper, the assassination produced a national (external) crisis in contrast to a personal crisis in a family or in an individual relationship or situation. In the case of a national crisis the *amount* of impact on a wider social group is important, and is, of course, relevant to the question of positive or negative outcome. When a crisis affects a great many people and, as in this instance, even the therapists working with these patients, there is both an increased "permission" to react and an increased opportunity to observe a wide range of different responses in the open. Our material shows that the impact on children was strong and cannot be discounted even in the very young age groups. The question of longer-term positive and negative effects needs further study, but one would suspect that many factors, including the observability of reactions to the same crisis events among other "significant" people, may be important. It is clear that this widespread crisis had some immediate effects on the two-person relationship of therapist and child, increasing both disruptive reactions and opportunities for new adaptive resolutions of bereavement responses.

In our material there are: (1) cases in which the crisis was attenuated—it was not experienced as a crisis in the two-person relationship for many reasons; the contact may have come too late or the issue of Kennedy's death was not a compelling one; (2) those cases in which the crisis and crisis work did lead to a new degree of communication; and (3) those in which there was a decrease in communication—session was canceled, interrupted, etc.

The issue of crisis and crisis work is complex and a few general comments seem warranted:

(1) The fairly general absence of crisis-oriented teaching and thinking in psychotherapy contributed to the confusion of therapists attempting to cope with an unfamiliar situation where the reality event, the crisis, had a powerful effect not only on the patients but on the therapists as well, and transgressed any known rules regarding transference and countertransference. Often it precipitated a secondary "therapeutic crisis."

(2) For those therapists who were able to utilize this as an opportunity for open discussion with or without verbal expression of their own feelings, this mutually experienced crisis seemed to lead to increased therapeutic communication. The actual crisis work itself might be described as the therapist's appropriately dealing with the crisis rather than immediately probing, digging deeper, or switching attention from the event in many other ways. Full mutual use of the immediate situation often led into the past, provided that the relevance of the current crisis, in its own right, was not disregarded.

(3) Hidden in the word "appropriate" is the fact that crisis work must be appropriate to the age and the ego development of the patient. In this material we have the opportunity to extend our knowledge of crisis reactions and crisis work to a wide age range of children. It would appear that the crisis stirs up age-appropriate and ego-appropriate underlying concerns but, by its very power-

ful and social nature, disrupts former methods of handling such situations and can readily lead to more regressive or more effective solutions to former problems.

VI. Summary

This has been a preliminary communication—a work in process. Hopefully, it has raised more questions than it has provided answers. Nevertheless this work on children's reactions to the assassination of Kennedy has provided us with the opportunity to expand our knowledge of grief reactions in children and in their parents. Grief reactions occur ubiquitously, but they are often hidden, scattered in time and occurrence, and responses to very diverse situations, making observations, collection of large numbers, and comparison difficult. In this instance the severity of the stress caused affective, defensive, adaptive, and other important reactions and patterns of child behavior and experience to emerge. Some of these grief reactions and patterns in several age groups have been described. Though strong affective responses were frequent among all ages of children and among adults, there was no marked correspondence in over-all level of affective expressiveness between parent and child.

In any crisis, action *must* be taken—positively, negatively, or by default. In a crisis, actions often are, of necessity, taken in haste. However, in any crisis, there is always the double potential, maladaptive or productive. It is not altogether clear what factors differentially affect these two potential directions of change. Our material on differences in behavior among therapists suggests that the wider and more visible effects of crises on a larger group of closely connected persons may provide new channels for a sense of mutuality or, on the contrary, may reinforce a sense of isolation and the utility of familiar defenses.

This research and the others concerning the assassination of President Kennedy were done in haste and under crisis conditions. There are various lacks and defects that can be easily seen. But we may hope that it has been possible to utilize the positive potentials of this national crisis in pressing several issues further. Grief and the research that evolved may then have led us to some better understanding of children and their parents.

NOTES

1. This study was done at the Judge Baker Guidance Center, Boston.

2. The author wishes to thank Dr. Marc Fried of the Center for Community Studies, Massachusetts General Hospital and the Institute of Human Sciences, Boston College, and Dr. Leonard Duhl of the National Institute of Mental Health for their ideas, support, and encouragement over the fateful and difficult weekend when this research was started. Then Dr. George E. Gardner and Dr. Elizabeth Makkay at the Judge Baker Guidance Center provided the necessary and invaluable support for the actual study to be done. This study was also aided immeasurably by my patient and untiring secretary, Mrs. Roni Shepard, who rose to the crisis requirements and rapidly put out the interview schedule and carefully organized and carried out the collection of the incoming interviews.

3. A large sample consisting of 1800 school children from early grades through junior high school in two different communities answered a specially designed sentence completion form. This form attempted to gather systematically, over an age and class range, the reactions to the assassination of children who were not patients.

4. Freud, S. (1917)

5. Greenacre, P. (1953)

6. Bibring, E. (1953)

7. Abraham, K. (1924)

8. Lindemann, E. (1944)

9. Spitz, R. (1945)

10. Bowlby, J. (1960)

11. Freud, A. (1944)

12. Rank, B. (1949)

13. Mahler, M. (1952)

14. Rochlin, G. (1961)

15. Rochlin, G. (1959)

16. Mahler, M. (1961)

17. Shambaugh, B. (1961)

18. Rochlin, G. (1953)

19. Johnson, A. (1949)

20. Lindemann, E. (1944)

21. Caplan and co-workers (1960)

22. Fried, M. (1963)

23. Erikson, E. (1959)

24. Bibring, G. (1959)

25. Zilbach and Stone, "Crises and Chronic Problem Families," presented at the American Orthopsychiatric Meeting, March 1963.

26. For one week following the assassination of Kennedy each child therapist was given a short open-ended interview questionnaire to complete on each interview with a child. This was followed one week later with a briefer follow-up questionnaire. The analysis of the follow-up material is not included in this report.

27. This was a preschool arts and crafts session.

28. These ratings were done on the basis of review of the questionnaire and then scored as to amount of expressiveness on a simple five-point scale. There is the possibility of some contamination since the judge did have some previous knowledge of the material. However, the main point is not one of the amount or intricacies of reliability about expressiveness but rather to remind us of the clinical complexities which are well known in noncrisis situations.

29. Webster, N. (1958)

LIST OF REFERENCES

Abraham, K. "A Short Study of the Development of the Libido, Viewed in the Light of Mental Disorders." 1924. In *Selected Papers of Karl Abraham*, Vol. 1, pp. 418–80. London: Hogarth Press, 1927.

Bibring, E. "The Mechanism of Depression." In Greenacre, P., ed., *Affective Disorders*, pp. 13–48. New York: International Universities Press, 1953.

Bibring, G. "Some Consideration of the Psychological Process in Pregnancy," *Psychoanalytic Study of Child*, 1959, *14*, 113–22.

Bowlby, J. "Grief and Mourning in Infancy and Early Childhood," *Psychoanalytic Study of Child*, 1960, *15*, 9–52.

Caplan, G. "Patterns of Parental Response to the Crisis of Premature Birth: A Preliminary Approach to Modifying the Mental Health Outcome," *Psychiatry*, 1960, *23*, 365–74.

Erikson, E. "Growth and Crises of the Healthy Personality." In *Identity and the Life Cycle*. Monograph, *Psychological Issues*, I, No. 1, 50–100.

Fried, M. "Grieving For A Lost Home." In Duhl, Leonard J., ed., *The Urban Condition*, New York: Basic Books, 1963.

Freud, A. "Infants Without Families," 1944, New York: International Universities Press.

Freud, S. "Mourning and Melancholia," 1917, pp. 243–58. In *The Standard Edition of the Complete Psychological Works of Sigmund Freud*, XIV. London: Hogarth Press, 1957.

Greenacre, P. Foreword, pp. 7–11. In Greenacre, P., ed., *Affective Disorders*. New York: International Universities Press, 1953.

Johnson, A. "Sanctions for Superego Lacunae," pp. 225–45. In Eissler, K., ed., *Searchlights on Delinquency*. New York: International Universities Press, 1949.

Lindemann, E. "The Symptomatology and Management of Acute Grief," *American Journal of Psychiatry*, 1944, *101*, 141–48.

Mahler, M. "On Child Psychosis and Schizophrenia: Autistic and Symbiotic Infantile Psychoses," *Psychoanalytic Study of Child*, 1952, *7*, 286–306.

———— "On Sadness and Grief in Infancy and Childhood," *Psychoanalytic Study of Child*, 1961, *16*, 332–51.

Rank, B. "Aggression," *Psychoanalytic Study of Child*, 1949, *3–4*, 43–49.

Rochlin, G. "Loss and Restitution," *Psychoanalytic Study of Child*, 1953, *8*, 288–309.

———— "The Loss Complex," *Journal of the American Psychoanalytic Association*, 1959, *7*, 299–315.

———— "The Dread of Abandonment: A Contribution to the Etiology of the Loss Complex and to Depression," *Psychoanalytic Study of Child*, 1961, *16*, 451–70.

Shambaugh, B. "A Study of Loss Reactions in a Seven Year Old," *Psychoanalytic Study of Child*, 1961, *16*, 510–22.

Spitz, R. "Hospitalism," *Psychoanalytic Study of Child*, 1945, *1*, 53–75.

Webster, Noah. *New International Dictionary*, 2d Edition Unabridged, 1958: G. & C. Merriam Company.

8

Patterns of Closure: College Students' Return to Political "Normalcy"[1]

CAROLYN PRATT under supervision of ROBERT E. LANE

A major issue in any democracy is that of succession in high office. The continuity of the nation's political life, and therefore the safety and well-being of its citizens, is dependent upon a smooth transition from one administration to the next. This has not yet become the norm in most of Latin America's aspiring democracies, or southeast Asia's. Among the Western countries, difficulties of succession have been most evident in the postwar French Fourth Republic. In general, it might be said that a change of political leadership requires loyalty and a sense of legitimacy about the new man by members of his own party; willingness to agree to the legitimacy of the new administration of the opposition; and a perception of the competence of the new administration by both. Normal transition from one leader to his successor is effected by the customs and institutions that create a psychological readiness to accept the change. In a stable system, most individuals have, since childhood, seen regular campaigns waged within bounds that grant legitimacy to the opposition; have seen regular elections after which the candidate with the most votes is proclaimed winner; and have imbibed from family or school the mythology of legitimacy—the history, codes, creeds, and heroes of the political system. Thus, early socialization is reinforced by the regular occurrence of events in the real world. To be sure, belief in the workings of democracy is not necessarily reflected in activism—e.g., campaigning, voting—but it forms the base of acquiescence upon which the continuity of the government depends.

Some pathological events that may disrupt succession in a usually stable system include hostility beyond the "rules of the game" on the part of the opposition or a continuing sense of loss of the old leader—political mourning, so to speak—which weakens allegiance and partisan support for the new. In the first case, a substantial part of the population may feel denied its goals beyond bearable limits, or a dangerous schism may have been created in the campaign. In the case of political mourning, the effects on the system may be more insidious. Lack of wholehearted support for the new leader may render his policies ineffectual, hard to administer, etc., in essence leaving the nation's business undone until the mourning has somehow been worked out. The latter may be the particular attribute of the crisis transition, such as that following the assassination of President Kennedy. There is no psychological preparation for the new leader: no campaign, no election day, no prior discussion of his merits or mobilization of his partisans. The suddenness of such an event is compounded by the fact of violent death, frightening and unfamiliar in the context of the stable polity. That the effects of the assassination were not going to disrupting extremes was soon apparent. Our research interest, then, was to probe the mechanisms that were used by individuals to deal with the assassination of President Kennedy and the succession of President Johnson, and to isolate the factors that could impede acceptance of the crisis succession.

The study originated with Professors Fred I. Greenstein and Nelson Polsby of Wesleyan University, who devised a questionnaire which was given to students in Political Science classes in various colleges in Connecticut within a week of the assassination (November 25–29). This questionnaire was modified by us and was administered during the first two weeks in January to students who had taken the first questionnaire at Yale, the University of Connecticut, and Albertus Magnus College for Women. We thus obtained November and January responses from 132 students between the ages of seventeen and twenty-one. Due to the *ad hoc* quality of the project, this group is not a random sample of the college population; the distribution of the response patterns we found may vary considerably from what would have been found in a random sample.

The Patterns of Closure

The concept we felt would be most applicable to the mechanisms utilized by students in dealing with the crisis transition is that of *closure*. While this term is usually applied to the effects of emotional drives on cognitive and problem-solving ability,[2] we have in mind something in which the problem to be dealt with is more emotional than cognitive, making emotion the most dynamic element. That is, closure would involve a lowering of affect and feeling of upset, an acceptance of the new situation, accompanied by decreased emotional and cognitive attention to the event that produced the disruption.

To operationally test this concept we employed two very simple forced-choice statements. In November, the statement read, "Even after the President's death was known, I sometimes found it hard to believe he *really* was dead." In January, this was modified to read, "Even now, I sometimes find it hard to believe that President Kennedy *really* is dead." The answers to each question were dichotomized into agree-disagree responses. Those individuals who expressed difficulty "believing" in both November and January we termed "nonclosers." These are the people who could not emotionally accept the loss of President Kennedy, who were still upset and bothered by the event. Those who expressed disbelief in November but not in January are "closers"; their original response was, we would say, appropriate upset and disorientation, but they, unlike the nonclosers, were able to handle the experience so that after a month their affective response was no longer salient. The students who were ready to "believe" within a week of the assassination and, of course, maintained this "belief" a month later, we have called "compulsive closers." This term is an adaptation of Dittes' "impulsive closure."[3] Those who fall in this category we felt might be "compulsive" in their need for closure, a deviation from the near-universal November response of shock and disbelief. The question of whether this is pathological will be discussed in greater detail below. Table I shows the classificatory scheme and number of respondents in each category.

TABLE I

January

	Yes	No
	NONCLOSERS	CLOSERS
November: Yes	58%	27%
	N = 76	N = 36
November: No		COMPULSIVE CLOSERS
		15%
		N = 20

Total = 132

November: "Even after the President's death was known, I sometimes found it hard to believe he *really* was dead."

January: "Even now, I sometimes find it hard to believe that President Kennedy is *really* dead."

We then looked at several other items to see if this measure was actually tapping the dimension of emotional closure responses. A rough index of emotionality was formed with answers to the statement "When I think about President Kennedy I feel: (1) Very upset; (2) Somewhat disturbed; (3) Not especially emotional; (4) Don't think about him." Answers (1) and (2) were designated "emotional," the remaining responses "nonemotional." We found, as expected, that the emotional of both sexes were more frequently nonclosers. These results are reported in Table II.

TABLE II

Emotionality in January

	Male		Female	
	Emotional	Nonemotional	Emotional	Nonemotional
Nonclosers	59%	16%	87%	50%
Closers	25	52	9	40
Compulsives	17	32	4	10
	N = 36	N = 25	N = 45	N = 10

"When I think about President Kennedy I feel: (1) Very upset; (2) Somewhat disturbed; (3) Not especially emotional; (4) Don't think about him."

It was also true that those who compared President Johnson unfavorably to Kennedy or distrusted Johnson more than the other groups tended to be nonclosers. Those with confidence in Johnson were also more likely to be nonclosers, which seems paradoxical. We suggest that this apparent sanguinity is an expression of great effort to make closure emotionally possible—apparently the less closure, the greater the effort. Those least likely to reserve judgment on Johnson are the compulsives, as shown in Table III.

TABLE III

Impression of President Johnson in January
(Coded responses to open-ended questions)

	Confidence	Compares unfavorably to J.F.K.	Distrust	Reserve judgment
Nonclosers	55%	90%	50%	47%
Closers	25	0	30	44
Compulsives	20	10	20	8
	N = 65	N = 19	N = 10	N = 36

There is also a slight indication that those who need to look on the cheerful side tend to be compulsive closers. Nineteen per cent of those who agreed to the F-scale item "When a person has a problem or worry it is best for him not to think about it, but to keep busy with more cheerful things" were compulsives, while only 13 per cent of those who disagreed were in this group.

We felt confident, then, that the measure was a valid one. Some intuitive reinforcement for this comes from the responses to the open-ended questions from the three groups. The emotional gulf between a noncloser and a compulsive is revealed in passages like these (written on November 26):

Noncloser: I had no thoughts [when I heard that the President was dead]. . . . My mind was washed out by the absolute horror that such a dastardly act could occur in a civilized nation. . . . The words "assassinated President Kennedy" began to haunt me as words for history books, not today's headlines. I became very depressed and pensive; an untold number of things left unfinished but so well articulated by President Kennedy had to be done . . . These three words still haunt me. Five times since Friday I have broken down and cried unashamedly. . . .

TWENTY-YEAR-OLD YALE STUDENT

Compulsive closer: [My feelings and thoughts upon hearing that the President was dead were] a medley of shock, disbelief, and irreverent thoughts—curiosity as to what effect it would have on the weekend . . . thought it was commentary on a civilized age, and then scolded myself for being absurd, as it was only an indication that this age is no better as far as basic human actions go than any other. . . . [Since then, I have felt] acceptance of the fact—and dismissal as a *fait accompli.* . . . I felt and feel that it was outrageous and a tragedy—but it has now interest only in its effect on the future.

TWENTY-YEAR-OLD YALE STUDENT

The Reference Group and Cultural Role

My feelings were sorrow at what had happened, and his being a Catholic, my thoughts centered around that, at his being given the last rites, and a sense of emptiness. . . .

CATHOLIC GIRL, NINETEEN YEARS OLD, NONCLOSER

Although the importance of the reference group is not often so overtly stated, its function for the personality, and most particularly for the personality feeling about and acting on public matters, is well documented.[4]

The reference-group attachments that are learned early, such as religion and political party, are significant models for who "I" am, how "I" feel. How much they guide thought and emotion may vary, of course, with the saliency of the group membership to the individual in a given situation. We know that religion gained unusual salience for Catholics in the 1960 Presidential election, evidenced by the fact that more Catholics voted for Kennedy than Catholics had voted for any other Democratic candidate in recent years. Party identification is, of course, made salient at election time when party symbols are forced on the individual's attention by the media. Region of residence has been salient in connection with public issues, particularly for Southerners, for at least a century. Given the exacerbation of regional tension by the civil rights crises of the past few years, we would speculate that "southern-ness" as a reference concept has achieved new, greater salience. The association of the Kennedy name with an anti-states'-rights position, which the polls show was interpreted by Southerners as an anti-Southern position, adds importance to region as a factor in our analysis.

In addition to the reference group as a source of identity in political matters, the cultural role assigned to the sexes is significant. It has been consistently found[5] that men and women differ with respect to candidates, issues, partisanship, political activity, and the like—women being more candidate-oriented and likely to personalize politics. The explanation lies in the cultural concept of woman's role as the affective element in society and the training in this behavior that follows from this role. These reference groups —religion, party, and region—and the roles traditionally accepted by the sexes, are the ones we would expect to explain much adult closure patterning around the crisis transition. Our hypothesis was that these would also be applicable to our late-adolescent population, given that the reference groups and roles discussed are internalized as emotional and behavioral guides in childhood. The results to be presented below largely support the notion that by late adolescence, at least, reference group and role utilization for politics is well established and operates in the same manner as on the adult populations that are the usual object of attention.

Nonclosers: The Meaning of "Political Mourning"

Those who had difficulty "believing" Kennedy dead in both November and January, who were saying, in effect, "I am still very upset and disturbed by this event," were predominantly female, Catholic, Democratic, or non-Southern. The independence of these attributes was established by controlling for religion, sex, and party. (It was not useful to impose controls for region due to the small number of Southerners in our sample.)

TABLE IV

Role of Religious Identification

	Male			Female		
	Prot.	Cath.	Jew	Prot.	Cath.	Jew
Nonclosers	30%	47%	*	70%	77%	*
Closers	44	40		24	20	
Compulsives	26	13		6	3	
	N = 39	N = 15		N = 17	N = 35	

* The number of Jews in any column was less than 10, so they are not presented in tables.

The tendency of Catholics of both sexes, as compared to Protestants, to fail to achieve closure, may be seen in Table IV. If religion is seen as a reference group, the meaning becomes overt: Catholics in America have felt politically underprivileged[6] and have chafed at the "unfairness" of the unwritten rule against Catholics in high office. Kennedy's election must have been a vicarious personal achievement for many, an increase in the stature of the self. His murder, then, became to a corresponding degree murder of part of the self. Hence, the continuing sense of irreparable loss by the Catholic respondents.

TABLE V

Role of Sex and Party

| | Republican | | Democrat | | Independent | |
	Male	Female	Male	Female	Male	Female
Nonclosers	26%	53%	54%	86%	50%	81%
Closers	43	33	46	11	25	19
Compulsives	30	13	0	4	25	
	N = 23	N = 15	N = 13	N = 28	N = 20	N = 16

Note: Those individuals whose party affiliation is classified as "other" are not included. N = 11

Females, of whatever political affiliation, are more often in the nonclosure category than are males. We have suggested that the typical politicization pattern of females in our culture is the explanation. This is supported by the data in Table II, where it appears that the women are more emotional in January than are the men. Another item in the January questionnaire, asking how much the respondent thought about Kennedy, also indicated that females more than males were devoting attention to the late President.

The female tendencies to emotionality and personalization differ from males chiefly over time, however. In November, males did not take the opportunity to mention Johnson or future political problems on open-ended questions any more frequently than the females. We suggest that the impact of the event was to reinforce the acceptable female response to politics and to disrupt the generally accepted political cultural role for the males. It may be that pressure to assume the accustomed pattern is a factor in greater male tendency to closure; conversely, the women would be under no such pressure to "pull themselves together."

On the latter point, it should also be noted that in our sample the females had the reinforcement of their community to continue grieving. They were preponderantly from a small Catholic women's college. The men from Yale and the University of Connecticut were in a more cosmopolitan environment. Thus no single set of reinforcing cues was available to them.[7]

Table V also indicates, as was expected, that Democrats of both sexes were much more likely to be nonclosers than Republicans. It is important to note that the use of party as reference group does not imply a well-structured ideology or even consistent policy preferences. This is also true of the adult population of our sample.

Very few students mentioned party or ideological prospects in either November or January. Nonclosure also does not imply lack of cognitive "confidence" in Johnson; 80 per cent of those who expressed confidence in the new man in January were Democratic nonclosers. The fact that partisans expose themselves to media featuring their party and not the other party means that Kennedy was probably more familiar to the Democrats than to the Republicans. Party as a reference group, then, has a personal more than a political meaning, even for men.

Even less political are the independents. Contrary to the myth of the informed, interested citizen who weighs his information and votes for the "best man" regardless of party, many independents in this country tend strongly toward political apathy. Without party identity, they must personalize their relationship to the leader. Personalization presupposes familiarity. That they had not been able to achieve this attachment to the relatively unknown new President is indicated by their lack of confidence in Johnson by January. (Of the independents who do not feel confidence in Johnson in January, 67 per cent are nonclosers.)

TABLE VI

Region

	South	Non-South
Nonclosers	33%	61%
Closers	33	26
Compulsives	33	12
	N = 18	N = 114

As is indicated in Table VI, non-Southerners were twice as likely as Southerners to be nonclosers. The special factors at work with the southern students will be discussed under compulsive closure.

TABLE VII

Dependency

"The government in Washington ought to see to it that everybody who wants to work can find a job."

	Agree	Disagree
Nonclosers	63%	54%
Closers	27	33
Compulsives	10	22
	N = 60	N = 67

"Sometimes politics and government seem so complicated that a person like me can't really understand what's going on."

	Agree	Disagree
Nonclosers	64%	55%
Closers	24	29
Compulsives	12	16
	N = 50	N = 80

The two items presented in Table VII are measures of dependency traits. Nonclosers tend to exhibit more of these than the other groups. Perhaps the loss of a strong leader is more threatening to these people, which would impede closure for them. They know that the old leader could "take care of things"—but what about the new man?

Compared to the other groups, the Republicans, Protestants, and males tended to have achieved closure by January (see Tables IV and V). As was noted in the discussion of nonclosure, the religious and party reference groups did not link these people with Kennedy, and the male role promotes closure after shock or grief. Cognitive as well as emotional attention shift is related to the process of closure. We find that the closers thought about Kennedy less than nonclosers even in November, and much less in January.

TABLE VIII

Attention Shift

"I still find myself thinking about Kennedy's death."

	November	January	
Nonclosers	85%	22%	N = 76
Closers	77	6	N = 36
Compulsives	42	5	N = 20

Also, as is shown in Table II, the closers are much less emotional than nonclosers, though more so than the compulsives. The picture presented by the closers is that of balance between affective and instrumental orientations, with perhaps greater ego strength, as indicated by their relatively weaker dependency trends. They do not fear the expression of emotion, but are able to work through their affective responses, thus freeing themselves for attachment to the new leader and support of the ongoing political system.

Compulsive Closers: Fugitives from Affect

Although most of the country was experiencing shocked disbelief in the days immediately following November 22, there were some students—15 per cent in our sample—who had already accepted the *fait accompli*. Their reference group and role characteristics were much like those of the closers—they were male, Republican, and Protestant. Most of the Southerners were also in this category. Several possible sources for compulsiveness were considered to explain the differences between these people and those with similar identifications who displayed more affect. Since grief generally involves disbelief, it may be true that the need to believe and accept quickly means a pathological inability to grieve or mourn. A desire to believe, a latent wish fulfillment in the murder, could be expressed in immediate acceptance. A response set to accept everything uncritically could be responsible or might indicate a need to end ambiguity, worry, and doubt.

We found little evidence of wish fulfillment in the open-ended responses in the questionnaire; however, given the cultural prohibition against expression of gladness at a murder, it is unlikely that such feelings would be made manifest. A somewhat ambiguous indication of hostility by this group is evidenced by its over-whelming agreement to the November statement, "There has been too much attention paid to the President's death. One man's passing should not be allowed to disturb the life of a great nation."

Of the nonclosers, 21 per cent agreed with this; of the closers, 33 per cent; and of the compulsives, 74 per cent. Some inability to express grief or admit painful affect is indicated by the compulsives' tendency to "look on the cheerful side" mentioned above, and may also show intolerance of ambiguity.

Southerners had an almost three times greater chance of being compulsives than non-Southerners. This is *not* due to beliefs on integration—relatively fewer compulsives than any other group believed "Negroes have been pushing for too much." There is a possibility here of guilt feelings by identification; the recent racial violence in the South, the well-known attitudes of the region toward Kennedy, and the scene of the assassination might create a pressure to shunt the incident to the background and "move on" rather than endure painful feelings of responsibility.

In summary, there is only tenuous evidence that the compulsives are pathological; our questionnaire included too few personality measures to support this. It is possible that, out of the group whose role and reference identifications predispose toward closure, the compulsives were the most self-consciously independent and fact-oriented.

Conclusion

This report has supported the previous findings with regard to the important role of reference-group identifications and cultural roles for the individual in dealing both cognitively and affectively with public matters. Our findings indicate that reference-group identifications and culturally assigned sexual roles are well established as part of the self by late adolescence, at least for dealing with public matters, and are utilized by young people in the same way as by mature adults. Moreover, these identifications appear to override the effects of individual personality traits for the most part. The failure of our personality measures to differentiate between closers and nonclosers may be attributed to the greater effect of reference groups and sex, and those whose attributes should predispose them to nonclosure were almost entirely absent from the closure group. Personality seemed to intrude most among those compulsive closers whose response was more extreme than that of the majority of those with similar attributes. We would speculate that, had the assassinated President been Republican, Protestant, and a Southerner, these students would have moved to the closer or even noncloser category.

The political and, in the long run, personal consequences of stable reference-group identifications and cultural roles, given the way in which these provide orientation even in crisis, awaits further investigation. The first question to be answered refers to the action potential of nonclosers, closers, and compulsive closers: Are those who continue to mourn debilitated for constructive leadership? Or are they the citizens who, by keeping the tragedy before them, will be more highly motivated to remedy the political and social ills they feel responsible for the event? Do the closers suffer temporary disability for participation in political life? And might not the compulsive closers—if they are the citizens with the greater instrumental orientation—be essential for the successful conduct of political life if others are unable to participate fully?

If nonclosure means low action potential, we must also ask what its limits are in the society after a crisis transition: How long may it last, and for how many, before it becomes dysfunctional for the whole?

Since, in actuality, there was no crisis other than the emotional one, no disruption of business or public life except for a one-day holiday, these concerns may seem extravagant. In our society the effects of the prevailing closure patterns should be more subtly reflected by, perhaps, lowered participation in the 1964 election by those whose reference identifications would predispose them to nonclosure or by increased support for legislation supported by the late President. But the larger questions may be relevant to other societies. It must be emphasized that our findings are very much the product of socialization into the *American* political system. The full nature of the formation of individual closure patterns in response to crisis transition requires study of such events in other countries in which cultural roles differ or reference-group identifications are more fluid.

NOTES

1. We would like to express our thanks to Yale University for the financial support which made this study possible. Grateful acknowledgement is also due to Professors Fred I. Greenstein, Nelson Polsby, and James D. Barber; Naomi Burns, James Eisenstein, Deane Neubauer, John Quinn, Marlene Stevens, and John Thomas, whose unselfish assistance was invaluable.

2. Allport and Faden, 1960.

3. Dittes, 1959.

4. See Hyman, 1958; Lane, 1959; Lane, 1962; Campbell, *et al.*, 1960; Berelson, *et al.*, 1954.

5. See Campbell, *et al.*, *op. cit.*; Berelson, *et al.*, *op. cit.*; and Lane, 1959.

6. Lane, *op. cit.*

7. The effects of community environment in the structuring and reinforcing of closure patterns has been dealt with in greater detail in James Eisenstein's unpublished paper, "Testing the Limits of Authority: The Hospital as a Microcosm of Society." In this case, reassurance and orientation for dealing with expression of affect by the staff in a psychiatric ward facilitated rapid closure for the patients; but closure was *not* reinforced for the staff, who continued to "mourn" throughout the week following the assassination. The lack of a unified community "working out" led to anomic or aggressive behavior on the ward, by which the patients tested the willingness of those in authority to maintain order. Eisenstein suggests that such behavior patterns might prevail in the larger community if the closure pattern of leaders and led were similarly divergent.

LIST OF REFERENCES

Allport, Gordon W. and Janet M. Faden. 1960. "The Psychology of Newspapers: Five Tentative Laws," *Public Opinion Quarterly*, IV, pp. 702–3.

Berelson, Bernard R., Paul E. Lazarsfeld, and William N. McPhee. 1954. *Voting*. Chicago: University of Chicago Press.

Campbell, Angus, Philip E. Converse, Warren N. Miller, and Donald Stokes. 1960. *The American Voter*. New York: Wiley.

Dittes, James. 1959. "Effects of changes in self-esteem upon impulsiveness and deliberation in making judgements," *Journal of Abnormal and Social Psychology*, Vol. 58, pp. 348–56.

Eisenstein, James. 1964. "Testing the Limits of Authority: The Hospital as a Microcosm of Society." Unpublished.

Hyman, Herbert. 1958. *Political Socialization*. Glencoe, Ill.: Free Press.

Lane, Robert E. 1959. *Political Life*. Glencoe, Ill.: Free Press.

——— 1962. *Political Ideology*. Glencoe, Ill.: Free Press.

9

Young Men and the Death of a Young President

FRED I. GREENSTEIN

One notable aspect of public reaction to President Kennedy's assassination was its generality: intense, deeply felt emotions seem to have been aroused in virtually every segment of the population. Even articulate Kennedy opponents, sometimes to their own surprise, found themselves swept up in the general state of mourning. To account for the extraordinary response to this event (after all, other public figures, and even personal acquaintances die without arousing comparable feelings), it is necessary to assume the existence of widespread *prior* attachments—albeit often unacknowledged—to the President and the Presidency. Evidently people come to relate themselves quite personally to the chief executive and to rely upon him as a symbol of social and political stability in a disorderly world.

Although grief was quite general, there were distinct quantitative and qualitative differences in response to the assassination from group to group in the population. These variations provide further insight into the public significance of the Presidential role and at the same time—because of the intensity of feelings aroused by the assassination—are a remarkable mirror of the groups themselves, a vehicle for understanding them in ways that might not otherwise be possible. Our concern here will be with several aspects of the responses of male college students to the death of President Kennedy, particularly as the responses seem to be selectively related to their status as young men and as members of a college community.

On the morning of November 23, 1963, my colleague Nelson W. Polsby and I conducted the first of four tape-recorded interviews, held on successive days, with "natural groups" of Wesleyan University students. Three of the groups were made up of volunteers from three different fraternity houses. Each of these groups included a number of individuals who had been together during various portions of the period beginning with the initial reports of the assassination. The fourth group consisted of members of a seminar. The average duration of the interviews was two hours.

In each instance the students were assembled informally in a room where they conversed with each other and with one or both of the interviewers. Questioning began by encouraging the students to describe in detail the circumstances under which they learned of the shooting, and their immediate and subsequent thoughts and actions. As the series of interviews progressed, attention was devoted to the unfolding events of the weekend, such as the shooting of Lee Harvey Oswald and the President's funeral.

It was clear that the students *wanted* to talk. The interviews had a cathartic, confessional quality. We were left with the impression that the group setting stimulated rather than inhibited response—that many of the statements that appear in our 100-odd pages of transcribed protocol would not have emerged in individual interviews and certainly would not have emerged from structured questionnaires.

Part of my purpose in what follows is simply to display portions of the interview material in their immediacy for their *prima facie* documentary value; in part, the quotations from the interviews serve as the basis for what is essentially an analytic, speculative discussion.

No claim can be made for the representativeness of Wesleyan students. Compared with the American undergraduate population at large, besides being exclusively male, the Wesleyan student body has a disproportionate number of students from relatively prosperous business and professional families, living largely (but not exclusively) in the suburban fringes of metropolitan areas in the New England and North Atlantic states. Further, Wesleyan is a small liberal arts college, with almost no commuting students. Rather stringent admissions requirements, a high faculty-student ratio, and a faculty oriented toward scholarship probably contribute to a more intellectual, politically liberal atmosphere than might be expected at most state universities, although Wesleyan is not characterized by the highly charged intellectuality associated with such small progressive colleges as Reed and Bennington. While the majority of students probably come from politically conservative families, the prevailing *Geist* on campus is moderate liberalism; for example, many of the students identify strongly with the Negro rights movement. Even though our interviews cannot be treated as an adequate sampling of the Wesleyan student body, the foregoing observations about Wesleyan are necessary background.

Before discussing the specifically student-related aspects of response to the assassination, it may be useful to summarize briefly a number of observations I have made elsewhere about the overall character of our respondents' reports of how they experienced the President's death.

Within a few minutes after the first reports that the President had been shot, the news seems to have spread throughout the Wesleyan community. Only a few students first learned of the shooting directly from the media; these initiated an almost instantaneous pattern of face-to-face communication, which spread the news. An important element in the rapid flow of communication was the need to establish contact with others in order to discuss the event.

Disbelief was the most commonly reported first response to the report, but the disbelief, rather than indicating skepticism, seemed to constitute denial—an attempt to ward off painful information. Especially during the first three of the four interviews, vivid memories were retained of immediate actions, thoughts, and feelings on learning of the assassination. In general, this jolting report had produced a sense of heightened awareness of one's own subjectivity, accompanied, to varying degrees, by thoughts and feelings such as the following:

A sense of "shock," often accompanied by physical discomfort (sometimes preceded by initial feelings of numbness and incapacity to absorb the message that the President had been shot);

A sense of the strangeness and unreality of the immediate environment;

The thought that "this sort of thing just doesn't happen in the United States";

A preoccupation with determining who had been guilty of the assassination;

Anger, sometimes taking the form of hostility toward more or less irrelevant objects in the immediate or remote environments;

Reflections about what the instrumental consequences of the assassination would be;

Associations with other deaths (it was commonly reported that similar or even more intense feelings had been evoked by Kennedy's death than by deaths of family members or friends).

Throughout the weekend following the assassination there were, with a few interesting exceptions which we shall discuss below, marked changes in customary behavior. Classes were canceled; studying came to a halt; the assassination was all that students could talk about; for hours on end they watched and listened to the news. Typical afterthoughts during this period were

Recurrent feelings of disbelief;

Fantasy reconstructions of how the assassination might have been avoided;

Occasional tension-relieving humor;

Feelings that "in spite of this, life will go on. . . . Life *is* going on."

The central objects of concern and preoccupation were, of course, the late President, but also, to a striking degree, Mrs. Kennedy, and to a lesser degree, President Johnson. President Kennedy's funeral and all of the ritual and ceremony connected with it served to allay many of the tensions of the weekend. Curiously, a somewhat similar function seems to have been served by various vague conspiracy theories which developed late in this sequence of events. These also seemed to lend a degree of order to the threatening, chaotic experiences of the previous days.[1]

Most of these aspects of response to the assassination are not especially distinctive of the late-adolescent, college-student status of our respondents. In some cases students may have been better able than many other members of the population to verbalize their feelings and perceptions, but feelings of disbelief and shock, attempts to assign guilt, immersion in radio listening and television viewing, and many other of the responses our students reported were generally widespread. Our survey of the more distinctly student-related aspects of their response begins with a rather trivial consequence of the physical setting of campus life and goes on to a number of more psychologically interesting observations.

An Effect of the Physical Setting of Campus Life

Student life in small, self-contained college communities is conspicuously groupy. Close circles of friends and loyalties to organizations such as residential fraternities abound. Individuals who are without a circle of intimates and who belong to no groups are in the minority and often are painfully aware of their minority status. The very physical setting of campus life—the communal nature of living, study, and recreational facilities, as well as the time spent with others in classrooms—discourages isolation.

Therefore one (in itself relatively trivial) consequence of student status was that the report of the assassination and the initial response to it were more likely to be face-to-face, interpersonal experiences than was the case in the general population. Studies of how information about the assassination was received indicate that about half of American adults first learned from the mass media that President Kennedy had been shot. All but two of the 50-odd students in our group interviews who described how they first heard of the assassination reported that they had heard of it from some other individual,[2] and the two exceptions were together when they learned of it. We get a sense in the following interview quotations of the group settings in which news of the assassination was received and the role of word-of-mouth communication.

> I was about to give a [student] lecture in a seminar, and people were filing in and one of the persons said, "Have you heard the news? Kennedy's been shot."

> I think it was about 1:30 or it must have been shortly after it came out on television. I heard of it by way of a person who had heard of it from our [fraternity house] cook, who was listening to the radio.

> I was . . . with about seven other fellows. We were studying and I don't know the person's name, but he came into the lounge and made an announcement. He said, "The President's been shot and so has the Vice President." And immediately you had to believe this because no one would just come into the lounge and make this announcement in front of seven or eight people.

Group and Subgroup Effects on Response

Throughout the interviews it was evident that group member-ships—both the immediate group setting in which the student found himself and his prior campus social experiences—were im-portant conditioning factors affecting response to the assassina-tion. The communal nature of student existence is a result of a variety of factors beyond the mere physical setting of the college campus. It has become a sociological commonplace to stress the ubiquity of informal primary groups in all types of formal or-ganizations, the importance of such groups as sources of emotional gratification and security, and their effects on members' behavior.[3] In the case of college students, who are not only physically sepa-rated from the family of origin, but also are in the process of setting themselves off psychologically from their parents, peer-group at-tachments are likely to be especially strong.

a. Dependence upon Peers for Standards of Response

Individuals often conform to group norms without being par-ticularly aware that they are doing so. On this occasion, sensitivi-ties to the responses of others sometimes were quite self-conscious: as has been noted, a great many students report that among their first reactions was a need to be in touch with others. They found themselves alternating between an examination of their own feel-ings and observation of the responses of others, and, in some cases, were conscious of a tendency to adjust their responses accord-ingly.

> Friday night sitting listening to the radio . . . the . . . feeling was that we were sort of sounding each other out on how to respond to the whole thing. How do you act about it, you know? You just didn't know how to react and you'd try on different reactions to see what they would do, and until you could really make it a part of you, you didn't know what your reaction should be.

> You know, just trying to see someone else absorbing the fact [that the President had been assassinated] helped you a little more in believing that it might be true.

> With everyone else having [a] concerned look on their faces, it was much easier to believe it—sort of self-reinforcing.

> The community TV set tends to cover up that kind of stuff [extremely emotional reactions to the assassination], you know—what you might do if you were in your own room watching your own television.

In the general population, the primary group to which most people oriented themselves at the time of the assassination seems to have been the family. The impulse of families to be together, or at least in touch, seems to account for the great increase in telephoning reported at the time. (The same tendency was observed at the time of Roosevelt's death and is also reported in the various studies of community disasters.)[4] Our students typically denied that they felt a need to be in touch with their parents; yet the phrasing of their denials—the degree of emphasis they placed on *not* feeling it necessary to share their feelings with their parents and their tendency to attribute this desire to *other* students—suggested that more was involved than a mere emotionally neutral realization that one had no reason to want to be in touch with one's parents at this time.

> INTERVIEWER: So you had no impulse to . . . call home?
>
> STUDENT: Because of this? No. Especially not. Other people talked about calling home and I said, "What in the world do you want to call home for?"

The two students who did report that they had called home were both from anti-Kennedy family backgrounds (one a Southerner and another a student who commented "Everybody . . . I know at home—they're all John Birchers"). Both report feeling relieved to learn that their parents and friends were equally disturbed by the assassination. A good number of the other students turned out actually to have called home and discussed the assassination with their parents, but their explanation was that they "just happened" to do so.

> I did call, but I was planning to anyway. I'd been planning for the last three or four nights. I was going to, but I always put things off.

> I tried to call home [Friday] night, but I tried to call the night before too.

These assertions provide an interesting contrast to the report by Dorothea Johannson (1946) that, when Roosevelt died, numerous girls at Skidmore felt the need to call their parents. "I just had to call my father," one of them commented. "I felt as though I had just lost *him*." It seems reasonable to suggest (even though the Wesleyan and Skidmore situations obviously differ in too many respects to make comparisons with much confidence) that the contrast in the accounts is a function of sex differences in the need to declare psychic independence from one's parents at adolescence.[5] Further, more than a trace of reaction formation seems to be present in the male stance of independence from the family.[6]

b. Effects of Contrasting Primary-Group Climates

There were notable differences between the reports of two of the fraternity-member groups we interviewed and those of a third—differences that seem to be clearly related to the kinds of individuals recruited into these fraternities and the resulting social climates. Fraternities A and B are a good bit more liberal and intellectually oriented than fraternity C, judging from campus mythology, as well as from a number of more reliable indicators such as voting in mock Presidential elections and the tendency of members to go on to graduate training in the humanities and social sciences. Members of fraternity C are more likely to be athletes, and this fraternity's social activities are closer than those of A and B to the popular stereotype of collegiate fraternity life.

Students in fraternities A and B tended to report more or less individualistic responses to the assassination—a need for solitude or, especially, the desire to be in touch with a particular close friend.

S_1: I wanted to talk to somebody, to try and verify this. . . . Well, my first reaction was to go up and ask [S_2]. To be consoled.

S_2: Yeah, even after it happened [S_1] wasn't there [at the dormitory television set] for a while. You know, we talk about politics a lot together and I had this feeling that I wanted to talk to him about it.

My reaction . . . was to call my roommate and tell him.

Immediately after dinner Friday night, I couldn't take it any more and [X] and I and another guy [went out for a drive].

Yesterday [Friday] my response was very, very emotional. . . . I walked down to the synagogue and sort of sat there for a half an hour waiting for an answer to come.

In fraternity C response to the assassination was more in terms of the entire fraternity group. Members headed for the house and clustered together around the television set.

> I was taking an . . . exam. . . . As soon as it was over the professor came in and said, "I've just heard that President Kennedy has been shot. . . ." So a few of us just took off. We figured the best place was our house—it's television-oriented, sort of. We figured the tube would be on and it was.

It was only from house C that we received reports of response to the assassination that contained overtones of violent retribution.

> When I went back down to the house and after the initial shock, which I think was what everyone felt, I think the most pervading feeling . . . was indignation.
>
> S: There was a great deal of talk about just what should happen to this Oswald character and a lot of that really shocked me, what some of these guys were thinking of.
>
> I: What were they thinking?
>
> S: Just nasty tortures for him.

Students in the other two houses were more likely to make such statements as

> I can't feel a real visceral anger toward the assassin for some reason. . . . [The] suddenness of it all keeps out the other idea. Of course, I hope they find the right guy and he gets what is coming to him, but I can't get involved as much with that as I can with just the suddenness of it.
>
> My sense of loss overwhelms my feelings for revenge.

The accentuation of tough responses in house C seems to have been accompanied by inhibitions against manifestations of tenderness. Crying (like the desire to telephone one's parents) was attributed to other people.

> There were a couple of guys, including myself, who were [showing emotion but] not actually crying because, you know, it wouldn't be right.
>
> I understand that there were places and people on this campus where this complete-dry-eyes outlook was not so true.

Contrast the following description of a gathering late Friday evening in fraternity B.

S: The whole room became filled with people smoking an [endless] number of cigarettes. . . . You just didn't know how to react. You'd cry a little. You know, I never cry or anything like that.

I: You changed your mind on this occasion?

S: Yeah, you know. I don't know whether I changed my mind or whether I just did.

I: Were a lot of people reacting that way?

S: I think so.

I: Was that everyone's observation? Was there some weeping?

S: Not weeping so much as just tears running out of eyes.

c. Two Cultures: Scientists and Nonscientists

Many students described the almost immediate consensus that led to the cancellation of classes and other scheduled activities as soon as the report that the President had been shot was received:

> For just a few minutes people [in a class] were sitting around in silence. And then they went out the exit.

> [A student entered a class which was in progress and reported the news] and then everyone filed out.

> [In one seminar, after the initial report that the President had been shot] the Professor said, "I'm going to give this lecture." . . . One or two people just got up and walked out. And then, after it was confirmed that [Kennedy] was dead, he just quietly said, "You can get the lecture after Thanksgiving" and everybody left.[7]

Students who attempted to study had difficulty doing so.

> I tried to do work. I tried to tell myself, if it's true, there's nothing you can do but just go on and try to keep on doing work, but I felt pretty sick about it.

> Most of the people I talked to had planned to study, since it was not a party weekend. As a result I know very few that did. Most people were right there around the television set the whole weekend.

Yet the behavior of some physical-science students seems to have been in marked contrast to this. Several students reported the failure to call off Friday afternoon science laboratories and the almost universal tendency of students in the sciences to continue their laboratory tasks.

> I was in the quantitative chem lab at the time it was announced. . . . [Dr. X] came in and said, "I'm not a politically oriented person, or

politically directed, but the President has just been shot." We went back to our experiments sort of talking about it. . . . I accepted the fact. I don't think I had much emotional reaction to it. We were all involved in something we had to get done at the time. Things started to slow up in what we were doing. We started making discussion points. One guy brought up the point, it seems rather irrelevant, "What's the Democratic image going to be for the Presidential campaign next year?" Somebody else brought up the point that "What's the succession of Presidential power?" I don't think anybody left only because of the incident. . . . A couple of guys left, but they were finished with their experiments.

I was in a bio lab. [No one left.] We had something we had to finish. We were in a sense totally preoccupied with our own obligations. We kept right on doing our dissection, but we talked simply of the political implications of it, not about the personality involved. . . . There were twenty [people in the laboratory] and everybody stayed until the conclusion of their work.

One element in this seems to have been that the laboratory tasks were manual and less likely to be interfered with by subjective distress (evidently athletic practices also were held on schedule Friday afternoon), as well as having a clear-cut set of steps to be followed. There also was a sense, however, that the science students were themselves less emotional, more apolitical than students in other fields, and that something about the context of scientific endeavor had muted student responses and turned their thoughts in coolly analytical directions. Indeed, one of the science students reported his irritation at the way the news reports were received in the laboratory during the afternoon.

S: The same things . . . repeated over and over again. There was no news and I sort of got a negative reaction to this.

I: Why would you say you did?

S: Maybe because I was in a scientific position and this was an inefficient waste of time, if nothing else.

d. Effects of the Campus Political Climate

I have characterized the over-all political climate at Wesleyan as one of moderate liberalism. There are, for example, no outspokenly conservative student organizations of the sort that have been publicized in recent years at other liberal arts institutions. It may be this general climate of opinion that accounts for the uniformity with which students immediately assumed that the President had been the victim of a right-wing assassin.

> Frankly I thought it was a segregationist because of the events that had happened in the South last summer. Especially I figured that if they could kill little children in church, they could [do this].

> The first thing that popped into everyone's mind was either racists or the far right.

For a number of the students this interpretation was fed by the memory that Stevenson and Johnson had been physically harassed by right-wing individuals in Dallas.

> [I thought that] in Dallas it would have to be a right-winger.

This, of course, is the interpretation that was speculatively advanced by many radio and television commentators after the first reports. In the general population relatively few people (about 12 per cent of the NORC national sample) reported that they had thought of right-wingers or segregationists as being responsible. In fact, Communism was referred to in the population at large with twice the frequency of conservatism, as a possible affiliation of the assassin.[8] Wesleyan University undergraduates, therefore (although inaccurate in their initial interpretations) were closer to the "informed" speculations of the press than was the general public.

On some other campuses, the presumption of right-wing guilt was not as common. A University of Massachusetts student who was present at one of the group interviews commented:

> All of you say that your immediate reaction was that a right-winger had done it. *Our* reaction was that . . . it must have been a Communist. . . . I walked into the [Massachusetts] Student Union where about a thousand people were assembled. The general reaction was, "Oh, my God, how terrible!" And "It must have been a Communist. . . ." Do you think [the difference in reaction is a result of] the intellectual status of the two different universities? . . . [Our] campus is more or less Kennedy-oriented—very pro-Kennedy. . . . But it's Catholic-Kennedy-oriented, rather than sort of liberal Democrat Kennedy.

Actually both conservative and liberal Wesleyan undergraduates reached the same conclusion, but with different feelings. Some conservatives report their relief in learning Oswald's identity—and some liberals, their regret; but in each case the cognitive assumptions as to who would be likely to shoot a Democratic President in the South were the same.

Student Perceptions of Kennedy, Mrs. Kennedy, and Johnson

On occasion the students quite consciously sensed that aspects of their response were a result of being college students and young men. This consciousness was especially evident in their statements about the late President, but was also evident in their responses to Mrs. Kennedy and President Johnson.

a. President Kennedy

A number of the students pointed out that their own interest in politics had essentially been coeval with Kennedy's campaign for nomination and election and his administration. Any teacher of political science cannot fail to be impressed by the short historical span of his undergraduate students' political memories: one of our respondents, for example, speculated about whether the death of President Eisenhower would have been as disturbing "if you were old enough to really take an interest in those days." Indeed the oldest of our students would have been fourteen years old at the time of the 1956 election; ten when the Eisenhower administration began. Memories of Kennedy, his actions and rhetoric, his family, his humor and the humor about him, made up a large portion of the political worlds of these students.

> S: If it had been somebody else I probably wouldn't have been so shook up, but just the fact that this man symbolized so much to me. . . .
>
> I: Why don't you talk a little bit about what he symbolized?
>
> S: For one thing, I always wanted to meet him. . . . I'd watched him. He was the first President that I ever really got to know as a President from his election right on up, probably because of age. This was the first man that I had seen his debates and everything else and I'd read so much about him—how articulate he was, his philosophies. I'd read a lot of what he wrote, his activities. . . . I'd seen him with Jackie and the kids which didn't impress me too much but it's still part of an image. . . . I thought he was on his way to becoming one of the greatest Presidents we have ever had.

Apart from the limitations of experience due to their age, it was the familiar elements of Kennedy's youth, as well as the ways in which he had become associated with intellectuality that contributed to the depth of their grief at his death. There seemed to be something more than a stereotyped use of jargon in the many references to personal "identification" with him ("There was an aura about him—something that someone my age could really identify with"). This was an individual who had come to serve ego-ideal functions—the students had, in effect, incorporated him within themselves. His loss, therefore, was truly painful.

Because of his age and everything, I always felt, you know, kind of pulling for him to do the right thing. He was young and maybe, although I had confidence in him and everything, it wasn't the deep confidence you might have in an older person and you wanted him to do well and were kind of just pushing for him, or at least I felt this way.

S_1: The realization began to sink in that not only would Johnson be President, but the whole Harvard-Yale axis around Kennedy [would probably be] dissolved.

I: Did you regret to see the Harvard-Yale axis [go]?

S_1: Even though we criticized them at the time, I began to feel . . . that we [students? intellectuals?] never had it so good.

S_2: You felt that there was a chance for—not an academic but a person who made . . . knowledge his business. . . . It gave him a chance to do something perhaps important.

I: Who do you have in mind when you say that?

S_2: Rostow or Schlesinger, McGeorge Bundy.

I was at a White House meeting for a bunch of guys who'd been working in Washington during the summer, I guess this was the summer before last, and toward the end of the summer we were all invited to the White House and there was really a beautiful spring kind of day at the end of summer, and Kennedy came out and stood up on a platform, there must have been thousands of us there, and you know, it's just so amazing, he had this tan—he'd been in Washington quite a while as I understand —but he had this beautiful tan on and he started there speaking in the clipped way he has and talking about the need for people to go into government service, and then right out of the blue he says, quoting a historian out of something or other, I'd never heard of the guy, said, he just quoted a paragraph, you know, just click, click. There weren't any uhs or buts and it was obvious that he was verbatim and then he went on with this tightly controlled sort of emotion saying, you know, we really need people in the government and it's a good life and our country needs it, and you got this idea of somebody who's completely dedicated himself to the service of his country who feels very emotionally about service and yet who controls it and guides it through intellect. This is the kind of person we'd all despaired of, a lot of us had, during the Eisenhower Administration. This is the kind of guy whom we could identify with, who was as we hoped we might be some day. This really deepened the emotion, I think, feeling the identification.

Even among students who had set themselves off politically from Kennedy, there was a consciousness that he had been *personally* attractive to them, and there was a degree of retrospective idealization.

> S: I was for Rockefeller and always saw Kennedy as more or less . . . too much of a politician. But now this morning [Saturday] . . . I sort of admire him, the day after. . . . I can still remember how I felt yesterday morning, but on the other hand it is more of an attachment to him than I had had for him before.
>
> I: An attachment to exactly [what] about him?
>
> S: It's partly his personality which was always attractive to me. . . . You associate Kennedy as a sort of . . . intellectual-type figure.

b. Mrs. Kennedy

Mrs. Kennedy also was responded to in ways that explicitly stressed the respondents' status as college students. There were numerous references to her "graciousness," her "intelligence," "cultivation," and "attractiveness." "This," one student commented, "is what the college guy would like to marry." There also were a good many straightforward statements of sympathy with her bereavement.

> Just seeing her standing there with those two kids after it happened—it's bound to touch you emotionally, no matter who you are, I think, if you have any feeling at all. And just before she was First Lady and everything and she's lost him, you know, she just practically lost everything, and so have the kids.

Yet in the students' responses to her there were indications of more complex undercurrents of a sort that do not emerge in such structured investigations of the assassination as the NORC national survey. It is not clear to what degree these responses are conditioned by the student status of our respondents. They include an ambivalent preoccupation with the details of her deportment and behavior, a concern (often bordering on hostility) with the genuineness of her feelings, references to her sexual unavailability —themes that, if evidence were available of responses at deeper levels of personality, might well prove to have oedipal significance.

> S_1: You know she is still very young and attractive and she's finished, really, as a woman. I really feel as though she's had it.

S_2: She won't be able to get married again—it would just be impossible.

I: No?

S_3: Maybe [after] ten years.

S_1: An announcer said, "Mrs. Kennedy is acting impeccably." Those were his words. "Impeccably," I remember that one, and I didn't like it at all. I thought she'd been acting impeccably far too long.

I: What did he mean?

S_1: Just the perfect social . . .

S_2: Stiff upper lip.

S_1: Right, and I didn't like a bit of it before and I thought if she had shown some emotion, I might have felt "Well, maybe she really is a real person." I don't know, I just . . . I never did like her.

S_3: I don't think the camera could show it that well. From their description she was fairly red-eyed most of the time and the tear is evident. Now she didn't break down sobbing, or anything like that, but I think if you'd ever seen anybody do that in a funeral, it bothers you even more than a person who can compose himself, stay fairly well composed, and I think she did and that's to her credit.

S_4: As long as I'm reassured that the emotion is there, I admire her for remaining composed. I had no desire for her to break down and cry and all.

I: How about responses to her from the very beginning? There were a number of pictures of her all the way through.

S_5: I felt admiration.

S_6: I think the most shocking picture of the whole day was when they unloaded the casket from the plane, and they showed her and they showed the blood on her skirt and her legs. I admit, though, that when I stopped to think about it I wanted her to take that blood off —I didn't want to see it.

S_7: What I think [S_4] said about reassuring yourself that she does feel the emotion . . . there was a picture in the *Times* of her standing next to President Johnson as he was being sworn in and she showed a great deal of emotion there. I think I looked at that picture and thought, well, I guess she is feeling something.

S_8: There were several close-ups of her . . . underneath her veil and you could certainly see emotion in her face.

S_9: What [S_4] said first occurred to me at the time . . . whether I wanted her to break down or not and then I decided I didn't because, I guess being somewhat of a romantic, or something, it seemed as though they were carrying this whole thing off in the only decent aspect of the whole thing.

It evidently still is true that Caesar's wife must be above suspicion.

c. Lyndon Johnson

Responses to President Johnson included profound feelings of reassurance that the institution of automatic Presidential succession had functioned successfully and a consciousness of how one's impressions of Johnson became immediately more favorable as a consequence of his assumption of the Presidential role. For a number of students an interesting further element in response to Johnson consisted of spontaneous initial feelings of resentment toward him as someone who had taken over Kennedy's position—feelings they acknowledged to be "irrational." All of these probably were generally prevalent sentiments, although the last (like the ambivalent responses to Mrs. Kennedy) would probably not be brought to light by survey research.

Most specifically student-related was the problem of reconciling new respect for Johnson with the obvious differences between his style and manner and those aspects of Kennedy that were most appealing to college students.

> He doesn't fit the traditional New Frontier image . . . that we've been living with for three years.
>
> Not quite as crisp and not quite as direct [as Kennedy].
>
> [He has] a sort of a heavy Southern accent.
>
> They had an interview with Johnson taken about a week ago at his ranch and he came out with things that if Kennedy had not been [killed]. . . . Stuff like "America is great and strong. . . ." That sort of thing. I would normally think, "What are you? Come off it man!" You know. However, listening to it now—I listened and sat there. Just the fact that he was in the Presidency gave him a sort of deification.

Statements such as these lead one to feel a shallowness in the instantaneous support of Johnson—to suspect that, if the 1964 Republican nominee had been a Scranton or a Rockefeller his support among student Kennedy followers would have been considerable.

Retrospect

We did no follow-up interviewing, but the impression one had from observing students informally was that behavior and feelings quickly returned to normal and that, three or four months later, many of the students would have found it difficult even to remember the intensity of their feelings during the weekend of the assassination. A sidelight of interest is that for at least some students there was a conscious reaction against the more extreme public acts of celebration of Kennedy—the naming of public objects after him, for example. Indeed a certain amount of undergraduate humor seems to have developed on this score. Without further evidence not much can be said about this, but my impression is that these later reactions were fully consistent with the students' distress at Kennedy's death—the humor helped to ward off painful memories, but it also was more of a piece with the aspects of Kennedy that attracted students to him than were the sentimental tributes that the students derided.

Summary and Conclusion

We have been concerned with analyzing and illustrating a number of ways in which the age and student status of a group of young men seem to have influenced their response to the assassination of President Kennedy. In many respects, of course, reactions to the President's death cut uniformly across population groups. Nevertheless, responses also mirrored individual and group characteristics.

Beginning with the effects of the physical setting of the campus itself—which made it highly likely that the assassination would be learned of in a face-to-face social context—there were a variety of ways in which membership in a college community shaped the weekend's experiences. Students felt a need to be in contact with their peers rather than their families and, in some cases, were conscious of a tendency to depend upon peers for standards of response to the assassination; response was influenced by the student's location in the subgroup structure of the university, both the situation in which they found themselves at the time of learning of the assassination and their prior group attachments (we noted differences in response between fraternity houses and differences between science and nonscience students); the campus political climate of moderate liberalism seems to have made for the common assumption—shared by conservatives and liberals—that the President's assassin had been a right-winger.

The age and student status of our respondents colored their perceptions of and responses to Kennedy, Mrs. Kennedy, and Johnson. In the case of the late President, this was especially striking: his youth and intelligence (and many of the other familiar aspects of his style and career, including his appearance, the electric quality of his public performances, his humor, his war record) made him a compelling figure for admiration and emulation. "He was as we hoped we might be some day." The brutal, sudden termination of Kennedy's life—particularly, at a point at which few solid accomplishments could be shown for his administration—was therefore disturbing in a profoundly personal way. One consequence of the assassination was to reveal even to students who had opposed Kennedy's politics—who would not have voted for him—the strength of their *personal* attachment, their fascination with him.

To all of this must be added a consequence of the timing of American politics—the quadrennial election cycle, as it relates to the individual life cycle. In 1956, apart from the lack of intrinsic interest to young people of the second Eisenhower election, most of these students were at an age when few Americans are especially politically concerned. The 1960 election, which brought Kennedy to power, constituted a political coming-to-maturity for this generation of students. They, in effect, were a Kennedy generation. The loss of a figure so closely connected with their own development was perhaps, to return to the image of Caesar, "the most unkindest cut of all."

NOTES

1. For an expanded discussion of these points, see Greenstein, 1965a, which draws upon some of the same illustrations presented here, as well as additional material from our Wesleyan interviews.

2. Compare Delbert Miller's 1945 study of how news of President Roosevelt's death was transmitted on a small college campus. Only about 15 per cent of Miller's respondents learned of the President's death directly from the media. On transmission of reports of the Kennedy assassination in the general population see Sheatsley and Feldman, 1964, and Greenberg, 1964.

3. See the discussion by Edward Shils, 1951, of the "rediscovery of the primary group."

4. On response to Roosevelt's death see Orlansky, 1947. Hill and Hansen, 1962, discuss family behavior in disasters.

5. For evidence of such a sex difference during the college years see Komarovsky, 1950.

6. For detailed and ingenious research findings which are consistent with this assertion see Kagan and Moss, 1962.

7. One student relates that he found the change in routine resulting from the assassination emotionally disturbing. "There was a feeling among four or five people in the class that the class should be called off. And I remember reacting to that suggestion with something awful close to, you know, almost anger. The idea that we can't let this thing upset us that much. You know, we've got to have our class. There's no point in letting this destroy the social order."

8. Sheatsley and Feldman, 1964.

LIST OF REFERENCES

Greenberg, Bradley S. 1964. "Diffusion of News of the Kennedy Assassination," *Public Opinion Quarterly,* 28, No. 2, 225–32.

Greenstein, Fred I. 1965a. College Student Reactions to the Assassination, in Greenberg, Bradley S. and Edwin B. Parker, eds. *The Kennedy Assassination and the American Public: Social Communication in Crisis.* Stanford, Calif.: Stanford University Press.

———— 1965b. *Children and Politics.* New Haven, Conn.: Yale University Press.

Hill, Reuben and Donald A. Hansen. 1962. "Families in Disaster." In Baker, George W. and Dwight W. Chapman, eds., *Man and Society in Disaster.* New York: Basic Books.

Johannsen, Dorothea E. 1946. "Reactions to the Death of President Roosevelt," *Journal of Abnormal and Social Psychology,* 41, No. 2, 218–22.

Kagan, Jerome and Howard A. Moss. 1962. *Birth to Maturity: A Study in Psychological Development.* New York and London: Wiley.

Komarovsky, Mira. 1950. "Functional Analysis of Sex Roles," *American Sociological Review,* 15, No. 4, 508–16.

Miller, Delbert C. 1945. "A Research Note on Mass Communication," *American Sociological Review,* 10, No. 5, 691–94.

Orlansky, Harold. 1947. "Reactions to the Death of President Roosevelt," *Journal of Social Psychology,* 26, second half, 235–66.

Sheatsley, Paul B. and Jacob J. Feldman. 1964. "The Assassination of President Kennedy: A Preliminary Report on Public Reactions and Behavior," *Public Opinion Quarterly,* 28, No. 2, 189–215.

Shils, Edward. 1951. "The Study of the Primary Group." In Lasswell, Harold
    D. and Daniel Lerner, eds., *The Policy Sciences*. Stanford, Calif.: Stanford
    University Press.

Conclusion

In the days immediately following the death of President Kennedy, a major feeling we had was one of unanimity. There was the sense of a great and terrible event, which had affected us all, and of grief shared throughout the nation and the world. This feeling of all being joined in a common emotion has been voiced recurrently when a nation suffers the loss of a great man. In his "Ode on the Death of the Duke of Wellington," Tennyson wrote:

> Bury the Great Duke
>   With an empire's lamentation;
> Let us bury the Great Duke
>   To the noise of the mourning of a mighty nation.

The sense of all joining in a common response has much emotional value for the mourner. He is not alone in his suffering. There is general acknowledgment of great cause for distress. Feelings flow more freely from the awareness of re-enforcement from others. The mourner experiences a sense of increased poignancy and at the same time assuagement from this sharing of emotion. Also in a culture like ours, where mourning for private losses tends to be curtailed, the national mourning for the President probably released many feelings for past griefs incompletely expressed before. "Then can I drown an eye, unus'd to flow."

It is undoubtedly true that in such a circumstance the individual finds some of his feelings echoed to an exceptional degree by a great number of other people. However, the assassination and its sequels constituted a series of complex events, from which different individuals could select and on which they could elaborate according to their varying susceptibilities. The most comprehensive generalization we can make about the studies in this volume is that they all deal with differences in reactions: differences between children and adults, between younger and older children, boys and girls, normal and disturbed, upper and lower class, science

students and liberal arts students, as well as a great variety of individual differences. In this concluding chapter we shall attempt
to sum up the major differences that were observed. We will also
try to show basic themes running through our material, common
motives, which manifested themselves in a variety of ways.

Let us start with differences between adults and children. Adults
acknowledged more outspoken grief than children did: more
adults said that they had wept. There is also the impression that
adults underestimated children's reactions. We have to do here
with differences related to age, and also with the complicated interchange between children and their elders. In situations of emotional stress generally, communication between children and
parents is often disrupted. Or perhaps we should say that at such
times their usual difficulties in understanding each other become
more noticeable. Adults tend to find distress in children hard to
bear. Parents often try to protect their children from the impact
of grievous events by suppressing information. Children, on their
side, are subject to certain inhibitions in expression of emotion,
and also tend to mask their feelings in the presence of adults. Thus
distress in children may be both muted and disguised, while adults
more readily overlook it because of their need to see their children
as untouched by suffering.

The general questions may be raised: when is emotion infec-
tious, so that one is drawn into feeling what another feels, and
when does the expression of emotion in another stimulate a different reaction? We know that anxiety is readily communicated
from mothers to their young children.[1] How is it with grief? On
the weekend of the assassination children saw their parents in an
unaccustomed state of distress, sometimes weeping, generally depressed, and less able to respond to the children's demands than
usual. We would suppose that, rather than stimulating grief in the
children, these manifestations in their parents would have provoked anxiety and some resentment. This would vary with the age
of the children and the degree of their dependence on the parents.
Our findings show much greater anxiety in younger than in older
children, which we would ascribe in part to the effect of seeing
their parents in such an unusual emotional state.

Differences in tempo of emotional response also set parents
and children at odds. Children cannot tolerate distress for long,

while adults can sustain more protracted grief. We have reported on children who cried briefly over the President's death but were then anxious to pursue their usual amusements during that weekend. This precipitated conflicts with their parents. Parents' impressions that children were unfeeling may be related to the short sadness span in children.

The fact that adults more frequently acknowledged weeping than children raises interesting questions. We touch here on the little understood psychology of crying in relation to phases of the life cycle. Infants and small children cry readily at any physical or psychic distress. Later an inhibition against crying sets in. This inhibition extends through the latency period well into adolescence.[2] There is also a strong conscious feeling of shame associated with crying. In our studies, young adolescents repeatedly mentioned that when other children cried over the President's death, when they themselves finally broke down and cried, they were not ashamed. It was as if feelings of shame had to be overcome before they could permit themselves to cry.[3] College boys who admitted that they and their friends were moved to tears had to qualify this by saying "not weeping so much as tears coming out of eyes." The marked sex typing that prevails in our culture in regard to weeping is evident here. It is more permissible for girls and women to weep than it is for boys and men. Thus among our subjects boys denied crying (sometimes contrary to what their parents reported) more than girls did. For either sex it is considered brave not to weep over personal misfortune. We may recall how often people praised Mrs. Kennedy for being brave in not weeping openly at the funeral ceremonies. The strong sentiment in our culture that it is brave not to weep and shameful to give way to tears interferes with the free expression of sad feelings.

How do we account for the fact that adults acknowledged weeping more than children did? Our studies of reactions to a death in the family have shown that while adults manifest outspoken grief, children and adolescents tend to suffer from an affective inhibition.[4] It is our impression that the capacity for a protracted mourning reaction develops only after adolescence. In response to the death of a beloved leader we would expect this capacity for mourning to be more manifest in adults. Also the struggle for control over emotions and impulses is less severe in adults than in children. The long childhood restraint of sexual impulses has subsided; there is greater freedom for emotional release generally. While children contend against their impulses and feelings, adults have gained the sense that they may under appropriate circumstances give free expression to their emotions. When it comes to sad feelings, it is particularly permissible to express them when the occasion is one that involves sympathy for others rather than personal misfortune. We did not find adults speaking of feelings of shame when they acknowledged weeping for the President. The less frequent acknowledgment of weeping on the part of children may have been due in some instances to their being ashamed to admit it. We would suppose, however, that there was a greater affective inhibition than in adults. Also for both adults and children who did not acknowledge outspoken grief there may well have been lesser emotional involvement with the President.

In the introduction we spoke of the phases of reaction to loss: protest, disorganization, and reorganization. We would like to see now from our various findings how these appeared in reaction to the President's death. Protest appeared in the feeling of disbelief, which was the most common initial reaction in all age groups. There was a strong unwillingness to accept the reality of what had happened. Related to this were frequent thoughts and fantasies of how the fatality could have been prevented, undoing it in imagination. Feelings of anger also characterize this phase. Lindemann has pointed out the component of rage in grief.[5] This rage is initially inchoate and objectless. It is a primitive reaction to being frustrated and cruelly deprived. Subsequently it seeks an object on which to vent itself. Following the President's death it took the form of vengeful feelings against the assassin, of directing blame against various groups and agencies, of disputes between people who had different interpretations of the events.

The phase of protest was variably prolonged in different age groups. It was most protracted in adolescents. Younger children achieved a quicker acceptance of what had happened because they had not as yet become so emotionally involved with the President. Adults underwent a process of mourning, which, however, was accomplished in a much more condensed time span than mourning for a personal loss. Distress of an acute nature tended to subside relatively quickly.[6] However grievous the loss was, it required less massive reorganization of emotions, habits, and expectations than does the loss of a person with whom one is intimately involved in one's daily life. Feelings of affection, admiration, and regret no doubt remained attached to the dead President. But the initial sense of protest, of inability to believe it, gave way to an acceptance of what had happened.

It was in adolescents that the sense of disbelief persisted longest. We can relate this to their unreadiness, in their phase of development, to carry through the work of mourning. They felt a continuing sense of not being able to accept the loss of someone to whom they had become so attached. But also we would suppose that our youngest President had a particularly strong appeal for this age group. He seemed close to them, someone who could understand them; for the younger adolescents, an ideal parent figure, for the older ones, the model of what they should strive to become. This applies particularly to young men. For young girls we may suppose that the President figured more as a love object than as an ego ideal. Among older adolescents, the girls found it even more difficult than the young men to reconcile themselves to his loss.

The phase of disorganization is difficult to observe. It consists of inner turmoil, inchoate distress, anxiety, restlessness, thoughts in disarray. The process of putting feelings into words is a step toward reorganization. Our subjects, in talking with us, in writing about what they had experienced, in responding to structured forms of inquiry such as questionnaires, were by these very activities getting reorganized. Probably we ourselves in pursuing research in a time of crisis were partly motivated by a need to bring order out of chaos.

We may observe nevertheless many indications of emotional disorganization. Anxiety and apprehension of other bad things happening were widespread. Generally those who have experienced a sudden disaster become fearful that it will be repeated.[7] This apprehension has no realistic relation to the future. It is rather a continuing reverberation of the disaster already undergone, which has not yet been assimilated. Also deep-seated, often unconscious beliefs in benevolent, protective powers keeping us safe from harm are seriously shaken. The apprehensiveness occasioned by a disaster, like the rage in grief of which we spoke, may at first be without definite object. Then it attaches itself to more specific dangers. Following the assassination young children frequently expressed the fear that the assassin might be lurking in their neighborhood. This sinister figure became condensed with the attacker in the night who already had haunted their fantasies. Other young children, most impressed with the fact that the father of children like themselves had died, became anxious about separation from their parents, or fearful that something might happen to them. Many adults, as we know, expressed apprehensions about bad things happening to our country, or the outbreak of another war. We might say that the President, as a good father figure, was trusted to keep aggression under control. The fact that he himself was killed showed that he was unable to do this; hence the fear of the outbreak of aggressive acts, whether the child's fear of the lurking assassin, or the adult's apprehension of a nuclear war. Younger children more than adolescents or adults were subect to anxiety following the assassination. We would relate this to their greater susceptibility to separation anxiety and their greater fear of aggression (their own and that which they project onto others) getting out of control. These vulnerabilities, combined with the unsettling effect of seeing their parents weeping and distraught, occasioned much anxiety.

Among the defenses noted against the anxiety thus provoked were regression and a massive blanking out of the events. Young disturbed children were observed to revert temporarily from games of fighting and killing to more infantile behavior: sucking their thumbs, clinging to a favorite toy which had previously been given up, wanting to sit on the therapist's lap. Other disturbed children showed a tendency to ward off the alarming stimuli, not to react, to take in the facts in a detached rote manner, later to forget everything connected with these events. It was observed conversely that the children who could tolerate an emotional response were better able to retain knowledge and understanding of what had happened.

Feelings of malaise also characterized the phase of disorganization. Children and adults alike spoke of feeling sick. This referred both to diffuse feelings of psychic distress and somatic reactions. On the large-scale questionnaire study, younger children acknowledged more somatic disturbances—difficulty in sleeping, loss of appetite, headaches—than adolescents. This may be related to the higher anxiety level in the younger children. But it may be also that the alternatives offered in the questionnaire did not cover the range of somaticized reactions. Thus in more spontaneous reporting, adolescents spoke, for instance, of an empty feeling in the stomach, feeling as if the breath was knocked out of them when they heard the news.

Feelings of helplessness were expressed, sometimes of wishing to do something, but there being nothing one could do. There was a sense of inability to carry on usual occupations or complete loss of interest in them. This again varied with age, younger children pursuing more readily than adolescents or adults their usual activities. It is characteristic of a true mourning reaction that the disturbing sense of loss permeates the mourner's mind and makes everything else unimportant. In younger children, their lesser involvement or their intolerance for protracted distress facilitated a greater isolation of the event; its effect was not all-absorbing. There is also evidence that among adolescents it was the more disturbed ones who tended quickly to push the event aside. Even if they had been very upset immediately following, they were anxious to have fun that weekend. In their inability to sustain painful feelings they resembled younger children.

Some college students spoke of not knowing how to react, of watching those around them to get cues. We may suppose that they were in conflict about expressing or restraining unusual emotions. Also there may have been some persisting sense of unreality, entailing a postponement of reaction. Confused thoughts and conflicting feelings were probably frequent, but difficult to observe. We see this kind of inner turmoil in the young adolescent girl who wanted to kill the assassin and also felt like killing herself. She seems to have suffered a diffuse rage reaction, without knowing how to direct it. We could also infer that feelings of guilt were stirred up, which may have motivated the suicidal thoughts. An older adolescent girl, when she heard that the President had been shot, found herself praying that he should not die. She had for some time before this ceased to believe in God. Under the stress of a great threat, older feelings, which she thought she had given up, came to the surface.

Adolescents and adults both reported that they felt compelled to think intensively about what had happened. This thinking often took the form of propounding a question to which there appeared to be no answer: how could such a thing happen? It seemed that the murder of the President had shattered basic assumptions about how the world is arranged. It constituted an appalling discrepancy. We suppose that on a deeper level there was horror at the violation of an awesome taboo, a sense that perhaps the laws of conscience are not laws of nature. Feelings and fantasies from deeply repressed levels were stirred. The intensive effort to think represented a struggle to reorganize the moral and rational surface structure of the mind, shaken by confused and alien feelings from the depths. In the phase of disorganization angry feelings also persisted. These now found many different objects of attack. We shall consider particularly vengeful feelings against the assassin.

We have spoken of the complexity of the assassination and its sequels, and how different individuals could select as the focus of their response the aspect most related to their emotional preoccupations. Two major aspects of the sequence of events were: loss of a loved and admired leader and a series of crimes of violence. For some people, grief for loss appeared to be the predominant reaction; others seemed preoccupied with murder and retribution. Our studies suggest that these two kinds of reaction tended to be mutually exclusive. For those who mourned, punishment of the assassin seemed relatively unimportant. Those who were filled with vengeful feelings seemed less susceptible to grief. Perhaps, however, these contrasting emotions occurred in the same subjects over time. The impression of their mutual exclusiveness may derive from our having tapped subjects at moments when one or the other emotion was temporarily in the ascendant.

Absorption in the crime and its punishment was expressed in the wish that the police would have shot Oswald down immediately, in many fantasies of cruel tortures that should have been inflicted on him, and in approbation of his being murdered by Ruby. We have found a number of variables related to these vengeful feelings. Younger more than older children expressed the wish for immediate and often cruel vengeance. Talion punishment dominates their moral outlook. The severity with which they condemn the aggressive impulses in themselves, with which they are still waging dubious battle, is readily turned against others. An external conflict is substituted for an internal one; the force of their primitive and cruel conscience can be directed against another, who has carried into action the bad wishes they themselves are holding in check.

Within a given age group (young adolescents) disturbed children were found to be more vengeful than normal children. In their lesser capacity to solve problems of aggression, they resemble younger children. With increasing age (on the level of high school seniors) lower-class children showed greater persistence of vengeful feelings than upper-class children. We would suppose that they, like the younger and the more disturbed children, have achieved less sublimation and moderation of aggression.

Among college students, a striking difference appeared between athletes and those more intellectually oriented. In the latter group there was weeping. As one of these young men put it, "My sense of loss overwhelms my feelings for revenge." The athletes were dry-eyed, and rather scornful of other students who were not. They were occupied with thinking up and discussing gruesome tortures that they would have liked to inflict on Oswald. From this predominance of vengeful feelings in the athletes, we would infer that they also are far from having solved the problems of aggression.

Children's understanding and acceptance of legal procedures are related to the exigencies of their emotional development. Intelligent, normal children in latency and prepuberty told us that Oswald should not have been given a trial, he should have got immediate death because he killed a very important man. They seem to see a trial as a postponement of punishment in cases where the crime is not too grave. We may find a counterpart to this in what they have probably experienced as reactions to their own misdeeds. If they commit a minor misdemeanor, their parents may palaver about what is to be done. This corresponds to a trial. If they do something really bad, their parents are provoked to immediate chastisement. A trial would thus mean a delay of retribution, which is allowed only for minor crimes. We may also discern deeper motives behind the demand for immediate punishment of the murderer. Theodor Reik has pointed out that when a murder has been committed, members of the community tend to feel an urgent anxiety to identify the criminal.[8] While he remains unknown, suspicion may attach to all. In the case of a particularly horrible crime a similar urgency may be felt to confirm the guilt of the culprit by his prompt punishment. Then doubts as to the innocence of others may be set at rest. The tendency of younger children to say that Oswald should have been shot down immediately may derive in part from uneasy feelings of vicarious guilt. With increasing age, as we move into adolescence, there is a progressive acceptance of the necessity for fair trial. This greater tolerance for the law's delays would seem to be related to reduced intensity of inner conflicts about aggressive impulses.

Speculations about a possible conspiracy represent another aspect of response to the crime and feelings about justice. Children were much less inclined than adults to consider that there might have been a conspiracy. For them it seemed clear that the assassin did it. We would suppose that this is partly due to children's having fewer concepts of intricate and indirect social connections, and less concern with the sifting of details of evidence. Also their fantasies of aggression tend to focus on direct interpersonal action. For the considerable number of adults who believed in a conspiracy, we would think that an underlying motive was a sense of disproportion between cause and effect, between the mad impulse of an insignificant man and the fall of the leader of a great nation. Children, whose fantasies and stories are full of small protagonists overcoming big giants, would be less likely to feel this discrepancy. While children had little doubt that the assassin did it, they were less ready than adults to commit themselves as to possible reasons for his act. In this know-nothing attitude we see their need to dissociate themselves from the crime.

That oedipal impulses and related guilt were activated by the assassination is evidenced, or may be inferred from clinical and other findings. In one group of adolescent patients, the boys in contrast to the girls avoided mention of the assassination in the first therapeutic session following it. This avoidance was ascribed to the arousal of vicarious guilt for a crime that bore the latent significance of parricide. Other clinical reports, of later responses, showed that manifest parricidal fantasies emerged. Some boy patients also produced fantasies in which they assumed an assassin's role.

With the President's death, many thoughts and feelings were

turned toward his young widow. College boys who were interviewed were scrupulous about denying that she could be thought
of as a possible love object. In praising her they acknowledged,
"This is what the college guy would like to marry." But they went
on to say that she could never marry again; it would just not be
possible. They were concerned about whether her emotional restraint might have meant less than total devotion to her husband.
It seemed as though they wanted her to assure them that she was
forever taboo, dedicated to perpetual mourning.

While the parricidal significance of the assassination was the
most disturbing on deeper emotional levels, incestuous impulses
were also stimulated. These appeared both in provocative behavior
of child patients toward their parents and in fantasies about the
President and his wife. Some boy patients reported amorous fantasies about Mrs. Kennedy. It was striking that some girl patients
acknowledged similar daydreams about Mr. Kennedy. An event
corresponding to the male oedipal crime had been translated by
them into feminine oedipal terms. We would speculate that if a
couple, emotionally equated to the parental couple, is separated
by death, either partner may seem available as a love object. Daydreams, as we know, override barriers of both convention and
reality. It should be added that where such amorous fantasies were
admitted it was likely to be with compunction and shame.

Negative feelings toward the dead are generally repressed or
suppressed. *De mortuis nihil nisi bonum.* When Lois Murphy pro-
posed to include in her questionnaire on the assassination a question about criticisms of the late President, her colleagues were
censorious. There is no doubt that following the death of President
Kennedy a strongly intensified idealization of him was widespread.
We shall have more to say about this presently. However, there
were minor indications of negative feelings. In reports of reactions
in schools to the announcement of the assassination, there were
recurrent references to some child who laughed. This was generally viewed with reprobation. A child patient who had laughed
reported how he had suffered from the vindictive behavior of his
schoolmates, and that he really felt terrible. This momentary
laughter may be related to the frequent thought at first hearing
the news that it was a joke. It may also be taken as a reaction to
extreme tension. But we are struck by the fact that this incidental

laughter was so repeatedly recalled. The sick jokes about the Kennedy family that appeared later reenforce the impression that there is a theme here of some significance.

Fenichel has said that persons who feel like laughing at a funeral are expressing mastery over anxiety and triumph over the dead.[9] Strong scruples militate against such feelings of triumph. Nevertheless a covert sense of how the mighty have fallen may make itself felt. In a democracy there are many defenses against envy of those who attain high position. Since the race is officially open to all, citizens cannot feel if they are low and others high that this is divinely ordered as it is in a hereditary monarchy or aristocracy. The ancient Greeks believed in *hubris,* an inevitable retribution against the great who vaunted themselves too highly. This may be interpreted as a projection of the envy of their fellow citizens. In our democracy we have many defenses against envy of the great. Among these are vicarious pleasure in their success, diversion of antagonism against their opponents, an emphasis on the sufferings of the great, a leveling view according to which a man in high office is just doing another job. The Kennedy family, with their many extraordinary advantages and successes, strained the usual defenses against envy. This was why there was so much joking about them. We suggest that this was also why the minor note of someone laughing at the news of the assassination remained memorable and Kennedy jokes began to reappear in the guise of sick jokes.

The phase of reorganization includes reduction of distress, perpetuation of the lost person in memory and in other internal and external ways, transfer of some feelings to substitute figures, and assimilation of what has happened into a coherent view of the world. Since our data were gathered shortly after the President's death the signs of reorganization that we can indicate are necessarily incomplete. Following disasters generally there is a recurrent wish that out of evil good will come. The thought is expressed that grievous things happen for a purpose. The survivors resolve that they will hereafter strive to do better. Both adults and children expressed some positive expectations that we would become better, that our country would become better, as a consequence of the President's death. These ideas tended to be vague, without concrete content. We might see in them the positive counterpart to the conspiracy theories, which generally lacked any specification of what the plot was. In both these views, of plot and positive purpose, we see a striving to find a meaning, to integrate a disturbing event into an organized view of the world. That these efforts to find a larger meaning, for good or ill, remained incomplete suggests the obsolescence of teleological thinking in our time.

On a deeper emotional level, there is the tendency to idealize a lost love object and to identify with it in various ways. It is evident that affection and admiration for President Kennedy were intensified by his death. Our studies show that children and adolescents felt more positively toward him than they had before. Those who had had some negative feelings tended to change over. Those who were already attached to him experienced a strengthening of this attachment. This is similar to what we have observed in children who have lost a parent, but we would expect it to have different consequences in relation to a national leader. When a parent dies, children tend to idealize him and intensify their attachment to him. In their own secret thoughts and feelings, they refuse to give him up and reject possible substitutes. No one else can compare with the idealized lost parent to whom they cling. Idealization and strengthened feeling for a national leader who has died would seem to have more positive effects. He has not occupied such a unique personal position in the emotional life of his followers. There is less resistance to his being replaced. Feelings of resentment toward Johnson for replacing Kennedy were expressed by some children and adolescents. However, this was a minor theme, whether because it was little felt or because it was considered inappropriate to express it. The opposite sentiment was also voiced, of gratification that our country was so arranged that we had a new President ready to take charge and with whom we could face the world. Also estimates of Mr. Johnson rose almost immediately on his assuming the Presidency. This has been regularly observed in response to any new incumbent.

A major way in which someone who has died is perpetuated is through those who live on identifying with his traits and aims. The superego and ego ideal of children are initially modeled on their parents as they perceive them. As they develop they turn increasingly to other models, from life or fiction, who seem to them to embody ideal qualities. These admired figures enter into the further formation of the ideal image that the young person strives to realize. A President, in life, appears generally in an idealized light. He is one of many from among whom the young may choose models. With his death, and particularly a death that resembles martyrdom, he not only becomes still more idealized, but there is a strong tendency to want to perpetuate him. There is considerable evidence that children and adolescents have become much occupied with the life of John F. Kennedy. This is partly an effort to recapture a valued person whose sudden loss has evoked strong regret. We would suppose also that his idealized image may enter into the formation of the ego ideal in those in whom it is still developing. It is difficult at this point to know what the image is or how lasting its effect will be. We would suppose that for young boys it is a hero image, of the sort they so prize; for adolescents, perhaps one of dedication to a career that is not merely self-seeking.

The murder of a leader, according to Freud, evokes strong posthumous obedience in his followers. They feel that they must take it upon themselves to carry out his behests. We would speculate that following the murder of the President a sense of this imperative was widely felt in the adult population. In the time between the assassination and the election of the next year, President Johnson became established in people's minds as dedicated to helping us carry out what President Kennedy had wanted done. The fact that he received an unprecedented popular majority in the election may be ascribed in part to posthumous obedience to the murdered leader.

How the death of President Kennedy will be remembered later is again a matter for speculation. Personal memories of such an event are difficult to preserve since they become overlaid with many publicly repeated versions of what happened. However, we would predict that for young children, to the extent that their personal experience survives, it will be remembered as an isolated event of an uncanny nature. The world around them, at school, at home, was in an upset state such as they had not known. Even their familiar television programs were suspended. What they watched was disturbing and bewildering. Their incomprehension of the grown-up world was intensified, with a sense of things being radically out of control. They were distressed, but they fell back on the resources of their age for escaping distress. They went out and played. Of course much was explained to them. They got some organized idea of the sequence of events, varying with their age and health of mind. But if some twinges of their own feelings from that time are revived later they will evoke something strange, something that intruded into the usual round of life and could not be quite assimilated.

For young adolescents we would predict that it will be remembered by many as their first experience of grief. It was for them an initiation into the experience of painful loss which none escapes in life. Perhaps this experience of grief, which they were helped to bear by sharing it with so many others, will have prepared them to some extent to tolerate later losses.

For older adolescents it meant the sudden tragic end of a career with which they were much identified. There was a young President to whom they felt unusually close. They wanted him to succeed; they felt empathic hurt in his fall. He would never achieve all that he had set out to do. Perhaps in later years, when they think back on the high hopes of their youth, which for them, as for other generations, will be incompletely fulfilled, their nostalgic regrets for lost youth will be mingled with their feelings for their young President cut off in mid-career.

We should like to add a few methodological reflections. A wide range of methods was used in the different studies in this volume. It does not seem necessary to recapitulate here the advantages and limitations of each of them.[10] Comparisons, for instance, between what can be obtained from questionnaire studies of a large population and more intensive studies of a limited number of subjects, based on interviewing or clinical material, are familiar to students of the social sciences. Nor shall we repeat well known arguments pro and con as to how much can be extrapolated from clinical findings that is applicable to normal subjects. We shall confine ourselves to a few methodological points raised by our studies, which may be of use to other researchers.

A problem was posed for all our investigations by a character trait that generally prevails in our culture, namely, inarticulateness, especially in spoken words, about strong feelings. Our tendency is toward understatement rather than verbal exuberance.

We have delegated to public speakers, such as television commentators and political orators, the role of expressor of what the majority cannot themselves articulate. We also often rely on music to evoke what we are unable to say. This is typically exemplified in the use of the musical sound track in films. For instance, in *High Noon*, Gary Cooper carried out his fated and lonely role with a look of tragic determination on his face, while on the sound track one heard the moving song, "Do not forsake me, oh my darling," which expressed what he felt and could not say.

Articulateness about feelings varies with the medium of expression. We would compare particularly what our subjects were able to express in spoken and in written words. It is our impression that on all age levels spoken words were inadequate to express much of what was felt. A young boy voiced what were probably massive feelings of distress on hearing the news of the assassination by saying, "I didn't like it a bit." His elders were not much more articulate, frequently experiencing a painful sense of the inadequacy of words. Often more could be expressed in writing than orally. A ten-year-old boy wrote, *"Please Lord, please. Tell me this was a publicity stunt. Please."* It seems unlikely that he could have spoken such words either to age-mates or to his elders. Among adolescents particularly, at an age when considerable mastery of written expression has been achieved, we found a strong striving to evoke and record in writing what they had experienced, and they produced moving documents. This finding suggests the importance of the written medium for obtaining expression of strong feelings.

In evoking the experiences of our subjects another alternative was whether we were asking for recall or recognition: that is, whether we asked for a spontaneous recapitulation of events, as in an essay, or whether we tried to elicit various details by a series of questions, on a questionnaire or in an interview. The relative effectiveness of these methods varies with the age of the subject. The less directive method has the greater possibility for eliciting unanticipated responses. However, it presupposes a considerable capacity to organize and formulate one's experiences. Younger children as compared with adolescents were less able to do this. The stimulus of specific questions, in questionnaires or interviews, facilitated their expression of the range of their reactions.

We have had to do throughout with the problems of young people communicating with their elders. Such communication varies with the age of the child, the person with whom he is communicating, and the medium of communication. Particularly relevant here are children's changing images of adults, and their preferences at different ages as to whom they most want to communicate with. A case in point is the group interviewing of college students, which proved highly evocative. It seems possible that these adolescents could not have talked as freely in individual interviews as they did when interviewed in groups of familiar age-mates. They were at an age when they were most anxious to talk with each other about their thoughts and feelings. They felt the need to check their responses against those of their peers, and having done so could move from more tentative to more outspoken statements. Confronted with a highly structured questionnaire, adolescents seemed to play down their feelings. They may have felt that the preconceptions of the adult questioner hampered their freedom of expression. With their demand for autonomy and their powers of introspection and organization they were able to report more intense emotional reactions in more open-ended communication. Young adolescents were able to confide anonymously in writing to unknown adults whom they could imagine to be sympathetic and understanding. We do not know whether this mode of communication would have appealed equally to older adolescents, who feel less longing to confide in an ideal parent figure.

The way in which the adult shared or failed to share the child's experience was of particular importance in therapeutic situations. Therapists found themselves in a relatively unprecedented situation in which they were agitated by an event that affected them as much as, or more than, their patients. Since they had little or no preparation for confronting such a crisis with their patients, procedure varied widely. We can readily suppose that whether the therapist dismissed his patients on the afternoon of the assassination, or listened to the news reports with them, had significant effects for subsequent communication. In the reports from the children's home, we saw how the staff lived through the crisis and its aftermath with the children. Over a period of time the children moved from idiosyncratic, mutually unrelated reactions to some assimilation of what had happened into a unifying group experience. Initial tendencies toward avoidance and withdrawal were counteracted. The children gained some sense of an event that had become history, and were then moved to ask about the past and future of the institution of which they formed a part, to add an historic dimension to their own lives and those of the adults who cared for them. In this instance, as in therapy generally, the responses observed were in the process of being modified by the observers.

It has been brought out in connection with clinical studies how important it is in assessing the impact of an event to know what was going on in the subject beforehand. For instance, fantasies about killing and rescue operations, which followed the assassination, might have been ascribed to its impact if there had not been observations of the child's previous preoccupation with such themes. At times it seemed as though the assassination only provided children with a new cast of characters for their habitual fantasies. However, comparisons of the functioning of child patients before and after the event showed some shifts in the breakthrough of impulses and in the marshaling of defenses against what were felt to be threats from without and within. These observations suggest the importance of antecedent knowledge of our subjects in assessing the effect a major event has on them.

We have had to do with an event that produced much emotional disorganization. A major problem for our studies was to get an adequate picture of this state of mind, in which the individual is assailed by confusing and opposite feelings. Probably we were not very clearly aware of this problem at the time of starting our researches. As we have said, the very fact of responding to a formal inquiry may make the subject present a coherent account that is at variance with his inner turmoil. We would say that the less structured the method of investigation, and the more it enabled one to obtain expressions of the subject over time, the more disorganization could be observed. In interviews, conflicting emotions, contradictory attitudes, and feelings of bewilderment and confusion were manifest. Essays revealed similar material. Clinical observation showed many shifts of reactions over time, initial avoidance yielding to intense preoccupation, or a nonchalant attitude giving way to painful guilt-ridden feelings. As to more structured methods, we would suggest that, when applied to subjects who may be expected to be in a state of disorganization, they should include questions that make possible the expression of a number of opposite feelings and opinions.

Those studies in which the subjects could be observed for some time after the event had the advantage of following them into the beginnings of reorganization, showing in some instances positive acquisitions from the mastery of what they had experienced. We would suggest that wherever reactions to an event may be expected to manifest a series of phases, as here, it would be desirable to provide for observations over time, or follow-up studies.

We are aware of the limitations of our investigation. As far as regional distribution is concerned, our researches were carried out only in the East and Middle West. It would have been interesting to have had observations of southern children, about whose negative feelings toward President Kennedy there were many rumors. Another limitation is that we have relatively little observation of parent-child interactions. All our studies had to be improvised in haste in the effort to observe the impact of an unexpected event closely following its occurrence. These investigations had few precedents, and there was little time for the preparatory reflection and planning usual in research undertakings. We have tried, however, to understand something of what the death of a national leader means to his people, and, for the first time, how such an event affects children.

NOTES

1. Janis, 1951.

2. Unpublished research on children's reactions to the death of a parent, conducted by the editors of this volume, in the Division of Child Psychiatry, Albert Einstein College of Medicine. Inability to weep in response to loss was frequently reported by children of an age range from latency into adolescence. Somatic distress sometimes appeared in place of weeping, as in the young adolescent boy who said he felt nauseated on the way home from his father's funeral because of having swallowed his tears.

3. The psychoanalytic literature on weeping has stressed the unconscious association of weeping with urination. This association would be relevant to the shame about weeping and the need to control it. Cf. Lewin, 1933; Fenichel, 1936, 1945; Greenacre, 1945.

4. Unpublished research on children's reactions to the death of a parent, cited above.

5. Lindemann, 1944.

6. Sheatsley and Feldman, 1964.

7. Wolfenstein, 1957.

8. Reik, 1945.

9. Fenichel, 1945.

10. Methodological statements about the uses of different kinds of material in the study of children may be found in Mead and Wolfenstein, 1955.

LIST OF REFERENCES

Fenichel, O. 1936. "The Symbolic Equation: Girl = Phallus." In *The Collected Papers of Otto Fenichel,* Second Series, pp. 3–18. New York: Norton, 1954.

_____ 1945. *The Psychoanalytic Theory of Neurosis,* pp. 319, 354, 492–93. New York: Norton.

Greenacre, P. 1945. "Urination and Weeping." In *Trauma, Growth, and Personality,* pp. 106–19. New York: Norton, 1952.

Janis, I. 1951. *Air War and Emotional Stress: Psychological Studies of Bombing and Civilian Defense.* New York: McGraw-Hill.

Lewin, B. 1933. "The Body as Phallus," *The Psychoanalytic Quarterly,* II, 24–27.

Lindemann, E. 1944. "The Symptomatology and Management of Acute Grief," *American Journal of Psychiatry,* CI, 141–48.

Mead, M. and M. Wolfenstein. 1954. eds. *Childhood in Contemporary Cultures.* Chicago: University of Chicago Press.

Reik, T. 1945. *The Unknown Murderer.* New York: Prentice-Hall.

Sheatsley, P. B. and J. J. Feldman. 1964. "The Assassination of President Kennedy: A Preliminary Report of Public Reactions and Behavior," *Public Opinion Quarterly,* XXVII, 189–215.

Wolfenstein, M. 1957. *Disaster: A Psychological Essay.* Glencoe: The Free Press.

Appendix

I

Questionnaire for School Children Used in Dr. Sigel's Study

(See Chapter 2)

MY NAME IS _____

I am a BOY ____

I am a GIRL ____

I am ____ YEARS OLD

I am in the ____ GRADE at _____ SCHOOL

1. Who is President of the United States now? _____

2. How long has he been President? _____

3. Who was President just before him? _____

4. What happened to him? _____
   _____

5. How did this happen? _____
   _____

Now we want you to think of American Presidents in general and not about any particular President. What do you think Presidents are really like? For each question below mark an X beside the sentence which is most true.

The President of the United States

6. ____Would almost always want to help me if I needed it.
   ____Would usually want to help me if I needed it.
   ____Would seldom want to help me if I needed it.

7. ____Knows less than most other men.
   ____Knows more than most other men.
   ____Knows about the same as most other men.

8. ____Is always a leader.
   ____Is more often a leader than a follower.
   ____Is usually a follower.

9. ____Can punish anyone.
   ____Can punish many people.
   ____Can punish no one.

10. ____Works harder than most other people.
    ____Works about as hard as most other people.
    ____Doesn't work as hard as most other people.

11. ____I like him more than anyone else.
    ____I like him as much as I like most people.
    ____I like him less than I like most people.

12. ____Protects me more than anyone.
    ____Protects me as much as most people do.
    ____Protects me less than most do.

Now let us once more think about President Kennedy. Just how was President Kennedy killed? (Put an X beside the one that is true.)

13. ____In a plane crash.
    ____By pistol shots.
    ____From a knife wound.
    ____By rifle shots.

14. Tell us, in a few words, just how you felt when you first heard that President Kennedy was dead. _____
    _____

    Do you remember if you ever felt that way before?

    ____Yes
    ____No

    If your answer was "Yes," what happened that time that made you feel that way? (Tell us in a few words.) _____
    _____
    _____

15. Now let's think a bit about President Kennedy *when he was still alive. Finish the sentence.*
    What I *remember* most about President Kennedy is _____
    _____

16. *Finish the sentence.*
    What I *liked* about President Kennedy was _____
    _____

17. What can you remember that President Kennedy *did* as a President? Write of the things he did in his job as President, not of what he did in his private life._____

_____

_____

18. Who is to blame for Kennedy's death? _____

19. John F. Kennedy
_____was a Republican.
_____was a Democrat.
_____belonged to no political party.
_____I don't know.

20. Below on the right are the names of eight people. On the left, six people are described. Draw a line from the description on the left to the name of the person on the right which you think fits the description.

Description	*Name*
The police officer who was shot	Jack Ruby
The Governor of Texas	Lyndon B. Johnson
The man who killed the President's alleged killer	J. D. Tippit
The man who they say killed the President	John Connolly
The President who was killed	Lee Harvey Oswald
The President of the United States	Will Fritz
	John Fitzgerald Kennedy
	Robert McNamara

21. What kinds of things can people do to make sure that President Kennedy is remembered?_____

_____

22. Did you watch any of the events on TV which had to do with the President's death?
_____Yes
_____No
_____I can't remember.

23. What do you remember most about what you saw on TV about the President's death? _____

_____

24. How much time do you usually spend watching television?
_____A lot every day.
_____A little bit every day.
_____Hardly at all.

25. The three days after President Kennedy's death all the TV programs were about him. All the regular programs were canceled.
Do you think
____It was O.K. to have only programs about President Kennedy?
____They should have had some children's programs?
____They should have continued with most regular programs?

26. During those three days, did you
____Watch TV more than usual?
____Less than usual?
____About the same amount of time as usual?

27. The death of the President happened in
____Washington, D.C.
____Arlington, Virginia.
____Dallas, Texas.
____Ft. Worth, Texas.

28. Some people say a man named Lee Harvey Oswald killed the President. Why would any person want to kill an American President? _____
_____

29. What happened to Oswald? _____
_____

30. How did you feel about that? _____
_____
_____

31. Now let us once more talk about Presidents in general and the government, not about any one particular President.
Which do you think is the most true?
____If you write to the President, he cares *a lot* what you think.
____If you write to the President, he cares *some* what you think.
____If you write to the President, he cares *a little* what you think.
____If you write to the President, he does *not* care one bit about what you think.

32. Who does the most to run the country? Put an X on the line beside the *one* you think does the most to run the country.
____Congress
____President
____Supreme Court
____I don't know.

33. When a President dies
   ____There is no government for a while.
   ____Government goes on just the same.

34. Make a guess.
   ____America has had Presidents who did their job well and Presidents who did not do a good job.
   ____American Presidents have almost all done their job very well.

35. Here are some events that took place in our nation's history. Some happened when President Kennedy was in office. Check those with which he had something to do.
   ____Signing a peace treaty with Japan.
   ____Forcing Governor Barnett to let James Meredith go to the University of Mississippi.
   ____Making the Russians take their missiles out of Cuba.
   ____Greeting the astronauts when they came back from outer space.
   ____Signing a test ban treaty with Russia.
   ____Dropping the atom bomb on Japan.
   ____Setting up the Peace Corps.
   ____Signing the Versailles Treaty which ended World War I.

36. Put an X beside the sentence which comes closest to telling what your father's job is. (If your father is dead or not working now, mark the kind of job he did when he was working.)
   ____He works in a factory or mill, or as a truck driver, janitor or some other job where he works with his hands.
   ____He works with his hands in a job that takes a long time to learn— like a carpenter, an electrician, a plumber, a TV repairman, a machinist, etc.
   ____He works in an office or store as a salesman or clerk.
   ____He owns a service station, laundry, restaurant, or small store or small business.

   My father's job is:
   ____He is a policeman, fireman, soldier, or works for the government.
   ____He is a manager or executive.
   ____He is a doctor, lawyer, teacher, an engineer, or some job like that.
   ____He owns a large business, like a factory or a big store.
   ____I don't know what my father does.

37. Different people felt differently when they heard that President Kennedy was dead. *How did you feel?* Read each line below and check how you felt.

WHEN I HEARD THE PRESIDENT WAS DEAD I	This is how I felt	I did not feel that way
Felt the loss of someone very close and dear.	_____	_____
Was so upset and mixed-up, I did not know what to feel.	_____	_____
Was mad that anyone should do such a terrible thing.	_____	_____
I cried.	_____	_____
Worried about what would happen to our country.	_____	_____
Felt sorry for his wife and children.	_____	_____
Hoped the man who killed him would be shot or beat up.	_____	_____
I did not feel bad.	_____	_____
I did not feel like eating.	_____	_____
Worried what would happen to our relations with other countries.	_____	_____
Felt in some ways it was the President's own fault.	_____	_____
I had trouble getting to sleep.	_____	_____
Hoped the next President would be better.	_____	_____
Felt ashamed that this could happen in our country.	_____	_____
I had a headache.	_____	_____
Worried how the United States would get along without its leader.	_____	_____
I had an upset stomach.	_____	_____

38. If you could vote what would you be? (Choose one)
____Republican
____Democrat
____Sometimes a Democrat and sometimes a Republican
____I don't know what Democrat and Republican mean.

39. Is killing an ordinary person as bad as, worse than, or not as bad as killing the President of the United States?
____As bad
____Not as bad
____The same
____Worse
____I don't know.

40. If Oswald really did shoot the President, then
____It was a good thing of Ruby to shoot Oswald.
____It was still wrong of Ruby to shoot him.
____It didn't matter whether Ruby shot him or not.

41. Since everyone saw Ruby shoot Oswald and since Ruby confessed doing it, will he still be tried in court?
    ____Yes
    ____No
    ____I don't know.

42. Is it necessary to try him in court?
    ____Yes
    ____No
    ____I don't know.

43. Oswald was shot in the police station while a prisoner there. Do you think the police protected him enough?
    ____Yes
    ____No

44. If your answer to 43 above was NO, do you think the police should be punished?
    ____Yes
    ____No

What do you think would have happened to Oswald if Ruby had not shot him? For each part below mark the statement with which you agree.

45. Someone else would have shot him.
    ____Yes
    ____No
    ____Don't know

46. He would have been sent to the electric chair.
    ____Yes
    ____No
    ____Don't know

47. He would have had a trial but it would not have been much of a trial; everyone knew he was guilty.
    ____Yes
    ____No
    ____Don't know

48. He would have had a fair trial.
    ____Yes
    ____No
    ____Don't know

49. In a trial Oswald might have been found innocent. Maybe someone else did it.
   ____This is true.
   ____This is not true.
   ____I don't know.

50. What is *your* opinion? Do *you* think Oswald killed President Kennedy?
   ____Yes
   ____No
   ____I don't know.

51. If you think he killed him, why do you think he wanted to do such a thing? _____

52. Do your parents think Oswald shot President Kennedy?
   ____Yes
   ____No
   ____They don't know.
   ____I don't know what they think.

53. Does your *teacher* think Oswald shot the President? (If you have more than one teacher, tell about the teacher who discussed the shooting the most.)
   ____Yes
   ____No
   ____Teacher does not know.
   ____I don't know what the teacher thinks.

54. Do you think the man who killed the President
   ____Planned it by himself.
   ____Planned it with other people.
   ____I don't know.

55. If you think he planned it *with* others, who do you think planned with him? _____

56. What do you think?
   ____President Johnson will be *just about as good* a President as Kennedy was.
   ____President Johnson will *not be as good* a President as Kennedy was.
   ____President Johnson will be a *better* President than Kennedy was.

57. My father votes as a
      _____Republican.
      _____Democrat.
      _____Sometimes a Democrat and sometimes a Republican.
      _____I don't know.

Thank you for your help and thoughtfulness.

II

Essays of junior high school students in a suburb of New York, written January 29, 1964, on: "What I Remember about the Weekend when President Kennedy was Assassinated."

(See Chapter 3)

How I felt about President Kennedy's Assassination.

When I found out about President Kennedy's assassination I was full of sorrow and I was very worried.

When this drastic event took place I was sorry because I did not think anybody could stoop to such a low thing to do as murder. When I heard that our President was dead, I just could not believe it. I felt just like crying. To think that our President was dead, struck down by an assassin's bullet, made me burn up inside.

I was worried about our country. Maybe it was just for a little while but I was worried because for a while we did not have a President. Some question kept flashing through my mind. What was to become of our country? Why should anybody do such a thing? Would Lindin Baynes Johnson be as good a president as the late President Kennedy? These are questions to be answered in the future. Maybe not even then.

I wish President Kennedy was not taken away from the world, his family and his country.

What I Remember about the Weekend President Kennedy was Assasinated

I was walking into my homeroom class when I heard that the President of the United States was shot. I just didn't want to believe it. I walked home from school wondering if it was true. Then, I heard another bulletin when I got home. It went, "Ladies and Gentleman the President is dead." I was dumbfounded. When I heard the bulletin I couldn't believe it, yet it was true. He died in a Dallas Hospital. I never thought I would ever live to hear about an assasination of a President really happen. I just couldn't believe it. I just couldn't bear the thoughts of having someone take away the life of the heroic John Fitzgerald Kennedy. He was so living at first and then 'poof' he's dead. I was grief-stricken when I heard he was shot. I was thinking that it isn't even safe to take a walk anymore. I hope I will never have to witness anything like that again.

BOY   AGE TWELVE   GRADE SEVEN

My feelings from the day of November 22, 1963.

I was in my school when they announced the new. The announcement told that the president was dying. It was anounced after my 6th period class at 2:45. At first I thought it was a prank of some radio station.

Then it became real because every station was giving the news. I couldn't believe that the president was dead. I went home around me everything seemed sad and crestfallen. Everything usualys so chereful when you get out of school on a friday. I got home and saw movies of the proceder.

The movies gave an even more shocking feeling and feeling of utter disbelief then did the radio. One minute this man who was so full of life was standing there smiling and the next picture shows a coffin coming out of a hospital.

It's a thing like this that you think will never happen so when it does happen its unbelievable. You just cannot conceive the meaning in your mind that the president is dead.

BOY   AGE TWELVE   GRADE SEVEN

What I Remember about the Weekend When President Kennedy was Assassinated

I was stunned. As I walked through the corridor people kept telling me this horrible happening. I kept telling myself that was just a joke. My teacher then told the class. President Kennedy was assassinated.

How could anyone do such a thing! I was filled with remote sadness. On the way home from school I could see people walking around in a daze. All the happiness of his family was gone in a few horrible minutes. I felt terrible.

Even now as I think about it, it seems too cruel to really have happened. But it did. Such a good man gone because of one half-crazed man. I give my deepest sympathy to Mrs. Kennedy, and her family. Her loss was also mine. As the years go by that day will seem dimmer and dimmer, but I will always have a place in my mind, and remember the day that President Kennedy was assassinated.

GIRL   AGE TWELVE   GRADE SEVEN

My first impressions on Nov. 22.

When I first heard those terrible words, I didn't think they were true. I just couldn't face reality. I happened to be in Mrs. ————'s class. She is my social studies teacher. When she turned on her radio all was a blur until, suddenly those words came as clear as anything. The president of the United States is dead. As I walked through the halls with my girlfriend, I saw many other girls and teachers crying. I was wondering why I didn't cry. I never found the answer. When I went home my mother was waiting for me. I dropped my books off and we went to the supermarket. Today we both walked very silently. When we came home I turned on the television nothing came but news. I listend for a while and then went to do my homework.

My sister were all cring. My mother and father didn't speak much that night, but I knew how they felt. The next few days were very dull, boring and sad to me. As I watched the funeral I started to cry, when I saw little John, John and Caroline. Mrs. Kennedy stood up the best. Those were my impressions.

GIRL   AGE THIRTEEN   GRADE SEVEN

How I felt when President Kennedy was assassinated.

I was in school when I heard of President Kennedy's assassinatiion. I felt very sad and very angry at the person who shot our president. When school was let out I went home and watched the news.

All day and night my family watched the news. When the television said they have found a suspect, I hoped they found the right man.

Poor John Jr., Caroline and Mrs. Kennedy. The casket was laying in state for everyone to come and pay their last respects.

Then the funeral began. When the casket went to the church my eyes filled with tears. His burriel was simple, but my heart broke.

I can not see how a man can go and kill one of the world's best friend and America's greatest president.

When his death was being announced and the showing of the latest films for days, the networks were right.

BOY   AGE FOURTEEN   GRADE SEVEN

How I felt when the President died.

At first I could not belived that he was shot. But when they told us he was dead something was inside me that I wanted to kill who ever did it. When all the programs were off I felt that it wasn't fair but when they showed us his life story, I was ashamed that I wanted to see T.V. When Oswald was shot I didn't want him to die. because I just wanted him to susfer. And be coveted by a jury fair and square. But the man who shot him shouldn't be punished because he just did his duty. I think its a dam shame that president Kennedy died. We lost a great man. I hope we get more men like him.

BOY   AGE THIRTEEN   GRADE EIGHT

What I Remember about the Weekend President Kennedy was Assassinated

Normally sunshine means happiness, but for me on that Monday on which the President was buried the sun was around and the cool crisp air was around but it really meant nothing it was just a cover up. If one relates feelings and weather, the Saturday when he was brought back to the White House sumed up my feelings for the whole weekend. The day was gray, raining, and cold and while watching his aids and friends file in I first realized he wouldn't make another speech like he made in West Berlin or wouldn't be back to his family in Ireland every ten years as he promised nor would he address us on a televised speech as "Dear Fellow Americans". I too thought about how the Kennedy Family had lost their baby only four months before and how John John was just beginning to do things with his father for example the trip to Arlington they made eleven days before, but also I felt with deep pride how the American people and the government changed its course so fast without complications and our forefathers had provided a means if something as traject as this happened we would not fall to foreign influence. A great country like we have is able to take a trajaty in step give the proper mouning and go on trying to make this country greater than we already are.

GIRL   AGE THIRTEEN   GRADE EIGHT

What I Remember about the Weekend President Kennedy was assasinated.

The tragic news of President Kennedy's death was at first unbeliev-able to me. It seemed as if I was having a terrible nightmare and hoped

I would wake up to find it all untrue. The weekend that followed that tragic Friday was to be the worst one in my life. All Saturday and Sunday as I watched television and saw over and over again the scenes of the assasination and highlights of President Kennedy's carreer I realized more and more what a horible thing had happened.

Things which I usually enjoy doing just weren't fun for me that weekend. I felt guilty if I found myself laughing or having fun, which I couldn't find very often. The whole world seemed upset and disorganized. It seemed as if it would take a very long time to get things back to considerable normality.

During the days which followed, gradually the world started taking shape. Now, when situations are normal again I know I will never in my life forget the sad weekend that started with January 22 [sic].

BOY   AGE THIRTEEN   GRADE EIGHT

What I Remember about the Weekend President Kennedy was Assassinated.

I was in mathe class, at the time my teacher made the frightful annoucement. Everybody was scared and upset in one way or another. Some girls just broke out crying while others didn't believe it. Even the boy's had a tear or two in their eyes. Everybody forgot about everything at that moment, and went home in a daze, still hardly believing it. But when I got home I saw the television and I knew this ill-fated accident was true. I can remember how all the people around me felt, the same as I. This turmoil of sadness went on for a weekend on television and for the people in the world, all their lives. I can remember how brave Mrs. Kennedy was at the time, and how she showed her courage and wisdom. I think half of the world's suffering was for Mrs. Kennedy. Although this terrible action occurred, Washington kept right on going and swore in a new president, the thirty seventh president. Not only Washington, but the whole world kept on going, through this terrible crisis. I remember how foreign dignities from all nations came to see the president, lying in his coffin and his wife. I think I will remember this all my life, although I wish not to.

GIRL   AGE FOURTEEN   GRADE EIGHT

What I remember about the Weekend President Kennedy was assassinated.

Were the tears hurt, anger, or may be alarm? Was it all these tied together? Oh, my G-d who could let this happen. Who in the world would do such a thing.

We, my class and I, were in Math class. We were taking our Friday weekly exame. I knew something had happened, because our teacher kept leaving the room and talking with other teachers outside the door-way. I thought a teacher was going to get married or something joyous, for I couldn't see their faces. I wasn't too interested at the time, because my test seemed to be important to me. Our test papers were collected a few minutes early. Then! yes then we were to find out. The president had been shot, he was rushed to hospital, the doctors did everything they could, everything but . . . . . but . . . . . nothing helped. He had died a few minutes ago. We couldn't even pray, or may be praying wouldn't have helped. Is there a G-d? If there is why did he let this happen? Why? Can you tell me? Somehow I remember these words were in my mind a few years ago, too. Someone so very close and dear to me died. Everyone told me it was for the better, because she had suffered a long time. Well, then, why didn't G-d make her well instead of letting her die? What is the better in this case. President Kennedy wasn't suffer-ing before he was shot.

I remember that tears came in my eyes and I just couldn't control myself. "Oh!" you may say that a fourteen year old girl doesn't know to much about things like this. Well, may be not. I really didn't know why I cried. I didn't know President Kennedy very well. President Ken-nedy wasn't my father. I just can't answer the question, "why?" I walked home with some of my friends and my only words, were words of violence. However as the hours passed by my attitude seemed quite different.

GIRL   AGE FOURTEEN   GRADE EIGHT

What I Remmember About the Weekend President Kennedy Was Assassi-nated.

It was a sunny and beautiful day, November 22, 1963. The air was chilled with a slight breeze, but there wasn't a cloud in the sky. For al-most everyone on the earth there was no anxiety or fear of and unex-pected tradgedy. It was a normal Friday and everyone went about their business as usual, but, the day was brought to an abrupt standstill.

Our class was in math our sixth period class. We were in the middle of the test when a neighboring teacher came in and handed our math teacher a note. A sudden expression of horror filled her face. She fol-lowed the other teacher into the hall, leaving us unattended. I began to feel uneasy and quite nervous when the teacher returned. She had a look of utter disbelief and shock on her face. At once the thought of another World War came into my head. I got very fidgety and was dis-tracted from my work on the test. For the next five minutes or so she just sat staring into space. Then she stood up and kind of moped around the classroom watching us. Almost immediately after she stood up the test was discontinued. There was a piercing silence in the room as we passed forward our papers. I think we all knew something was wrong.

Then she told us the horrible and tradgedy filled event. "The President had been killed." I was standing almost frozen stiff with shock and disbelief. Presently I began to move again and I found my seat. The school was dismissed very shortly. We all moved in silence back to our homeroom where we gathered our books and coats. The halls in school were never so quiet. We went home and tried to console ourselves but it was too much. Most of us cried. I shed one tear I couldn't allow myself to cry although I certainly felt like it.

That whole weekend you were glued to the television. It showed from the tragic moment until his casket was lowered into the ground. I never felt so empty in all my life. I felt as if he was one of the family. Never could such a thing happen I said to myself. It's just impossible.

I'm Catholic so Monday night our church had a Mass said for him. When I walked into church and saw the imposter casket sitting in the middle of the isle I almost died. My sunk to my knees.

From that Black day to this day I still can't bring myself to really believe deeply inside my heart what had happened that day President Kennedy was assassinated.

BOY   AGE FOURTEEN   GRADE NINE

What I remember about the week end President Kennedy was assassinated

Well, when I first found out about the assassination I was in science. My science teacher was giving us a quiz when another teacher walked in and wispered something to him. He became sort of weak for a moment. Then he told us to go to the projector room and the television was turned on. A reporter said what had happened and all of a sudden I had a funny feeling. A feeling of insecurity. For about ten minutes I was actually shivering. The thought that did this was a feeling of insecurity of the country. For the rest of the day I walked in this kind of daze. To me it had a psychological effect. I was feeling the world is about to collapse on me. After the swearing in of President Jhonson, it was like a burdon load was lifted from me. I am sure I can truthfully say this was the most horrifying day of my life.

BOY   AGE FOURTEEN   GRADE NINE

What I Remember about the weekend President Kennedy was Assassinated.

During the weekend of John F. Kennedy's assassination I along with an entire nation sincerely mourned the death of a great, youthful president. The shock was great when I first heard the reports that the president died. However, an even greater shock was the killing of Kennedy's assassin, Lee Harvey Oswald. Oswald, the suspected killer of Kennedy, was convicted, accused and hated before a trial, which might have revealed evidence in favor of Oswald, was made. Unlike the majority of people in the U.S., I grieved the death of Oswald because he died a hated man not given a chance to defend his life. I think that the weekend of our loss showed the world what a savage and waisted nation we live in.

BOY   AGE FOURTEEN   GRADE NINE

What I remember about the weekend President Kennedy was Assassinated.

When I first heard that the president was shot I didn't believe it, I even joked a little but when I found out he died this was even harder to believe. It came as a shock to me. Everywhere you went you heard about his death, on the radio, television and in the newspapers. The topic of discussion for most people was how he was killed and by whom. The story was the same with everyone, it must have been a mainiack or a communist. Well it was a communist. Lee Oswald was the man who had killed the president and sent the whole country into a state of mourning. It was the most tragic event I had ever heard of in my life. The pitiful part of it was his little children. They are now fatherless and his wife is now a widow. This great man killed, for an unknown reason, now he's beneath the earth acclaimed as one of the greatest men of our times. All the stations played music in memory of the president and all the information recorded was publicised for 84 hours. When the program comes on again I shall be sure to watch this report on him.

GIRL   AGE FOURTEEN   GRADE NINE

What I Remember About the Weekend Pres. Kennedy Was Assinated.

When we first heard of the news, we were in Spanish. My subject teacher was called out of the room by another teacher which was not unusual. She came back into the room, and told us to clear our desks, and find something to do, she could not go on with the class, "The President was shot, and he was rushed to a hospital." My first reaction was, "Well, the next thing Miss ——— is going to say is the martians have landed, or Mr. and Mrs. Kennedy have just been divorced." Then she proceeded to say that it is the truth, and the teacher that told us would keep us informed. I got "goose bumps" all over; I bowed my head in prayer for his life. My subject teacher left the room, and the kids that I was sitting next to began to talk. Across the room one boy, and about five girls were cracking jokes. The girls were flirting, and the boys were enjoying it. I also prayed for them. When we heard the news of his death, I broke out in tears, uncontrollable tears. To think what our country is coming to.

That weekend the family got together, my Aunts wearing black. We gathered into the living room, and watched T.V., the funeral march. The part that really broke me up, was when the person that I really idolize, my aunt cryed. I couldn't control my feelings. My uncles were cracking jokes to change the mood. Even now, people that are reading this, I am almost crying.

GIRL   AGE FOURTEEN   GRADE NINE

What I Remember About the Weekend President Kennedy was Assassinated.

We were told about the assassination while we were in our Spanish class. At first we thought it was a joke and everyone started to laugh. Then we realized our teacher wasn't kidding. When the story was confirmed, everything stopped. All work was stopped in the classes. We girls were all crying, and the boys had to hold themselves back.

That night I had planned to go to the movies, but after what had happened, I didn't feel much like doing anything. I stayed in all day Saturday and Sunday and listened and watched the reports. I still couldn't believe what had happened. I felt ashamed. Just the night before I was wondering if I could go to the show, or what I was going to do this weekend. They had all seemed so important to me then. Then when I thought of what happened, they seemed so small and insignifant. Sunday, I watched the march and the funeral services on television. I was seeing what was going on, but I still couldn't understand it. Even now, after it's all over with, it's still hard to believe and understand.

GIRL   AGE FOURTEEN   GRADE NINE

What I Remember About the Weekend President Kennedy was Assassinated.

I was in the gym when I heard. The gym teacher came in and said the President was shot in the head. It sounded rather funny and a few girls laughed, but then who could believe it. There was a lot of whispering around the gym. No one was sure whether it was true or not. We finally got a radio. It was turned on and the first words I remember were, "The President is dead." At the moment, I just couldn't believe it. Things like that just don't happen in this day and age and in this country. A few girls started crying. I couldn't. I was really dumbfounded. When I got home, I cryed. I couldn't hold it in anymore. That whole weekend was a nightmare. My eyes were glued to the television. I don't know how Jacqueline Kennedy stood it. She was always so poised. And Caroline and John-John what was to become of them? Sure, they have money, but to live with memories of that weekend, it's the third child they lost. All the time and love that was put into their son was lost because of an insane assassin. Even afer two months, I still can't believe those events did happen but then we must believe them, and Jacqueline Kennedy, Caroline, and John-John have to go on living.

GIRL   AGE FOURTEEN   GRADE NINE

What I Remember about the Weekend President Kennedy was assassinated.

That weekend was something I shall always remember. There was deep mourning and national grief thruout the U.S. and the world for our beloved ex-president. I clearly remember being told in gym 6th period. After being told we were all in sort of a daze especially the teachers. People were crying but something as serious as this did not make me cry; it made me stop and think seriously about the world & the future. The world seemed as if it was the year when Lincoln was shot and people were just so astounded they didn't know what to do. That weekend I'm sure the entire U.S. was glued to their T.V. sets. You didn't feel like eating or talking or anything when you turned on the radio there was beautiful music that made you feel so sympathetic as if someone in your family had died. There was a feeling of togetherness & Brotherhood when Kennedy died. It seemed as if the world had come together at last. There was no feeling of copetition but a feeling of warmth to love your fellow man. People, for once started to appreciate the people around them. You did not think of it as a Roman Catholic or a Capitalist dying but as a human being. Jews, Catholics, Negroes, Socialists and even Communists, our worst copetotos, worshipped together. I don't think Pres. should have to dye to create such an atmosphere, but I think there wouldn't be such violence and depression if there always was such an atmosphere.

Most important of all it stopped, if even for 2 days, the horrid rat race we live in.

III

Transcript of tape-recorded interviews by Dr. Gilbert Kliman with children ages seven to twelve in a suburb of New York, November 23-25, 1963.

(See Chapter 6)

Date of interview: November 24, 1963.

DR. KLIMAN: Do you want me to explain to you a little more about what I want to know? You see what I want to know is how children feel about what happened to President Kennedy. That would help me to understand better how to help children. . . . We don't know too much about how children think and feel about it so could you tell me how you feel and what you think about it?

THOMAS: It's pretty hard to think about this—and I just can't say anything about it because it is bad just being a President. I wouldn't like to be a President because sometimes they get shot—what I don't like about this mostly is why the person would want to do this, because he should have a reason or something like that and I feel sorry for him, for President Kennedy, because there was no reason for him to do it. So everybody should wish that there was a time machine so we could go back and we'd know about it and then we could get ready for it, but that couldn't be done, so we just have to keep going on. We don't have any witnesses now because Oswald is dead and what I think about this is that it shouldn't have happened because everybody likes to see the planned shows that are on and even though that they still wouldn't wish that this happened because he was a good man, a good President and that's what I think about it for right now.

DR. KLIMAN: You certainly have a lot of thoughts and I'd like to ask you about one that you told me already—that is that you wouldn't like to be President now. When you were younger did you sometimes wish that you could be President?

THOMAS: Well, I really didn't think about anything like that—I really was wishing that I was going to be a carpenter and that's what I think I'm going to be—I'm going to try to be it instead of President because there are a lot of jobs and I think I would like to be a carpenter because that's one of the things I'd like to be. But, I can't be any one of the things I want to be and I have to be a President maybe. And what I think now is that why it all has happened because this just shouldn't have happened on a nice day—why would a person do it to a nice man like him? There is just no reason why he should and nobody can really make a good reason out of it.

DR. KLIMAN: Now we can't know any more because Oswald is dead, but do you have any guess why he did it?

THOMAS: Well, it might be because he—maybe he wanted President Johnson to be President instead of President Kennedy. So he shot him so President Johnson could get to be President and that's what I think about this.

DR. KLIMAN: Where were you when you found out the President had been shot?

THOMAS: We were at school—Ted and I were the helpers at school who were lowering the flag down when someone at school told me and I saw Ted lowering down the flag at half-mast.

DR. KLIMAN: What did you think when you heard?

THOMAS: I thought this was pretty bad because why would a person want to do it to a good man like him.

DR. KLIMAN: Did you believe it right away?

THOMAS: Yes, but there still can't be any reason why without him because they didn't get much time to question him—because he is dead now when they were taking him to the court. So we can't really have any reason for it.

DR. KLIMAN: Thomas, did you get excited or upset in any way after you heard the news?

THOMAS: Well, I did get upset a lot because nobody should have done it and there was no reason why on a good day—maybe they could do it some other day—if they had to do it. And maybe not even some other day but I'd really want them not to do it at all.

DR. KLIMAN: But maybe another day would have been better—what kind of a day was it that day?

THOMAS: Well, it first came out very happy for everybody there for the President coming and then one shot and the happy day was over—and all the days are going to be unhappy now—practically.

DR. KLIMAN: Have you been feeling very sad?

THOMAS: Well, when I think about it I do—and when I don't I just keep my mind on the things I'm doing—but when I get to think about that it gets very sad and I can sometimes—when I think about it—I just can't get my mind off of it.

DR. KLIMAN: Does it make you feel like crying?

THOMAS: No, but it makes me feel unhappy very much.

BOY: AGE NINE.

Date of interview: November 25, 1963.

DR. KLIMAN: Well, like I just explained to you I am asking you to help me by telling me what you felt and what you thought about all the things that happened since Friday afternoon. . . . I would like to understand better what children think about these things. Maybe I could help some other children better if you would explain to me how you took it and what you have in your mind.

LARRY: Well, whoever did assassinate President Kennedy sure had the nerve and if he's from the Fair Play of Cuba I thought that Castro had made up with President Kennedy and that was the end of the fight. But now since he has come from the Fair Play of Cuba and assassinated President Kennedy I think it is going to start another war. And uh . . .

DR. KLIMAN: Have you been thinking about what might happen?

LARRY: Well, no I haven't that much. But I am wondering if President . . . or if the new President can stop a war like President Kennedy did and not . . . and prevent a war that is going to come up with Cuba or Russia and the United States.

DR. KLIMAN: Did you have some ideas about what the first thing would be that might go wrong?

LARRY: Well, no I haven't but if somebody else assassinates another person that's going to start a war, I think. Cause maybe one person assassinated is enough, two persons are . . . well that's too much especially if it is the President of the United States.

DR. KLIMAN: Where were you when you heard the news?

LARRY: I was in school.

DR. KLIMAN: In class?

LARRY: In my arithmetic class. I was going down to the bathroom and I heard somebody scream out "President Kennedy was shot" and when I came back up I told the class. They thought I was fibbing cause nobody thought that that could happen to the President but it did and it was true.

DR. KLIMAN: How about you when you heard somebody shout "President Kennedy was shot." What was going on inside you when you heard that?

LARRY: I thought, well, at first they said "He's shot" and I said "Who's shot?" "President Kennedy." Somebody . . . some other person, and I said, "That couldn't happen." And when I heard it I was shocked. I just couldn't believe it.

DR. KLIMAN: But you did feel that your class had to be told. You must have had some feeling that it was very important, too.

LARRY: I know and I was wondering then how Johnson would be if President Kennedy is dead, how the new President is going to be. Is he going to be like him or different, better or worse to the country?

DR. KLIMAN: Do you have some ideas about how he would be?

LARRY: Well, after he made his speeches he . . . well I thought he would be pretty good but it all depends in the future what happens.

DR. KLIMAN: So first you couldn't believe it and you were shocked?

LARRY: Right.

DR. KLIMAN: And then what went on inside as far as feelings and ideas?

LARRY: Well, first I wondered how his wife felt in the car. Was she faint, did she faint or did she cry very much and what happened to the rest of the people in the car, like when Mr. Connally got shot, the governor of Texas, in his back and what went on inside his friends and everybody that he knew personally.

DR. KLIMAN: You were imagining all that. Many, many thoughts. Did some of the children in the class show their feelings right there in the first few minutes?

LARRY: In arithmetic class? Well, Ernest did. Uh, Harvey didn't really bother. He didn't care; he just didn't care. He was laughing and saying, yelling out, "The President is dead, the President's dead!" But our French teacher, I could see, I could see it in her tears she was very much upset. I could see how she felt about a good friend of Charles de Gaulle's and she came from France and she liked the President very much.

DR. KLIMAN: Did you notice some of the children were crying?

LARRY: Well, I didn't notice, I didn't see anybody crying at first but when it was time to go home I saw quite a few people crying.

DR. KLIMAN: Even children?

LARRY: Yeh.

DR. KLIMAN: Yeh. How about yourself, was there any crying at some time over the weekend?

LARRY: No.

DR. KLIMAN: Or that day?

LARRY: No.

DR. KLIMAN: Sometime children feel crying inside. Do you know that feeling?

LARRY: Well, they start to cry but they keep it in and ah the hurt is within themselves. I don't really know what it is like. It never happened to me.

DR. KLIMAN: Did you ever have anything like this happen before?

LARRY: No. Not in my life.

DR. KLIMAN: Nobody you knew, that you knew well, died in your life?

LARRY: Oh, yes. My uncle did and I was very young when that happened and I cried and cried and cried. And if somebody else died I wouldn't cry. I wouldn't bother to cause he wasn't related to me. And I wouldn't know what it meant to other people that he was related to, his loved ones.

DR. KLIMAN: How old were you when your uncle died?

LARRY: Oh, seven or eight. I don't know really.

DR. KLIMAN: It was just a year ago then?

LARRY: Yes.

DR. KLIMAN: Do you remember the first thing . . . let's go back to the time that your mother told you. What did mother say?

LARRY: Well, she said, I quote, "Larry guess what? Your Uncle Everett in the hospital he died. He died from flu." I said, "What, what?" I said what two times and then I started crying. Just couldn't imagine it.

DR. KLIMAN: How about that evening, did you have anything special going on in your mind later on?

LARRY: Well, besides my uncle's death I was anxious for Mr. W——— to come over to tell me more about this trip.

DR. KLIMAN: To Africa?

LARRY: Yes, the Congo.

DR. KLIMAN: Yeh. And did you have any trouble in your sleep that night?

LARRY: No.

DR. KLIMAN: All right. Did you think anything special might happen?

LARRY: Well, that's hard to say. Half and half. Half the time I was thinking about my uncle and then I just turned over and forgot it. . . . I forgot all about it. Cause something special was going on. It was a holiday. I didn't have to go to school and I was anxious to go outside and play with my friends. Uh, uh, I was a little older then cause it was about a month more when I recovered the sadness.

DR. KLIMAN: Were you very close to your uncle?

LARRY: He was a very close friend of mine. I just called him Uncle Everett and then I felt how Aunt Nora and her child felt. It's like the Kennedys and Mrs. Kennedy heard the shocking news that her husband—

DR. KLIMAN: What do you think the Kennedy children felt?

LARRY: Well, uh, it was very shocking for them too. As they were the same as Mrs. Kennedy. She was very brave. She had enough courage to walk up to the catapult, kneel down and go back without crying with the children. They were very brave. [Pause] And if a little child like that could go up to his father or her father without crying that's very very brave. If I–I couldn't do that. They were so young and I was a little bit older than them and I didn't even see my uncle and I cried and I cried. So they have lots of courage to do that.

DR. KLIMAN: Yes, I wonder what might have been going on inside their minds that they didn't show on the outside. They were very brave.

LARRY: Yes.

DR. KLIMAN: But maybe they had other thoughts and feelings.

LARRY: I had one thought that when Mrs. Kennedy got home, uh, that she would dream that her husband would come home and the next day when she woke up she would feel so sad because he was not there. And she would remember that he was assassinated and feel very bad and so would the children.

DR. KLIMAN: Have you had any dreams lately?

LARRY: Well, no.

DR. KLIMAN: How about when you went to bed on Friday night, did you have any thoughts as you were in bed?

LARRY: Well, I lay there awake thinking what will happen, what will become of the assassinator or Oswald and what will Mrs. Kennedy feel like in the future. Will she forget or will she remember. And will the people of this country remember it or forget it. And will Oswald get death or life in jail.

DR. KLIMAN: When you first heard about it what did you feel toward Oswald?

LARRY: Well, first I thought that it was a maniac but then later when I heard it was Lee Harvey Oswald from the Fair Play of Cuba Committee I thought about Castro and his hatred of Kennedy cause he stopped their missiles from coming—from being shipped from Russia to their country.

DR. KLIMAN: What did you think right away when you heard the President had been shot, what did you think should be done about it? What should be done to the person who shot him?

LARRY: Well, I would think they just [have] no trial if he shot a President— a person but a President. He shouldn't get a trial whoever he is. He shouldn't get a trial 'cause he shot a very important man and killed him so he should just get immediate death, immediate.

DR. KLIMAN: Who should have killed him?

LARRY: I . . .

DR. KLIMAN: Who should have killed him then?

LARRY: Well, I really don't know. They just should have hanged him or maybe the electric chair.

DR. KLIMAN: Right away?

LARRY: Right away.

DR. KLIMAN: And then when you heard that the man in Texas named Rubenstein, Jack Rubenstein, you heard I guess that he shot him and killed him, how did you feel about that?

LARRY: Well, he shouldn't have interfered with something that is none of his business. He was not like me. I don't have anything to do with it. I'm just one of the uh, mourning people . . . uh, of President Kennedy. And Jack Rubenstein should have been one of us but when he went over and shot Oswald they could have gave him a lie detector test or questioned him some more and that would have made a lot of sense. But since Jack Rubenstein went over and killed him now we can't get anything out of him 'cause he was the uh, he was the uh, he was the man who thought, who the people thought that assassinated President Kennedy, and if it was somebody else he could have told them. But now that Jack Rubenstein killed him you just can't know anything else about President Kennedy or Lee Oswald.

DR. KLIMAN: Is there anything else that has been on your mind that happened to you since then?

LARRY: Well, after I was thinking how Mrs. Kennedy felt. I heard on the radio that J. D. Tibbets the policeman was shot. And I was thinking about her wife and children and how they would get along in the future.

DR. KLIMAN: Hm-hm.

LARRY: And they had enough courage like Mrs. Kennedy or they just couldn't stand it.

DR. KLIMAN: What would happen to children if they couldn't stand it?

LARRY: Well, I would think they would cry and cry. They could cry for a month and not forget it. They could cry every night when they went to bed and dream about and dream about and the tears roll down their eyes and they won't know it and they were thinking about it and tears just running down their eyes at night while they are dreaming. And they keep on doing that and doing that until somebody took them some place for a vacation and had lots and lots of fun. That would make them forget all about it. Or if they wanted to go somewhere very much for a long time and you took them there and they weren't going yet but they were having—but they had it on their minds that Christmas was coming and they were thinking what they would get then probably they would forget about it.

DR. KLIMAN: So the problem they have is how to forget?

LARRY: Right.

DR. KLIMAN: They might even in their dreams be thinking about it and re-membering. I wonder if that happened to you.

LARRY: Well, no. Only for about two days I remembered my uncle's death then I forgot about it.

DR. KLIMAN: I'm not clear whether you were thinking about your uncle at night when you were sleeping.

LARRY: No, I wasn't.

DR. KLIMAN: No dreams about your uncle?

LARRY: No, no dreams at all.

DR. KLIMAN: Sometimes when children are upset they show it other ways.

LARRY: I know another way. They don't want to eat supper; they don't want to go to school 'cause at school they are afraid they might remember it and just cry and cry in school. They don't want to eat their dinner be-cause they are so sad and they don't want to go anywhere. They just want to be alone and sit and think about it. And try and forget and try and forget but they just can't do it because it is too much of a shock for them.

DR. KLIMAN: And maybe even some other way some children might show that they are upset, like they might get very excited.

LARRY: Yes. That is possible but not that often. Most of the time they show it in crying or just going in a corner and just sitting there, thinking about it.

DR. KLIMAN: Did you or anyone you know have any worries or fears since Kennedy died?

LARRY: I don't think so.

DR. KLIMAN: And what you mention about appetite and not wanting to eat, did you have a touch of that?

LARRY: Well, yeh. When President Kennedy died my mother said "Time to eat" so I came to the table and I was just sitting there when she put the plates down I just couldn't do it—eat—and she told me to eat, she ordered me to eat so I had to. After I ate I just sat there just wondering and thinking about the President and what such a good man he was and would his efforts be continued by Johnson or will they not be or will the whole future be changed.

DR. KLIMAN: What did you especially like about Kennedy?

LARRY: Well, that's hard to say. Uh . . .

DR. KLIMAN: The good things you said he did, what a good man he was.

LARRY: Well, he made good speeches about physical fitness and when he said that all children should pass their tests he was telling them to try to help them not to make them do their exercises. He was trying to help them. He wasn't trying to order them to do something, he was trying to ask them to—to ask them to do something. And it wasn't for his good it was for their—for the people's good for that person not passing the test in physical fitness.

DR. KLIMAN: What do you think about talking about it this way? What do you think it does when you talk about these things with me?

LARRY: Well, it proves the knowledge of boys and girls and it makes them understand a little more how people feel when something comes over them like that.

DR. KLIMAN: Well, I thank you very much for helping me.

GIRL: AGE ELEVEN AND A HALF.

Date of interview: November 23, 1963.

DR. KLIMAN: Karen will tell her feelings and thoughts in the first day and a half since her learning of President Kennedy's shooting and death. It's now about ten minutes after six the day following his death.

KAREN: When I first heard that Kennedy had been shot but before he was killed, when I was told I couldn't believe the person who told me and I was sure that this was a joke but then when I looked into it, turned on the television, I found out that it was true, and this was very terrible to me, and when I found that he had died, I just couldn't believe it and I was waiting to wake up from this terrible dream and even though I heard all these things going on I just still couldn't believe it—I don't think I even can now.

DR. KLIMAN: Where were you?

KAREN: I was at school because it was two o'clock—no—it was about 1:35, 1:45, about fifteen minutes after he had been shot, and I'm not quite sure but this was in school, before he died, about fifteen minutes before he died I heard.

DR. KLIMAN: What were the other children in your class doing when they heard?

KAREN: Well the whole class was having a discussion and ironically this was in social studies and my teacher had been talking about—even though you killed a person who had an idea, even if you killed him the idea would still go on—the idea could never die—it might be replaced but the idea would never die—and this was before we'd even heard of it. And then while we were in the middle of the discussion a boy who had been out came in and told us that while we had all been discussing this—

DR. KLIMAN: How did your class react to this when the boy came in and told you?

KAREN: At first none of us believed it. And we thought it was just a very stupid practical joke and then one of us suggested that we turn on a television which we have in the classroom and we did so and we discovered that this was true.

DR. KLIMAN: Were any of the children upset in the first few minutes after hearing the news?

KAREN: We all were upset—even those who had from their parents' views been Republican, and those who shared my opinion, all of us did, we were all shocked and we were all upset by it.

DR. KLIMAN: How did they show it?

KAREN: Well, at first we just grew silent and no one said anything and then after a while started whispering how could this be done—how could anyone do this thing—I didn't think anything like this could happen—when I was alive . . .

DR. KLIMAN: Were there some people in the class who believed it right away?

KAREN: Well, at first when this boy told us we believed him but then after thinking we thought well we were just being taken advantage of and that this was just a practical joke. So when first we believed him and then we figured that it couldn't be true. Anyway this was most of us, including me.

DR. KLIMAN: Were any of the children crying in the first few minutes?

KAREN: Well I don't know—nothing that could be heard—but after a while people—I suppose were doing it to themselves and saying aloud to people around them, saying I just can't work or I can't go to the movie tonight or I can't go to after-school sports, it would be wrong—I can't do anything. This was of course a difficult time—'cause we were all expecting um report cards and most of us expected something good so it came just at a difficult time, of course any time would be.

DR. KLIMAN: How did that make it difficult about the report cards?

KAREN: Well most of us expected good marks. But then it didn't seem to do much good in a way—well—you have good marks but then even though we had been told, the shot was in such a vital spot that we knew he couldn't live. And losing the President, in a way it didn't seem quite as important as a good mark. It sort of spoiled the whole day, the whole week for us.

DR. KLIMAN: It didn't seem as important as a good mark?

KAREN: No. The good mark didn't seem as important. 'Cause the shooting of the President meant so much to the whole world. It was just overwhelming.

DR. KLIMAN: Did you get good marks?

KAREN: Yes, I did. It didn't mean as much to me. Because the idea was just spoiled. I couldn't think about the report card even though I had gotten good marks because of this attempted assassination which turned out to be assassination. The report card couldn't mean as much to me any more.

DR. KLIMAN: Some of the children—when they are nervous—sometimes they do strange things—puzzling things. Did you see any things which you felt were puzzling?

KAREN: Well, I didn't at all look at the rest of the class—I just felt so down —I stopped my work and I was just looking straight ahead without looking around at anything. It might be. I don't know.

DR. KLIMAN: Did anyone make jokes?

KAREN: Well, a couple of the people I think tried to say a couple of things that made them smile a bit. But the smiles stopped right away.

DR. KLIMAN: Do you remember some of the things?

KAREN: No, I don't. I just remember a few wisecracks. I don't think about the President himself but I think just trying to make himself more cheerful.

DR. KLIMAN: Did you walk home?

KAREN: Yes I did. With my brothers. One of which didn't know about this at all. The younger one and I felt a little bit badly about it. He had gotten wonderful marks and he came up to us saying all these wonderful things and I felt badly about it—about the death of Kennedy, which he didn't quite understand. And both my brothers were asking quite a few questions, a lot of which I didn't know the answers to.

DR. KLIMAN: What happened to your feelings then as you were getting home?

KAREN: I was just miserable. Nothing else. I felt like crying but I couldn't. And I couldn't until I got home and my mother and I both asked "Do you know?" at each other at pretty much the same time and I just sort of went upstairs and she came up and we just started crying a lot on each other. But I couldn't in class and I couldn't walking home. Maybe it was because I was afraid to then, in front of my brothers and my class . . . well it was strange—when I first got home and I went up into my room I cried on and off for fifteen minutes—then my mother had to go somewhere and I went into L.'s room and we talked over it and I got a little bit calm and then we both started crying—and then we calmed down . . . well every time we talked about it it seemed I burst out crying again. So if every time you really start talking about it—every time I thought about it more deeply I started crying again.

DR. KLIMAN: Did you have any other trouble that day?

KAREN: No, the day was perfect until that.

DR. KLIMAN: After, did you have any trouble inside yourself besides the crying?

KAREN: Well, I had a little bit of trouble with my brother who was upset in a different way, but other than that, and the death of Kennedy, and my misery about that, there was nothing else—I didn't have any troubles if it wasn't for that.

DR. KLIMAN: And did you get any fears later that day?

KAREN: Well yes. I have been studying the history of many countries who had great power and then when something came up they came to the fall of that country and became sort of slaves to other countries. I didn't think of slaves, but Kennedy I think even though he hadn't gone too far he was a strong leader and much of the world depended on him. I was afraid now with a new President who wasn't thought quite as much of that the country might start to collapse in a way, never to become slaves but to lose its power in the world, which would be difficult because our country is now in such luxury it would be sort of difficult to go through what so many European countries are going through now 'cause most of us—the children anyway—have had no experience with living as in the European countries.

DR. KLIMAN: Did you have any more personal fears about your own safety that day, last night?

KAREN: I don't think—I don't think I did but I was just thinking really of the countries that depended on the U.S. and the U.S. itself as a whole. I wasn't afraid for myself, I don't think.

DR. KLIMAN: You didn't have any fear of being in the dark or being in your room alone or outside by yourself?

KAREN: Well, no, I don't think so. I felt very much that if this itself wasn't a nightmare I was going to have it that night but that was the extent of it.

DR. KLIMAN: Did you have a nightmare that night?

KAREN: No, I don't remember having one. I had my cat with me and she very often calms me down quite a bit when I am frightened—that might have helped. But I don't remember having any nightmares. Only thinking what this whole thing was.

DR. KLIMAN: And how about other changes? Did you have any change in your appetite?

KAREN: Yes, last night I usually am quite hungry when I get home and I'm usually quite ready for dinner and last night I didn't have anything to eat when I got home. I didn't feel hungry when supper came and I didn't feel hungry the whole day after that though I had been rather hungry in the morning and at about 1:15 I had been quite hungry. But then when I was told—I lost all sense of appetite.

DR. KLIMAN: And how about today?

KAREN: Well, I—it's just been a sort of a day—that I feel the whole world doesn't want to eat and it's no real loss of appetite. It's just one of those days when you don't feel like eating. It might be just a coincidence— though it's more likely to be the problem itself.

DR. KLIMAN: Do you have any thoughts about the fellow who assassinated Kennedy?

KAREN: Yes. I wonder how he could go to such extremes even though he might have disagreed with him and I wonder if he feels guilty now the way the whole country and much of the world is crying over Kennedy or whether he has a sense of achievement. I can't understand how he could. But I just wonder how he does feel.

DR. KLIMAN: What do you think ought to be done about him if he is caught and is actually the one who did it?

KAREN: Well they do have a suspect now. But I believe he is—well with something like this—in ordinary things very often they put a murderer to death—but in—I never feel that this is—I always feel that something like this is just too good for a murderer but—you know to be put to death—and then we have nothing to worry about after that—but somehow I feel even a life imprisonment or death wouldn't make any difference to him if he has a sense of achievement. So I just don't know. Because if he was put in jail he would just become very hard, feeling that "They put me in here because I did something that I have been wanting to do for so long" and he wouldn't feel that he was right and if he was put to death he would never have a chance to feel sorry for it. He could die a thousand deaths before he could make up for this.

DR. KLIMAN: Is there anything else you can add that might help me understand how children feel about the President dying?

KAREN: Well, I never met him and I never thought I would but somehow when he's gone it's sort of like I lost someone in my family and it's impossible to believe, it left a big hole in my life even though I've never even met him or even come near him.

DR. KLIMAN: Thank you, Karen.

BOY: AGE TWELVE.

Date of interview: November 24, 1963.

DR. KLIMAN: What I am trying to do is to learn how children feel and think when something terrible happens—because I think that probably it is very hard for grownups to understand what a child feels. . . . It may help me to understand more about them if you would tell me about yourself—what you felt and thought when you heard about Kennedy.

TERENCE: Well, at first I didn't believe it because I thought that it was a joke that this kid was playing on me; but then I heard everyone else say it —then I wanted to find out if he was just shot or dead. Then I found out that he was dead. I went home on the bus a little bit dazed and when I came home my mother asked me how I felt about it and what I said was, "I hope they catch the guy who shot him"—and now this Lee Oswald who they think shot him, was shot by someone else and he was killed. And so this is a form of justice. Now they're going to do something to this Jim Ruby, or whatever his name is.

DR. KLIMAN: What do you think should be done to Ruby?

TERENCE: Well, he just murdered him. It was the same way as Oswald killed Kennedy, if he did kill Kennedy.

KLIMAN: Oh, then you're not certain that he did kill Kennedy?

ERENCE: If he did kill him, then it's the same thing. The same sort of trial should be given to Ruby as they would have given to Oswald.

DR. KLIMAN: Did you feel that way right away when you heard Kennedy had been shot—were all your thoughts about the trial or did you have some other thoughts?

TERENCE: No, I guess I felt just about the same way. At that time nobody had any idea who did it—they then thought it was two men—I just hoped that they would catch the man who did it and that justice would be done.

DR. KLIMAN: You know I'm very interested about what you felt inside. First you said you couldn't believe it—it is a very hard thing to believe.

TERENCE: In some ways I still believe he is still alive.

DR. KLIMAN: How did you notice that—in what way do you still kind of believe he is still alive?

TERENCE: I don't know—it takes some time to get adjusted to things, like when the Dodgers beat the Yankees in the World Series four straight, I didn't get adjusted to that for a whole month.

DR. KLIMAN: Some of the other children had a very difficult time adjusting to it. What would you say was the worst part of your difficulty?

TERENCE: In the beginning, when they said he was dead, I asked the person who told me and other people if they said he was shot and what really happened. I was in French class, my last class, and our principal came in and said the French class couldn't go [to] something outside of school. So I thought that they meant something happened to somebody at Columbia. But then when we walked out and heard shouts that the President was dead—he was shot and was dead, I asked somebody if he was just shot—or is he dead or what and they said he really was dead. When I came home I just turned on the TV because everyone else was doing it.

DR. KLIMAN: What do you think about the school not telling you? What in your opinion was the best thing to do?

TERENCE: I think they should have told us right out—because it keeps us in suspense. We got out a few minutes early—and I didn't know why. What could have happened—something terrible happened—and finally I found out what did happen.

DR. KLIMAN: Did you have some idea of something different that would have been terrible that might have happened?

TERENCE: Maybe there was a fire at Columbia or something. My grandmother lives there and I got extra scared because she could see Baker Field if she stuck her head out the window and I thought maybe there was a bad fire and her place might have been on fire and something may have happened to her.

DR. KLIMAN: Who was the first person who told you Kennedy was shot?

TERENCE: I don't know. I think his name is ———. He was in school—we were walking down the hall, I heard some of the girls crying, some people were shouting—the President was shot, the President is dead, things like that.

DR. KLIMAN: Did you cry?

TERENCE: No, my brother did, though.

DR. KLIMAN: Did you have anything going on inside you that felt like you were crying even though the tears didn't come?

TERENCE: No. I guess I didn't realize what they were saying until I got on the bus, 'cause I didn't believe it.

DR. KLIMAN: Well, first you were afraid that something might have happened at Columbia and your grandma might have gotten in trouble from it. Did you have any fears later in the day?

TERENCE: No, no, I guess not.

DR. KLIMAN: You weren't afraid of a war or something like that?

TERENCE: No, there was some talk of that, that Khrushchev might strike us now but I heard on the radio that he was sorrowful and I don't think he'd strike if he felt like that.

DR. KLIMAN: What else do you think might be helpful for me to know about so I understand more about how children feel about death?

TERENCE: About my cat—what happened when she died. She was sick for some time; we had taken her to a doctor in Bronxville—and he was pretty far away—we kept bringing her there—we'd been back and forth something like a dozen times—a little more than that—a dozen and a half or more—and finally she died. After about ten trips to this doctor we brought her to a doctor. We brought her for worms and he found out she had some intestinal disease or something like that—the doctor nearer to us said there was no help for her and my mother came home and she said there was no help for her and he just put her to sleep and so we were in front of TV—had tears in our eyes and we all cried—I saw my father cry a little bit. Luckily it was on a Saturday, I wouldn't have gone to school that day.

DR. KLIMAN: Did you feel bad the whole next day?

TERENCE: No, I don't remember because this was a year ago—ah, March tenth I think it was '62.

DR. KLIMAN: You certainly have a very exact memory for that.

TERENCE: I got a good memory for things a few years ago.

DR. KLIMAN: Have you had any trouble from the death of your cat?

TERENCE: No, no trouble. I just felt like you would feel when your pet dies. I've had to bury three animals. I buried my rabbit, I had to bury my rabbit, a bird of my brother's and my hamster.

DR. KLIMAN: Well, sometimes children get upset, have bad dreams, fears, trouble sleeping. Do you have any trouble like that?

TERENCE: No, I only dream about good things.

DR. KLIMAN: How about the past two nights—do you remember what you dreamt about?

TERENCE: Girls—I dream I'm grown up and have all sorts of girl friends and you know, we go along in life—tenth grade, college—then in the end we wind up getting married or something like that.

DR. KLIMAN: Are these pleasant? They sound very pleasant.

TERENCE: Sure.

DR. KLIMAN: How about Friday night—do you remember what the subject of the dream was?

TERENCE: The same thing—the death of the President didn't scare me any.

DR. KLIMAN: Do you remember the last time before that that you had a dream like that—about girls—and going to college?

TERENCE: Oh, I have dreams like that all the time.

DR. KLIMAN: I'm very pleased that you could tell me that—it really helps me.

TERENCE: Oh, that's okay—are you going to play it back so I can hear it?

* * * * *

Index

DATE DUE

GAYLORD			PRINTED IN U.S.A.